…l-town love and dedication…a timely …t part local football clubs play in their communities."

Jim White, *Daily Telegraph*

"If you don't think lower league football matters, then read *Because it's Saturday*…intelligent research and interviews yield chapter after chapter of evidence why they matter so much."

Douglas Alexander, *Sunday Times*

"Well written, well researched and fully experienced attendance of grassroot teams. A great read. I think any real football fan will enjoy it."

Ian Newell, Plymouth Argyle Supporters on the Internet

"An excellent read that taps into the DNA of an assortment of clubs…an outstanding publication."

Phil Butterworth, Forest Green Rovers vice chairman

"A vivid picture of football life a million miles from the riches and bright lights of the Premier League. For all the love for their club is not diminished by the lack of finance or success, it's all about their team and their local community."

Peter J Leatham, Chairman Accrington Stanley Supporters Trust

"Read it in a day, and really enjoyed it. Some excellent people and stories packed into it."

Pat Bell, Grimsby Town Fanzine Editor

"Reflections on the dark days at Blackpool may be uncomfortable reading, but Gavin Bell deals with these and many other issues in a sensitive, positive and entertaining way."

Jim Hastie, Past-President Queen's Park FC

"Prize-winning travel writing and journalistic skills portray love and joy, dedication and faithfulness to fuel hope for the future of the game in what, for many, might be its darkest time."

Gordon Wilson, Grimsby Town supporter

Because it's Saturday

A Journey into Football's Heartlands

Gavin Bell

pitch

First published by Pitch Publishing, 2020

Pitch Publishing
A2 Yeoman Gate
Yeoman Way
Worthing
Sussex
BN13 3QZ
www.pitchpublishing.co.uk
info@pitchpublishing.co.uk

A CIP catalogue record is available for this book from the British Library.

ISBN 978 1 78531 646 3

Typesetting and origination by Pitch Publishing

Printed and bound in India by Replika Press Pvt. Ltd

Fixture List

Gavin Bell is a former foreign correspondent of Reuters and *The Times* and award-winning travel writer whose wanderings from Antarctica to Zanzibar have failed to diminish his passion for football and supporting Motherwell FC. He is probably the only person who has cheered during heavy fighting in Beirut on hearing his team had beaten Celtic. This is his third book.

Also by Gavin Bell

In Search of Tusitala: Travels in the Pacific after Robert Louis Stevenson (winner of the Thomas Cook/Daily Telegraph Travel Book of the Year)

Somewhere Over the Rainbow: Travels in South Africa

For Claire,
the best match of my life

You never know what happens in football, it's littered with fairy tales

– John Coleman, manager Accrington Stanley

Even a bad day at the football is better than a good day at the office

– Keith McAllister, Queen's Park supporter

A football club will always be a thing of passion

– Pat Bell, editor of the Grimsby Town fanzine

Acknowledgements

I AM grateful to everyone in these pages who shared memories, insights and opinions on their clubs and the challenges of the modern game. Generous with their time and honest in their views, they were a pleasure and an inspiration to meet.

Special thanks to Jane Camillin and all at Pitch Publishing for bringing out this book in the dark days of the Covid-19 outbreak as a reminder of better days that will come again. Also to Duncan Olner for an inspired front cover, the artist Paine Proffitt for his great cartoon on the back, and to those who provided images that capture the essence of home-town football.

What a team.

Author's note

MODERN FOOTBALL is a carousel of owners, managers and players constantly hopping on and off teams in pursuit of fame and fortune. Every season sees new actors appearing on revolving stages and others bowing out, most of them leaving with more memories than medals. On average, managers in English professional leagues are lucky if they keep their jobs for 18 months.

The action and interviews in this book were recorded during season 2017/18 and since then team sheets and coaching staff have changed, but most fans remain as faithful as ever. They are the lifeblood of the game, and this book is a tribute to their enduring, defiant loyalty.

Kick-off

THE PUB was crowded after a couple of midweek games, the usual raucous assembly of celebrating, drowning sorrows and questioning the parentage of referees. A big guy I vaguely recognised detached himself from the bar, weaved his way purposefully towards us, and proceeded to regale my pal with a beery account of how his team had stuffed Partick Thistle.

Eventually he turned to me and said, 'Hey Gavin, I hear ye're a Motherwell supporter?'

'Yes, that's right.'

'Tell ye whit it is, the wife an' I are movin' house and we've got a three-piece suite we don't need. If ye fancy takin' it, ye can have an all-seater stadium.'

Needless to say he was a (Glasgow) Rangers supporter. It's the price you pay for not following a big club, you become the butt of jokes, an object of bemusement and sympathy, and more often derision. Fans of Crewe Alexandra and Scunthorpe will be familiar with the scenario.

This is no bad thing in Glasgow, a football-daft city fiercely divided by historic rivalry of blue and green, Proddie (Protestant) and Tim (Catholic), Rangers and Celtic. When the 'Old Firm' clash at Ibrox or Parkhead it's like a gathering of clans for battle, massed ranks of fans roaring defiance and sectarian abuse beneath blizzards of

Union and Irish Republican flags. They are not so much rival fans as warring tribes. It is a thrilling spectacle, and the imposing presence of Glaswegian constabulary usually averts serious trouble, but inevitably when the pubs close there are minor skirmishes. At such times it is good to be a Motherwell supporter. The Old Firm brigades just laugh at you.

It could all have been different. My family left Motherwell when I was seven to move to a council flat in Glasgow, barely a mile from Ibrox stadium, the home of Rangers FC, and it was assumed at my new school that I was, or would become, a 'true blue'. But it was too late. They say real supporters don't choose their team, it's either where they come from, or it's the team their dad supports. And I came from Motherwell. I'd already been to my first games at Fir Park, near huge steelworks that had endowed the team with its nickname 'The Steelmen'. In football terms, the die was cast. Motherwell usually manage to survive in the Scottish Premier League, but this doesn't mean very much. With crowds of around 4,000 and a team that costs next to nothing, we are hardly in the multi-million stratospheres of Chelsea and Manchester United. I suppose the likes of Burton Albion and Shrewsbury are more in our financial league.

I got to meet my 'Well heroes in the 1960s as a trainee sports reporter with DC Thomson, publisher of popular Sunday and weekly newspapers. One of them was Ian St John, who a few years earlier had scored six goals in a 9-2 'friendly' hammering of Brazilian side Flamengo at Fir Park. This was the era of the 'Ancell Babes', a team of gloriously gifted ball players managed by Bobby Ancell which produced no fewer than eight Scottish internationals. St John was one of them and later he recalled how times have changed. He was paid a pittance at Motherwell, and when playing for Scotland he went to Hampden Park by bus.

My fledgling career in journalism almost crashed and burned on my first assignment, reporting on a First Division game between St Mirren and Dundee. DC Thomson also published daily and evening newspapers in Dundee, and it was my job to provide a running commentary for half-time and full-time issues of the evening paper.

On arriving at St Mirren's ramshackle ground in Paisley, I found the wooden press box crammed with big men in bulky overcoats, and I had to scramble for a seat nearby. It struck me there was something odd about the teams when they came out, but I couldn't put my finger on it and duly phoned the team sheets to Dundee. Fifteen minutes in, Dundee scored, and I promptly filed this important news for the first edition. Then it dawned on me. When the game began the players' shorts had been dirty, and I couldn't for the life of me think why. Eventually I plucked up the courage to tap one of the big sports reporters on the shoulder and ask him. He looked at me incredulously, scowled, and turned away.

At this point my dad, a well-known and well-liked freelance journalist in the area, came unwittingly to my rescue. After a moment the reporter turned back, looked at me quizzically and said, 'Are you Gavin Bell's son?'

'Yes sir.'

'Whit time did you get here?'

'Ten to three.'

'Early kick-off son, this is the second half. It's 3-1 St Mirren.'

I don't think I cried, but I'm pretty sure my eyes were moist. My career was in ruins before it had begun, and was there even any point in going back to the office?

'Who're you writing for, son?'

'The Dundee *Evening Telegraph.*'

'Right, come wi' me.'

And with that he saved my life by striding to the press phone, catching the first edition in time and dictating a substitute story, supposedly on my behalf. Words can never fully express my gratitude to this good Samaritan who saved me from ignominy on a rainy day in Paisley.

Fast-forward to a lifetime roaming the world as a foreign correspondent and travel writer, and when Saturday came I invariably looked or listened for the 'Well result. I may be the only person who has cheered during heavy fighting in Beirut on hearing we'd beaten Celtic. At least now I'm back in Glasgow I'm not alone. The length and breadth of Britain from Elgin to Plymouth there is a brotherhood and sisterhood of kindred spirits who turn out week after week, more in hope than expectation, to cheer teams with little prospect of winning anything other than their undying devotion.

This is the world of the Pilgrims, the Mariners and the Ironsides, clubs whose nicknames are derived from the history, geography and industries of the communities that produced and sustain them. There is no logical explanation for why anyone travels from Grimsby to Carlisle on a wet Tuesday night in November to watch journeymen footballers having a go at each other with more enthusiasm than skill. It's easier and cheaper to stroll to a pub and watch the silky soccer of superstars on Sky Sports.

But they steadfastly follow their local heroes come rain or shine, in battles for promotion or dour struggles against relegation, and for many it is the highlight of their week. Theirs is the triumph of optimism over experience, and when they lose there's always next Saturday. I am informed by a German friend that there is a saying in the Ruhr area that is the classic response of a man when asked by his wife why he is leaving their home on a Saturday. He looks at her in bemusement and says, '*Weil Samstag ist*' – 'Because it's Saturday' (and he's off to the match). The lure of the beautiful game is universal.

If the stadia of glamour clubs are like gladiatorial arenas, those in the lower leagues are more like community playing fields where matches are social occasions for friends to catch up on local news and gossip over a pie and a pint. In an era of obscene wages and payouts to superstars, agents and hangers-on, men and women who follow the likes of Accrington Stanley are the lifeblood of the game. Theirs are the teams that hold up the pyramid of leagues, nurture young talent, and provide fields of dreams for the stars of tomorrow to hone their skills and attract big-club scouts. It is they who conjure the romance of cup ties in homespun grounds against giants of the Premiership, and fairy tales when they win. Some of their supporters remember the days when the local plumber was their team's centre-half. For them, the idea of being born and bred in Rochdale and supporting Manchester United is unimaginable, and I support this view. It goes to the heart of the matter, that football clubs rooted in their communities reflect and draw strength from them and become flag bearers for them and their aspirations. Never mind another factory has closed, the team's up for the cup on Saturday.

I remember reading a study that showed when Newcastle and Sunderland win, production in the North East rises the following week with a general sense of well-being. I can attest to this phenomenon. As a young lad I used to walk to my gran's for tea after games at Fir Park, wearing my claret and amber Motherwell scarf. Inevitably somebody would ask, 'Whit did we lose by the day laddie?' News of a win would bring an instant smile, and as often as not you'd see a spring in the man's step. Where Rangers and Celtic fans expect and demand victory every week, a win for a 'Well supporter comes as a pleasant surprise. The recurring prospect of relegation never bothered me much; I saw it as an opportunity to broaden my horizons in away games to places like Dumbarton and Brechin. And I'd stopped going to Ibrox and Parkhead anyway because of the intimidating atmospheres. Being forced by police and stewards to remain packed in our tiny corner of Ibrox after the match until the stadium has emptied of Rangers fans, supposedly for our own safety, isn't much fun.

Loyalty and devotion to clubs at grassroots level run so deep and span so many generations they could be in the genes. As a result, communities support their clubs and in return the clubs support their communities with extensive social welfare programmes, and the symbiotic relationship enriches both.

And sometimes it reaps unexpected rewards. The best hope of European football for most of us is probably a pre-season friendly in Ireland, but a few years ago, to general astonishment, Motherwell qualified for an early round of the Europa League and we were drawn against a team from the Faroes. The club chartered a plane from Glasgow and invited fans to help pay for the flights by joining them, and when we arrived at the wind-swept ground on a sea cliff our part-time opponents came out to greet us. There was a practice ground next to the little stadium, and the Faroese team generously provided us with a ball for a kick-about before the match. At one point I somehow managed to lay on a pass that led to a goal, and I heard a voice from the sidelines: 'Hey Gavin, didn't know you were that good, can I put you on the bench?' It was Alex McLeish, the Motherwell (and later Scotland) manager. You don't get that at the Emirates.

Nor do you get strikers hitting seagulls. This happened five minutes into the Faroes game when a wildly wayward effort soared over the bar, slammed into a startled bird and fell over a cliff into the sea where it was recovered by a fishing boat.

Another amusing incident in Motherwell's forays to far-flung, exotic places occurred during a cup tie at Arbroath. It was a wild, stormy day and the combination of gales, a high tide and the stadium's misfortune to be perched on the edge of the North Sea resulted in an Arbroath player being drenched by the spray of an incoming wave as he was lining up to take a corner. This was viewed as a natural if rare hazard of the Scottish game, and the referee's decision to abandon the match shortly afterwards was greeted with astonishment and dismay. 'Just for a wee bitty wind, the man's daft in the heid,' was one of the more polite remarks. So it goes.

The glamour clubs and their galaxy of superstars obviously have their place on Planet Football. We all marvel at the skills and artistry of players at the top of their game, even if they are preening peacocks like Ronaldo, seemingly determined to become a parody of himself. But it's on windy days at Arbroath and dark winter nights in Grimsby that roots are nourished which allow stars to flourish at the highest levels.

Increasingly, top clubs are reaping crops of promising youngsters barely more than children to bring through youth ranks, but few make the grade and most end up playing in empty stadiums for youth and reserve squads. For those who don't drift out of the game, their recourse is lower leagues where they can revive their careers and be local heroes to fans as passionate and committed as any in the Premier League.

The purpose of this book is to take readers on a season ticket to sparsely filled grounds where managers and fans are on first-name terms and players join them for a pint after the game. Along the way, I hope to find answers to a couple of questions – how do they survive on shoestring budgets, and for how long? While the big fish funded by billionaires gobble up worldwide television and sponsorship revenues, the minnows scrape along as best they can with crumbs from the Premier League table and the support of local butchers, bakers and candlestick makers. As I write this, Manchester City have just drawn more fans to a home game against Crystal Palace than all of the two dozen clubs in League Two combined to their weekend matches, and any one of City's superstars is paid more in a week than some teams earn in a season.

Inevitably, some clubs sink into the obscurity of non-league, and others simply disappear. I remember witnessing the sad demise of Third Lanark, originally the 3rd Lanarkshire Rifle Volunteers and founder members of the Scottish Football Association, at their last home game at Cathkin Park in Glasgow in 1967. Only four years before, they had beaten Celtic 2-1 to win the Glasgow Cup. Others like Accrington Stanley refuse to die, and against all the odds climb out of administration and the depths of regional leagues to rejoin the professional ranks. How do they do that?

My travels take me inevitably to the cradle and enduring heartland of the game in the North and Midlands of England, which produced the dozen clubs that founded the Football League in Manchester in 1888, the oldest such competition in world football. (Preston North End won the first league title undefeated and completed the first league and cup double by winning the FA Cup.) For me this is a whimsical odyssey to places long known but never explored. I know my way around Beirut, Seoul and Johannesburg, but I'd be hard pressed to find Mansfield and Rochdale on a map. They are in the outer limits of my geographical knowledge, along with Uzbekistan, and have existed since my youth only as names on Football League tables. English fans may have heard of Queen of the South, but ask them to identify and locate the club's hometown and they'd probably struggle (it's Dumfries in the Scottish Borders).

On the way I expect to encounter the homespun wit and wisdom that has enlivened my experience of the game since I was first lifted over the barrier at Fir Park as a wee boy to get in free. I recall years later a comment directed at one of our players, Stevie Kirk, who belonged to the hit-and-miss school of Scottish strikers. After one particularly abysmal miss from point-blank range, he was trotting by the main stand when a chap behind me called out, 'Hey Kirkie, ye're nae mair use than a chocolate fireguard.' It was an inspired metaphor, and to his credit Kirk looked up, smiled and applauded. He was accorded a rousing cheer. Sadly, at the time of writing, the author of this perceptive remark has recently passed away. He was a constant presence in the season ticket holders' section in the main stand, in the row behind me, and every time I look around I still imagine he's there.

In truth, he'll always be there when Saturday comes, rain or shine, supporting a wee club. Just like the rest of us. It's what Saturdays are for.

Accrington Stanley

You never know what happens in football,
it's littered with fairy tales.

Founded:	1893
Ground:	Wham Stadium
Average attendance:	1,979
Honours:	Unibond Premier League champions 2002/03
	Nationwide Conference champions 2005/06

IT IS said they used to make men as hard as the town bricks in Accrington. The bricks were the densest and strongest in the world and you'll find them in the Taj Mahal, the Empire State Building and the base of Blackpool Tower.

Local heroes include the Accrington Pals, otherwise known as the 11th Battalion East Lancashire Regiment, who went over the top in the Battle of the Somme on 1 July 1916. In less than 20 minutes, 235 of them were dead and 350 wounded, half the battalion was wiped out, and it was reported that not a man had wavered or turned back. Images of the smiling pals are prominently displayed on public buildings and an indoor market, ghosts of a proud past long gone along with a weaving industry that was the town's heartbeat. Accrington is a gaunt shadow of its former self. For a sense of pride now it turns to a football team.

I've been here before. A few years ago I came with my dog Patch for a whimsical newspaper series on travels with my dog. At the time, Accrington Stanley were plying their trade in the Unibond Premier League, light years in football terms from a return to the EFL. On a shoestring budget, they might as well have set their sights on reaching Mars.

Aficionados of the game may recall that the original club went bust and disappeared from the old Fourth Division in 1962 with debts of £60,000. But a team with a memorable name and an honourable past as successor to one of the 12 founder members of the Football League in 1888 was too proud to die, and six years later it was reborn in a working men's club and began working its way back up the non-league pyramid.

There was never any doubt that Patch, an enthusiastic cross between Border Collie and black Labrador, was born to be a footballer. The first time he saw a game in a public park, he was on the field in a flash. His pace and ball control were a joy to behold, but his skills were not universally appreciated and at subsequent matches it was decreed that his enthusiasm be restrained by a leash.

His passion for the game was undiminished, however, and it was only a matter of time before we went to watch one of the most famous names in British football in action. On our arrival I bought him an Accy Stan scarf, which he wore with pride and panache as we entered the Crown Ground for a match against Runcorn FC Halton, drawing an approving comment from the terracing: 'Well-dressed dog is that.'

Those were the days when a man and his dog could wander pretty much anywhere they pleased at Conference grounds, so we chose terracing behind the away goal. Patch quickly picked up the pattern of play, rising on hind legs with front paws on an iron rail and barking encouragement whenever Accrington forwards muscled into the Runcorn box. This was warmly appreciated by Accy fans, who suggested that Patch should consider becoming the club's mascot. A novel attraction of the Crown Ground then was pointed out in programme notes in Lancashire vernacular: 'Tha gets good crack and summat time tha con hear cherman swering is head off at corner where bogs are.' True enough, in the second half a strident voice was raised near a corner flag: 'Coom on, wake up ye lazy boogers, get stook in.' It was, as the programme promised, the chairman in full flow. Those were the days.

Accrington Stanley is more than a football club, it is a state of mind and an enduring symbol of northern grit. They call it 'the club that refused to die', and like a phoenix rising from the ashes of a post-industrial wasteland, it fought its way up through regional leagues to come freewheeling back into the English league in 2006. By the time I return they are realistic contenders for reaching the dizzy heights of League One for the first time in their chequered history. It is early in the season, but they are lying third with five wins and a draw in eight matches, and next up is Cheltenham, who are struggling at the other end of the table.

My trip begins unpromisingly when my car breaks down on the M65 a few miles short of Accrington. Fortunately, the sun is shining, and a grassy bank provides safe refuge while I await rescue by the AA. We end up at a nearby garage, where a dreary conversation about the unfathomable mysteries of modern car mechanics turns to football. The proprietor used to support Blackburn, but says he stopped going to games in the 1980s because of violence on the terracing. He recalls police having the bright idea of ordering fans to remove the laces of Doc Marten boots to curb fighting, and to prevent culprits fleeing from the boys in blue. Apparently, this did not prevent nutters from throwing darts in the direction of rival fans. I am shocked by the painful images, but he says, 'Don't worry, times have changed. At Stanley they'd have been more likely to be throwing paper aeroplanes anyway.'

I am pleased to find my guest house is little more than a paper plane flight from Stanley's ground, renamed Wham Stadium after the main business of the club's major shareholder and benefactor Andy Holt, which is plastic home accessories and storage boxes. I suppose you could call him the plastic box king of Lancashire.

The stadium is only a few minutes' walk from the town centre in a neighbourhood of solid, suburban terraced houses lining the main road to Clayton-le-Moors, so I begin with a stroll downtown. The club's sobriquet about refusing to die could apply to the town, but the team seems to be faring better than its home. Textile mills that once echoed to the clatter of 14,000 weaving looms are long gone, along with engineering works that supplied the machinery, and the community that sustained and relied on them is threadbare. High street chains have deserted shopping centres and only Costa Coffee and Sports Direct survive in a sad array of Poundlands, charity stores and betting shops. 'The town is on its arse,' Andy Holt tells me later with northern bluntness.

The *Accrington Observer* reports that a factory outlet clearing old stock – any three items for a fiver, including boots worth £50 – was forced to close after hundreds of 'frenzied' bargain hunters cleared the shelves. It looks as if the town centre itself is in a clearance sale.

Cutting its cloth for straitened times, Accrington has reverted to old ways, with local suppliers trading in basic necessities rather than designer fashions. Some have stalls in the Market Hall, a Victorian masterpiece of lofty glass ceilings and ornate wrought-iron pillars filled with light and memories of a prosperous past. When it opened in 1868, proud civic officials proclaimed it 'A building second to none in England for beauty and design', and one of the speakers expressed the hope that it would 'save many a life, preventing them from getting cold'.

It is a blustery day in late September, and I'm grateful for the warmth of the bustling emporium as I wander around shops and stalls selling everything from meat and veg to furniture, pet supplies, wool, old-fashioned sweeties and golf shirts for a fiver. There is a sense of stepping back in time to a slower-paced era before supermarket checkout tills, when service was more personal and there was always time for a chat with a butcher about his sausages and a greengrocer about her fresh sprouts. I'm enjoying the illusion of time travel, heightened by a one-room 'Heritage Museum' with a random collection of old domestic bits and bobs including a display of antique glass bottles and china collected by 'Jim Whittaker, Bottleologist (*talks can be arranged*)'. Next door the football club has a small store staffed by an elderly couple selling an array of red and white shirts, scarves and hats, and a treasure trove of matchday programmes for diehard fans. I emerge from this Aladdin's cave of souvenirs and memorabilia with a pen inscribed with the club's name for the princely sum of £1.

In the Accrington Pals Café a few steps away, beneath a huge Union Jack, hang photographs of the pals marching to the front and sheltering in trenches from shellfire, and of German soldiers manning a machine gun that probably dispatched many of them. The images are a stark reminder of the insanity and futility of a war fuelled by the patriotic frenzy of adjacent posters declaring: 'Women of Britain say GO!'

For light relief I stroll next door to the council information office to enquire whether there are any sights worth seeing. 'Tourism has died a bit of a death to be honest,' the lady behind the desk says. 'We don't even have a town guide.' They do, however, have interesting souvenirs. In a glass case there are slate coasters, one of which is inscribed with the legend 'Lancashire born and bred so tek mi' s thi' find mi' or bugger off!' Nice one for a guest house window I'd have thought.

Among brochures extolling the delights of Blackpool, Burnley and Morecambe, I find a leaflet for the Accrington Acorn Trail, a stroll around neighbouring streets of handsome Victorian buildings that have mostly survived the ravages of time and economic decline. The former Conservative Club, bastion of wealthy mill owners and landed gentry in a dyed-in-the-wool, working-class town, is not among them. Marble pillars still adorn the club's grand entrance beneath the imperial mantra *Dieu et Mon Droit* carved in stone, but the front door and windows are gaping wounds exposing a roofless ruin of smashed stones and timber evocative of a World War Two air raid. Around the corner the erstwhile Manchester and Liverpool Bank proudly bears the cities' elaborate coats of arms, but it's up for sale and overshadowed by the sweeping, futuristic lines of a glass and concrete supermarket across the road. It looks like a giant spaceship landed from planet Asda.

I stroll back up the road for a pint and a fish supper in the Crown pub at the entrance to the Wham Stadium, a venerable watering hole for Accy fans and weekend pilgrims from lower league citadels as distant as Crewe and Crawley. No club scarves or emblems adorn the walls, ensuring a neutral venue for visiting supporters who are as welcome in the pub as they are in the ground next door. It's midweek and there are no fans in evidence, but a woman who sees me reading a Stanley FC leaflet volunteers, 'You can go anywhere and say you're from Accrington, and they say "Accrington Stanley".'

Her husband nods his head in agreement: 'That's right, no matter where you go.' And they're quietly proud of it.

Malcolm Isherwood is the kind of supporter any club would love to have. A retired gas fitter, he is a lifelong Accy fan and former chairman of the supporters' club. Attending matches with his mates are social occasions, and the chances of him supporting Premiership neighbours Burnley or Man Utd are on a par with Cristiano Ronaldo signing for Scunthorpe. I first met Malcolm in the Unibond Premier days, when returning to the EFL was an improbable dream. His parting comment then was: 'We're just like lots of little clubs with big ambitions. A lot of it's dreams, they might never happen, but you can always hope.'

When we meet again in the club's Founder Members Lounge he says realising the dream hasn't changed the ethos of the team. 'We've moved on thanks to chairmen that have invested a lot of time and money in the club, but we've still got the non-league spirit,' he says. 'We're a good family club, everybody says we're friendly.'

We are sitting in red leatherette chairs embossed with the club badge, surrounded by framed shirts of the founding members of the English league signed by current and past players. Beside Accrington are the shirts of Aston Villa, Blackburn, Bolton, Burnley, Derby, Everton, Notts County, Preston, Stoke, West Brom and Wolves, all of them from the Midlands and North of England. All of them are from the working-class roots of the game when legions of flat-capped men crowded terracing in all weathers to cheer local heroes who earned no more than them. It is a modest lounge for club staff with a small bar in one corner and not much else. When I meet the team manager later he describes it cheerfully as a glorified portacabin.

Over cups of tea Malcolm recalls the days when the previous chairman went around turning off lights to save money. 'We had lads in the past playing with curfew tags, you could see them above their socks. Now we can afford to give decent players two-year contracts, but it's still a small club, you feel part of it. Matchdays are social events. You don't just turn up at quarter to three and go home at five, you come early to meet friends and stay afterwards in the club sports bar and the Crown. Win or lose, it's always a good day out.'

He has brought along Peter Leatham, a company manager and his successor as supporters' club chairman, and Rob Houseman the supporters' liaison officer, who earns his living as a supply teacher. Last time I was here Rob had just won himself a bride after taking his girlfriend to a Unibond away game at Pickering. After the match he asked her to say slowly the name of the team they had just played. 'Pick-a-ring,' she said. So she did, they were wed a few months later and Kerry was named Accy Stan female supporter of the year. His second favourite memory was when Stanley beat Gateshead at home in 1992: 'I remember crying because it was the first time we'd qualified for the first round of the FA Cup.' He was 21 at the time.

Rob stresses there's more to the club than football. 'We have a social responsibility, we have to look at social deprivation and help get kids off the streets. It's fine having the community working for the club, but the club has to work for the community.' The talk is of how to aim higher with the lowest attendances of the 92 members of the Football League. The club lost a generation of supporters when it disappeared for six years in the 1960s, and their last home league match on a Tuesday night against Grimsby drew a meagre crowd of 1,288. 'If 70,000 didn't turn up for Man Utd it would make no difference to them because of corporate revenues and sponsorship, but if a hundred don't come here it affects us,' Malcolm says. A vital source of funds is the transfer market. 'We can't sell players for a million, but a youngster rising up through the leagues can be worth a lot with sell-on clauses and add-ons. We sold a teenage lad to Blackburn for a pittance, but he's moved on to Bournemouth and earning thousands for us in appearance money.' In the close season three players stepped up leagues with transfers to Barnsley, Bradford and Shrewsbury. 'They didn't say what we got for them, but it'll be a lot of money for Stanley.'

There is a sense that Accrington Stanley is the epitome of northern soul with a gritty determination to survive against the odds. I am warming to a club that fosters companionship and romance, and makes grown men cry, and it seems fitting the badge on the shirts is the town crest bearing the motto *Industry and Prudence Conquer.*

Honest endeavour on the field and careful husbandry off it by successive benevolent major shareholders are key to Stanley's survival. Promotion and financial stability have allowed the club to offer players decent contracts, and Peter says, 'It means we're not at the beck and call of big clubs any more, we don't have to lose players for next to nothing. Now we only sell for the right reasons, for the club and the player.'

Peter is the most recent convert, having been a season-ticket holder at Bolton until a friend brought him to a match at Accrington. 'I found I was enjoying myself more here, so I gave up my Bolton ticket and I've been here ever since, I'm happy to say. As an outsider, I can say this town doesn't realise how lucky it is to have this football club.'

The conversation with the three Accy Stan stalwarts is like banter among pundits on *Match of the Day*, each adding pithy comments on the merits of their club: 'At big clubs you're just a number ... It's loyalty, there's not a lot of it in football ... the atmosphere's good, the players like it here, the crowd's very friendly and never get on their backs ... the manager keeps developing the squad, young lads come to Accrington because they know they'll be given a chance, more than at Man Utd.'

A recurring theme is that manager John Coleman insists on a passing game instead of hopeful punts up the field. 'Coleman has them playing decent football, so clubs are happy to loan us players because they'll be schooled in the right way ... the loan system is very important to us, we have a strong bench at the moment.' In fact, eight of the 22-strong first-team squad are on loan from the likes of Brighton, Hull City and Sheffield Wednesday, and from what I see of them playing a couple of days later they are enjoying being here. Only one player cost a transfer fee, a midfielder signed from non-league Southport for the princely sum of £7,500. But progress has its drawbacks. Malcolm laments that opposing fans are segregated under league rules that didn't apply in the days of non-league football, and Rob reminds me of the day I brought Patch to a Unibond game. Now he says four-legged supporters are no longer permitted – league rules again.

There have been improvements to the stadium since I was here last, but it's not quite Old Trafford. A guided tour begins with a visit to the boardroom, a small, sparsely furnished office with a few trophies on a sideboard. 'These are mostly trophies we've given ourselves,' Rob admits. The only one the team actually won is Unibond Premier champions 2002/03. Others include one inscribed 'Norway Supporters Club competition winners 1993', but Rob's not sure what it was for. 'We get a lot of fans from Scandinavia and Holland who come over to watch Liverpool on Saturday and then us if we're playing on Sunday. They drink a lot.' The idea of Accrington Stanley fans in Bergen and Rotterdam is not as far-fetched as it sounds. When the supporters' club organised a fundraising drive for a new scoreboard and video screen, donations flowed in from Australia, the US, Spain, Italy, France and Norway. This is a club that captures the heart at home and the imagination away.

When the foreign legions arrive, they enter the smallest stadium in league football, capacity 5,057, with views over hills and woodland. Seats were installed throughout the ground to comply with FA regulations when Stanley entered League Two, but the fans were not impressed and terracing with metal barriers was restored behind the goals after they voted for it. Malcolm supposes they were given permission in view of plans to build a new 1,500-seat stand opposite the main stand. This is known as the Whinney Hill side, where Rob informs me one of the largest rubbish tips in Europe lies over the hill in a disused brickworks. 'People come from all over the North West to dump rubbish there,' he says and I detect a hint of pride. Fortunately, it is a calm day with no ill winds. Malcolm says it's mainly away fans who want seats because presently they are allocated terracing open to the elements. 'Can't say I blame them,' he says. 'Last time Grimsby came here midweek they got soaked. I wouldn't want to drive home to Grimsby at night wet through.'

Needless to say, there are no fancy airs and graces at the Wham Stadium. The prawn sandwich brigade at Old Trafford scorned by Roy Keane would be an alien species here. The directors don't presume to have their own box and place their rear ends on the same red plastic chairs as everyone else, with only a striped ribbon denoting the section reserved for them and VIP guests. Like any self-respecting club, Accrington has an 'ultras' section that goes to every match, home and away, enlivening proceedings with chants of 'Come on ye Reds' to a steady drumbeat. Rob confides, 'They were louder when they were younger, but they're a bit older now, they've got families.'

Visiting teams are not afforded luxuries in a basic changing room with plywood walls, four showers and a single toilet. Modern leisure centres have better facilities, and Malcolm says it's best not to test the plumbing by using the showers and the toilet at the same time. 'We don't want to make them too comfortable,' he says. The home dressing room isn't much better.

A couple of first-team players are coming to the club sports bar tonight for a question and answer session with the supporters' club, and I'm invited. In the meantime, scurrying clouds threatening rain have gone so I go for a walk to the club's birthplace.

Accrington FC was founded in 1878 when a bunch of lads from around Stanley Street got together in a nearby hotel and formed a team nicknamed 'Th' Owd Reds'. Ten years later they were invited to join the newly formed Football League, where they played for five seasons until they went bankrupt and were reincarnated in the Accrington & District League under their present name. The place where it all began still bears the name 'The Black Horse', but now it's a coffee shop and 'food emporium' popular with ladies of the town. A plaque by the front door proclaims it is where the forerunner of 'the world famous Accrington Stanley' was founded, and inside there are images of teams from the 1950s wearing collared rugby-style shirts and big leather boots.

Stanley Street probably hasn't changed much since then. There is a supermarket at the bottom of the street, and rows of red brick and stone houses slanting up a hillside are festooned with television aerials and satellite dishes, but they would be instantly recognisable to lads who kicked around balls with cans and clothes as goalposts in streets empty of cars a century ago.

But time has taken its toll. Since my last visit the corner butty shop has gone, and Stanley Social Club is boarded up and for sale. The HQ of the Accrington Detachment of the Lancashire Cadet Force looks forlorn and abandoned, with metal grilles on its windows. A de facto *Upstairs, Downstairs* scenario seems to have evolved, with the lower end of the street showing signs of weariness and decay, while houses higher up appear better cared for, with smartly painted windows and doors, some with small gardens filled with flowers. I am reminded of Motherwell after its steelworks closed, a working-class town with not much work to be had, but where a wee boy felt safe in familiar streets with corner shops where people looked out for each other. I feel as if I'm rediscovering my roots, and I'm enjoying the experience.

At the top of Stanley Street, town gives way to country in Peel Park, a wooded hillside and open grassland of 100 acres dominated by a viewpoint called the Coppice, where the Accrington Pals trained before being sent to the hellfire of the Western Front. It is a delightful tangle of deciduous woodland, ferns and mosses, where orchids and wild primrose grow and sparrow hawks and tawny owls nest. Braving blustery weather, joggers and dog walkers offer greetings on footpaths that meander by rows of lime trees to a hay meadow and the Coppice, where you can see forever.

On maps, Accrington is sandwiched unpromisingly between Burnley and Blackburn in a tangle of motorways in east Lancashire. What the maps don't show is a small town in a green valley, with a canal running through it, surrounded by hills and moors and great country pubs. Up on the Coppice I am deep in hill country framing the town crouching darkly in the Hyndburn valley, its uniform rows of terraced houses like ranks of soldiers drawn up on a parade ground, the regiments that manned clattering mills now silent and empty. Glistening beneath wintry sunshine and passing showers, it is a quintessential panorama of northern life worthy of a poet or a landscape painter. In its industrial heyday it would have been a living Lowry painting. A few chimney stacks still stand like gaunt tombstones of the era when the town helped to build the Taj Mahal and the Empire State Building.

Scots may be bemused to learn the town also boasts what is claimed to be the oldest civilian pipe band in the UK and reputedly the world, formed in 1885 in an ex-serviceman's club by a local gamekeeper and a man from Stanley Street, whose pipers and drummers wore doublets fashioned from billiard table cloth. They still perform every year at the Royal British Legion's Remembrance Day parade in Accrington and Skipton Christmas markets. This is also the town that invented snooker tables and floating soap, and produced the composer Harrison Birtwistle, the runner Ron Hill, and a couple of *Coronation Street* actors who probably felt at home on the TV film set.

In the middle distance Wham Stadium is a postage stamp field of dreams. Previously Stanley played at Peel Park, where a photograph taken in 1921 shows a huge crowd of men standing around an open ground bordered by farmland. I am reminded of a comment by Malcolm: 'People forget we started from a field, there weren't even a rope round it.' In 1954 a friendly against Blackburn attracted a record crowd of 17,634 to Peel Park – more than three times the current stadium capacity. The town's future may be uncertain, but with brave men, hard bricks and passion for football it has history.

It is Thursday evening and about 30 supporters have gathered in the sports bar to meet two recent first-team recruits. They all seem to know each other, and it's like a family gathering to welcome home prodigal sons.

Malcolm insists on buying me a beer and the barman pulls a pint of Hen Harrier from Bowland Brewery. 'It's a good beer is this, we go through two barrels on matchdays,' he says.

Peter is in the chair and introduces Kayden Jackson, a striker signed from Barnsley after a loan spell at

Grimsby, and centre-back Ben Richards-Everton, who left Dunfermline in the summer with a knee injury.

Ben is asked if the game is more physical in Scotland. He reckons it's more physical in England because there aren't many players his size and physique north of the border. He's a big strapping lad is Ben, a traditional centre-half. He raises a laugh when asked what level Stanley would be at in Scotland, and he says, 'SPL of course,' though it's probably not far from the truth.

A wee boy who has to stand on a chair to be seen asks who their favourite players are. Ben says Rio Ferdinand and Kayden says Thierry Henry, but he'll never forget the day he was on the same pitch as Gareth Bale when Swindon played Spurs in a pre-season friendly. 'I just got a few minutes on the field, but to be on it with him was amazing. I'll probably never get the chance to play against a player like that again, it was like a dream.'

The boy wants to know if they like the manager and his assistant Jimmy Bell. Kayden says, 'They're straightforward. From the first day you know what you'll get from them, and I believe under the gaffer and Jimmy we'll be playing in League One next season.' Ben agrees: 'Their philosophy and the way they want us to play is good. No reason we can't get promoted. We can't underestimate any team but we've got nothing to fear from any team in the league, even in the big games against Luton and Mansfield.'

This is what the supporters want to hear and there is a buzz of expectation. Bring on League One Wigans and Scunthorpes is the mood.

'The team spirit is massive,' Ben says. 'Some teams have cliques but here everyone just gets on. Come Saturday we never fall out.' His best moment so far? 'Mansfield came out with a big fancy coach and dozens of staff and we turned them over and sent them on their way, it was great.' Stanley's facilities may be modest, but Kayden feels at home: 'I enjoy the pitch and the changing rooms, it's got a family feel about it.'

When the meeting breaks up I have a chat with Kayden, who tells me he got into the game when he won a football talent competition on Facebook that led to a contract with Swindon, followed by moves to Wrexham and Barnsley, with loan spells at Oxford and Grimsby. A lean, whippet-like 23-year-old with a turn of speed, he's happy to be where he is. 'Obviously we're not the biggest club, it is what it is. I think a lot of people turn up their noses at the ground and facilities, but for young lads it's a great opportunity to play league football. Most lads where I come from never get that chance.'

He was brought up in a Bradford council estate where he says it's hard to find work and lads end up involved in 'illegal stuff'. 'I'm lucky. I feel valued by the gaffer and the fans have been great, they always support you home and away. We know we're playing for a small club, but everyone thrives on it. I just want to repay them by scoring goals.'

So far he has been as good as his word, forming an effective partnership with top scorer Billy Kee, notching seven goals himself in ten matches and earning a nomination for League Two Player of the Month. Kayden comes across as a modest young man who loves the game and appreciates the support of those who help him play it, a credit to the values of his club.

Friday morning and I'm back at the club in the hope of meeting manager John Coleman. His assistant Jimmy Bell is in the Founder Members Lounge with a member of the coaching staff, watching a video of tomorrow's opponents Cheltenham on a laptop, analysing their play. Close attention is paid to their movement at corners and set pieces, and tactics to counter them.

I'm invited to join them and the conversation turns to poor attendances. Jimmy says he'd like to know where all the supporters have gone since the 1960s when the club went out of business for six years. The simple answer is that Burnley is six miles in one direction and Blackburn five miles in the other, and Man Utd's Theatre of Dreams is barely half an hour down the M66. In six years it's easy to form an allegiance to another club.

'Going out of business was massive,' he admits. 'But the town is poor, a lot of shops have closed, and people can't afford £15 or £20 to watch a game. It's cheaper to go down the pub and watch the big guns on Sky, and I don't blame them.'

Paradoxically he believes lack of support works in their favour: 'At least there's not a lot of pressure from them. With more fans come higher expectations. If we get promoted the games will be bigger and better supported, but I don't think the club will change our mentality. We're always striving to be better and we use the underdog mentality as a tool. We're like the mindset of Mourinho, who's managed the best teams in the world, it's us against the world.'

A stocky, middle-aged man walks in from the boardroom towards the bar and calls, 'Jimmy, does your pal want a cuppa?' This is my introduction to manager John Coleman, who brings me a cup of tea. Like Jimmy, he's a veteran of non-league football, a prolific striker who scored 200 goals for Morecambe in the Northern Premier and Conference leagues. He first came to Accrington as manager in 1999 and stayed for 13 years before committing what he calls an error of judgement. 'I went to Rochdale thinking it was a step up, but it wasn't.' After spells at Southport and in Ireland with Sligo he got the call to come back to Accrington in 2014 and he jumped at it. It was like coming home: 'When I came back here at first we had crowds of 300 and I probably knew a hundred of them.'

He points out that at bigger clubs you don't get to have a pint with supporters after the game, and he says he and Jimmy have been to more than one fan's funeral. The rewards of his job are sparse given the club's limited resources, but Coleman is aiming high. 'Every year we emphasise promotion. We never put a ceiling on ambitions, and in the short term we'll definitely get into League One. You never know what happens in football, it's littered with fairy tales.'

His other ambition is to take the club to Wembley – Accrington is the only club in the English leagues along with Crawley Town that has never played in the national stadium. 'It would be nice to get to Wembley before Crawley, I must admit. Reaching the play-offs this season is a realistic prospect. There's never been a better time to be at Accrington on and off the pitch. We've got a good squad and ongoing ground improvements, everything's going forward.'

All this with players' wages that are the second lowest in the league in relation to turnover, which is an improvement. Last season they were the lowest. 'I pay the lads what we can and I'd like to pay them more, but if the chairman told me we could pay them £5,000 a week I wouldn't want to, because then they'd not be playing for the club, just for the wages.'

It is heartening to hear this take on club loyalty in an era of agents tearing up contracts and millionaire mercenaries switching clubs for astronomical salaries.

Coleman has been offered jobs in League One but says leaving would be disloyal to his players. If ever a big club came in for him he believes he could leave with the blessing of the chairman, but in the meantime he savours memories that will never fade. The day Stanley beat Farsley Celtic in the Unibond Premier in the last game of the season in the spring of 1999 didn't feature on Sky Sports or *Match of the Day*, but for Coleman it was one of those football fairy tales. Stanley had been 17th in the league at Christmas but a good run had taken them to a game away from promotion. 'If we drew or lost we'd be third, but a win would take us up to the Conference. It was all or nothing. A lot of other teams were wanting us to lose. It was a sunny day, I was player-manager and I scored and we won. It doesn't get any better.'

Stanley has another claim to fame, as the only club in all of the English leagues without its own training facilities. Today they are preparing for the Cheltenham game with a workout on a plastic pitch at a local leisure centre and Coleman takes me along. Fortunately it's not raining.

The players are in high spirits and there's much laughter in one-touch passing warm-up drills, while Coleman tests his keeper with shots from outside the box. He still knows where the goals are, sending in full-blooded drives that produce flying saves and I have to duck to avoid being decapitated by a rare miss.

There is another spectator, retired lorry driver and Accy fan Callan Killeya, who often attends training sessions. 'You can't just turn up and watch players at Man City, can you?' he says. 'This is a good friendly club, they have time for you and the players speak to you, they don't look at you as if you're stupid.' On cue Ben Richards-Everton trots by and my companion asks him how the injury's going. 'Injury's 90 per cent there, I'll be back soon,' he says. Echoing an earlier comment by the manager, Callan says, 'The players we have want to play football, they're not just here for the wages, and they're doing grand. Be alright if the season ended now.'

On the field the laughing has stopped and a practice game is underway. It is fast-paced football with a repertoire of tricks and flicks, dummies and defence-splitting passes, with time and confidence to occasionally put a foot on the ball. Long balls are few and far between and as often as not find their man. Jimmy is in charge of the match, barking instructions on positional play while Coleman supervises from the sidelines. It is easy to see why the John and Jimmy double act is popular with fans. They are likeable characters, plain-speaking aficionados of the game who know it inside out from non-league grassroots where they forged their playing and management careers. I'm looking forward to tomorrow.

Saturday dawns bright and blustery, the kind of weather that's as unpredictable as the match. It would be misleading to say the town is buzzing in anticipation of the game. If it wasn't for a few flyers advertising it you'd never know it was on. So I go for another walk before lunch.

In the nearby hamlet of Church, a footpath leads past a 15th-century church with a medieval tower to the Leeds and Liverpool canal, where its halfway point is marked with Victorian precision on a white stone inscribed 'Leeds 63⅝ miles'. I am greeted by a noisy gaggle of ducks on the canal bank, and an equally gregarious bunch of cyclists out for a morning spin. They call out cheery greetings in impenetrable accents, the cyclists that is, and I don't understand a word.

Here the distance between town and country is the width of the canal. One side is dominated by industrial skeletons, textile mills crumbling into dereliction, and the other opens out to a patchwork of fields and common land grazed by horses, cows and a few bored-looking goats. At this point the towpath crosses a long-distance cycle route that passes over an old stone bridge and by a dilapidated farmhouse, heading invitingly for the hills. I find myself wishing I was on my bike.

Instead I stroll along a footpath by the canal, where I jogged with Patch years before. It's not the same without him; I still miss my faithful companion and best pal trotting beside me and barking encouragement at the Crown Ground. So as I meander along I have an imaginary chat with him about the fun we had then. Dog lovers, as daft as football fans.

The canal is a conduit through the past and present of the industrial heartland of England. Among the reeds and rushes I pause to admire hand-crafted Victorian stonework on quays and bridges, built on a scale and with artistic flourishes barely conceivable today. Long-abandoned mills and brick factories loom out of early morning mist, silent memorials to an industrial revolution that ran out of steam, but in their own way works of stark architectural beauty. Where steamers once plied their trade in textiles and coal, I pass only a couple of fishermen trying their luck with rod and line. In spring and summer the canal comes alive with swans and butterflies among banks of meadowsweet and willow herb, and gaily painted barges bedecked in flowers and proclaiming where they come from in ornate letters. Last time I was here cyclists were obligingly opening swing bridges for *The Great Escape* from Barnsley. But now it's autumn, the skies are clouding over, and kick-off is approaching.

By one o'clock the Crown is filling up with Accy Stan scarves and yellow shirts of Cheltenham, all sitting together and chatting amiably about past games, players' performances and prospects. The Robins have come a long way, but they're on home ground here among kindred spirits who share a love of lower league football with all its crazy ups and downs. It reminds me of Ayrshire poet Rabbie Burns's eulogy to the brotherhood of man:

'... *Man to Man, the world o'er,*
Shall brothers be for a' that ...'

Admittedly it was written before local mini civil wars between Kilmarnock FC and Ayr United.

Outside the ground I find Malcolm selling pin badges, and he points to a man in a woolly jumper, jeans and trainers. 'You might want to have a word with 'im, he's our MP.' Graham Jones, MP for Hyndburn constituency, says his family has been in the area for a century or more and are 'Accrington through and through'. But when he was a boy in the 60s Stanley didn't exist, so he went to Blackburn. 'It just goes to show that when a club dies, the consequences last for decades. People here come to odd games, but they've already pledged allegiance to other clubs,' he says sadly.

When Stanley was revived he came back and now he has a season ticket, though parliamentary duties prevent him from using it as often as he'd like. 'The future looks promising,' he says. 'The new owner is making every effort to make the club more successful. I'm optimistic, there is a fondness for Accrington Stanley, and whether or not it's based on nostalgia, it's famous worldwide. People have an affinity for the club and are proud of it, the challenge is to translate that into financial support.'

In the new fan zone, basically a covered catering section round the back of the William Dyer Electrical stand at the Clayton End, Ken Jefferson is doing his best to help fill club coffers by selling tickets for supporters' buses to away games at Port Vale and Forest Green. He has a steady stream of customers and hopes to send a couple of coaches to Forest's home in the Cotswolds next weekend. They manage to get to most games, and six coaches went to the Olympic Stadium in London last season for a League Cup tie with West Ham, which Accy only lost 1-0 with the last kick of the game.

I pick up a programme and find the anonymous author of *The Stanley Scene* is in a buoyant metaphorical mood: 'Once again under the guidance of John & Jimmy and the staff, the good ship expectation has set sail and we hope to dock in faraway places in early May. There will undoubtedly be choppy waters along our route but with our current captain at the helm, and with his capable lieutenants alongside, we appear to be set fair for a decent trip.' Beat that, Chelsea fanzine.

In 'Coley's Comments', the manager is upbeat: 'I think we've got strength in depth now ... it's going to be tough to pick a bench, let alone a starting XI ... as I say time and time again I will back this side on our home ground to give anybody a hard time.' Fighting talk from a wee team punching above its weight is what the fans want to hear, and hopes are high for today's game. The last time the two clubs met, Cheltenham came out on top 3-0, but now they're at opposite ends of the table, with Stanley third from top and Cheltenham fourth from bottom, and the home side starts 6/5 favourites.

The programme also has news that newly formed Accrington Stanley Girls & Ladies FC got off to a flying start in their first-ever league match by thumping Barrowford Celtic 13-0, including three hat-tricks. And the club's community trust is celebrating its seventh anniversary, having raised £2 million from the Premier League, National Lottery, Sport England and others for projects engaging 10,000 local folk in sports, health, social inclusion and education. At the last count more than 400 adults were playing in its seven-a-side football tournaments, and walking football for over-50s is proving popular. The town may be 'on its arse', as the chairman succinctly puts it, but it has a football club doing its best to lift it up.

I meet club secretary Mark Turner rummaging around electrical equipment in a shed, hoping he has enough power for the floodlights. It's still early in the season and the lights may not be needed, but the dark days of mid-winter are approaching. I ask if he's worried. 'Very,' he admits. It's ten minutes to kick-off, the skies are darkening and he is aware that beer pumps in the new fan zone and the electronic scoreboard are drawing power from a limited electricity supply. Chances are if he has to switch on the lights, and a player comes off early and switches on an electric shower in the changing rooms, the lights will fail. Last season one pylon failed before a match, and when Mark went to investigate he found a youth player who had joined the warm-up having a shower. 'Poor lad didn't know what he were doing, I just got him out of it quick.' Welcome to life in League Two.

When electricity was installed in the Crown Ground in the 1970s, nobody dreamed the club, then toiling in the Lancashire Combination, would reach the giddy heights of the EFL and need more than 200 amps to power floodlights and heat the pies. 'If you'd thought then we'd be in the Football League, the men in white coats would've taken you away,' Mark says. Now he says Accrington's rise up the league has drawn scouts from Hibs and Motherwell to today's game.

The ground is filling up but there are spaces in the terracing and the shed opposite the main stand, and the Robins have brought only about 100 fans, scattered on terracing behind the goal they are attacking in the first half. Malcolm has insisted on buying me a ticket and we sit together in the main stand, so close to the pitch we can hear every grunt and crunching tackle.

Cheltenham start well and the game is evenly balanced with chances at both ends, belying the contrasting league positions. The ball is played mostly on the deck with hardly any long balls or speculative punts and the crowd is appreciative, applauding every good pass, move and tackle.

'He's doin' alright is the lad,' goes a chorus of approval. 'They're playin' fast, that's what John wants.' From his demeanour it's not clear whether the manager is satisfied. In contrast with Cheltenham gaffer Gary Johnson, animatedly urging on his side from the touchline, Coleman is relaxed, arms folded, leaning on a barrier and watching impassively. Neither manager has the luxury of a sheltered dugout.

Eventually there is a lull in the action, prompting a disparaging comment from the row behind me: 'I could've been gardening this afternoon.' But Stanley are gradually gaining control of the midfield, and on the half-hour mark midfielder Liam Nolan rouses the crowd when he unleashes a ferocious strike from 20 yards that crashes off the bar. In the stand behind the Cheltenham goal the Accy 'ultras' are in full cry, filling the air with 'Come on ye Reds' to a rousing drumbeat. A few minutes later they're silenced when Cheltenham open the scoring against the run of play with a scrappy goal in their first real attempt on target. Within two minutes Accy are level when Kayden Jackson latches on to a through ball and fires low and hard past the keeper. It is a goal worthy of the Premier League, and Accy should have gone ahead before half-time when another well-timed pass splits the Cheltenham defence, but the ball is blasted over from point-blank range. I have been to matches where such profligacy raises loud queries about the legitimacy of a player's birth, but all I hear is, 'Brilliant move, he were very unlucky wi' that.' When the half-time whistle blows someone says, 'We could be three up, couldn't we?' and receives a pragmatic northern response: 'It is what it is.'

Malcolm says, 'There's no animosity, you haven't seen a policeman, have you?' League rules insist the game must be policed by stewards, but most of them appear to be huddled in a corner chatting and watching the game. Security duties here must be the least demanding in professional football.

Malcolm and I repair to the sports bar for a pint, where it seems word of my presence has spread. 'Are you the writer?' a man asks. This is Accy fan Rick Gater, who tells me a tale of good fortune, and the rewards of supporting a team that values its fans. After helping to sponsor the new scoreboard, he won a club competition that made him 'director for the day' for an away match at Chesterfield. This involved travelling with the team, a three-course meal with drinks before the match, and a seat in the directors' box. He was allowed to bring along his father-in-law, and together they had fish and chips at half-time, and more drinks after the match. 'It were brilliant,' Rick says. 'We won and the lads were singing on the way back, and we had Dominos pizzas on the bus, and John and Jimmy invited us for a drink when we got back. We love it here, they look after you.'

Malcolm is upbeat as the game resumes. 'Don't think we're playing that bad really, we're just not finishing them off.' And they don't, in a second-half, midfield battle full of honest endeavour largely devoid of goalmouth incidents. Unlike at bigger grounds, the crowd doesn't become restive and even an opposition move gets credit where due: 'Good ball lad, brilliant ball,' Malcolm says. 'To be fair they're not a long-ball team this lot, they're trying to play football.' Evidently, I'm among fans who appreciate decent football, no matter who is playing it. There is no industrial language, and the harshest criticism is directed at a winger who balloons a cross high over the heads of assembled strikers in the box: 'Oh come on, they've got red shirts on, they're not hard to identify, are they?' An abysmal miss is greeted with 'Good gracious!' and a crunching late tackle by a Cheltenham defender elicits only a mild rebuke: 'Stupid person.'

With 20 minutes to go Malcolm says, 'There's a case for putting McLeod on, he's got a bit of pace.' Coleman must have heard him as two minutes later the pacey winger is on and promptly overruns the ball with his first touch, prompting amused calls of 'take 'im off'. The game ends 1-1, and Malcolm concludes, 'That was one of our poorer displays.' The man behind me who had been thinking of gardening is philosophical: 'Oh well, I suppose if you can't win you have to make sure you don't lose.' The players are cheered off the field and striker Billy Kee gets special plaudits: 'Unlucky Billy, well played, well worked Billy lad.' Kee promptly trots over to say thanks and ruffle the hair of a young admirer.

Back in the bar Malcolm spots somebody he knows and calls out, 'Andy, will you have a word wi' Gavin, he's writing a book about us.' Andy Holt, major shareholder and bankroller of Stanley, is what you'd expect from a northern businessman, straight-talking and canny with his money but generous when he wants to be. Deep pockets, a big heart and an irrational devotion to a plucky underdog in league football make a powerful force for progress. The story goes that he used to have a box at Old Trafford, when he was invited to Accrington for a pre-season friendly against Burnley, and the bar ran out of beer because the brewery hadn't been paid. 'He likes a drink, does Andy,' Malcolm had said. A conversation took place and since then it's reckoned he has spent well over a million on the club. 'He liked the club and he got involved right away. It were a good day for us.'

Holt is no dreamer with fanciful ambitions for Stanley. Having built a successful business in plastic boxes, construction and other enterprises, he is determined to keep a tight rein on finances. 'We work to a budget,' he says. 'We're not in debt and I don't borrow. It's important not to grow too fast or too big. We've got to be sustainable or we'll go bust again, and that won't happen as long as I'm here.'

I ask why he decided to help the club, and he says bluntly, 'Somebody had to, they couldn't pay the wages.' Now they can, and are enjoying better facilities, including an impeccable new pitch with improved drainage. Plans are well advanced for the new stand and increased electricity capacity, and the word is that Holt has bought land from a farmer that would do nicely for a training ground. But much remains to be done. He admits that if they put the sprinklers on at half-time the showers probably wouldn't work, and Malcolm says flushing the changing room toilets has much the same effect.

So what does Holt get out of it? He says there's no answer to that, and then provides one: 'It's a great club, but it's not just a club, it's a community. Accrington isn't known for much else. I'll tell you what I get out of it, I get a lot of pride and job satisfaction. It's like when you plant bulbs in the garden in January, you get a good feeling when the flowers come out in March. It's summat I can do.'

Planting the seeds of revival in an economically depressed community requires careful husbandry. Holt is incredulous that a non-league club recently offered one of his players £2,300 a week. 'It's reckless,' he says. He confides that Accrington's first-team squad is paid a total of £15,000 a week, and says, 'We played Middlesbrough in a cup game and they didn't have a player earning less than that.'

He is particularly proud of the club's community involvement: 'There's no other way a thousand people can get together every other week for a drink and a chat, and we have a real good mixture of young and old. It's about dealing with social isolation and getting people out of houses. There's so many things about the club you don't see. Man United's community is the world, ours is Accrington.' A passing fan pats him on the back and says, 'You're doin' a brilliant job Andy,' and Malcolm concurs: 'Andy's taken us to another level.'

In the process he has incurred the displeasure of his lords and masters in the EFL for the heinous offence of buying burgers for the team when they win. He has been officially informed that giving them a couple of hundred quid to get 'McDonald's or the like' contravenes an EFL regulation that all payments or benefits must be included in standard contracts, and told he should ensure the club 'complies with all appropriate HMRC guidance in such matters'. In a series of tweets, Holt defended his 'right to buy anyone a burger with my own money', adding, 'You have to wonder what these folk would do with their lives if it wasn't for my errors of judgement.'

Holt and his predecessor Eric Whalley are largely responsible for taking Stanley to where it is now, local entrepreneurs applying business acumen to a hobby that rewards them with the satisfaction of giving something back to their community. But perhaps the underlying reason the club keeps bouncing back from bankruptcy and oblivion is the simple resolve of fans to support their hometown team, no matter which league they're playing in. Burnley and Blackburn may be just down the road, but they're not Accrington.

Star centre-forward Billy Kee wanders into the sports bar with his young son, and Holt offers him a pint and commiserations for not winning. 'Yes but it's a point, better than a kick in the face,' the player says matter-of-factly. Every club has its Roy of the Rovers, the striker who scores vital goals in the nick of time to win cups and championships, and Kee is Accrington's Roy Race, a cheerful, seemingly well-adjusted young man enjoying his football and racking up goals for the fun of it. As well he might, a happily married man on a decent wage, he is his club's top scorer and local hero.

What I don't know is that he is afraid of an imaginary rat running around inside his head that makes him want to drive his car into a wall. This shocking confession comes a few months later in interviews in which he speaks of crying through sleepless nights with severe anxiety and depression that threatened to end his career and his life. The trigger was an away game at Cambridge last season when he couldn't face taking a couple of penalties. 'I didn't want to be on the pitch the whole match … it all hit me and I just didn't want to play football ever again.' That's when the rat began running around his head, depriving him of sleep. 'You are at home not wanting to go in to work and crying. You start thinking, will I just drive my car into a wall? Why does someone with the best job in the world want to kill himself? That's the thing with depression, it doesn't make sense.' The worst of it was the effect on his family. 'The lads at the club probably thought I was okay as I was putting a brave face on it here, but my missus was going through hell at home and that was the worst thing. You don't want the person you love going through hell.'

Fortunately his manager was sympathetic and told him to take a month off, he moved back in with his mum and dad and spent his days working with his dad on a building site. The change did him good and Kee is now on medication that keeps the black dog of depression at bay and helps him cope with the unremitting pressures of the modern game. 'With football there are so many ups and downs and emotions. You might get injured, you might get subbed, you might be flying. You can't sleep after midweek games and there is a lot of pressure, and you have to maintain your level of emotions.'

Kee is lucky to have the support of a club that is aware of psychological stresses on players and does what it can to help. 'The gaffer and Jimmy have been good to me. I can come in in the morning and say "I'm really struggling today". They'll put an arm around you and they'll give you a cuddle. You don't get that in football. It's a lot of fronts, but with our team there are no fronts. They are so honest.' It was a brave, eloquent confession which Kee hopes might help others to understand and cope with the illness, and in a BBC sports report his manager agreed: 'It's a dark word, depression. People are afraid of the stigma. Until you've been depressed, you can't tell people who haven't been depressed what it's like. You can try and describe it but it doesn't make any sense really in your own head. One of the first ways to rectify anything is to admit that it's there in the first place and so Billy should take a lot of credit for the way he's done that. I think it will help other people in the long run.' Wise words and compassion, rare qualities in the fiercely competitive world of professional football.

And badly needed. Every season dozens of footballers in Britain are left without clubs, but with pressures of families to support and mortgages to pay that can lead to mental health issues. A 33-year-old defender who was released after helping St Mirren win the Scottish Championship tells a BBC interviewer he is getting 'twitchy' as he sees men he played with starting pre-season training. 'You hear of players without clubs struggling, they've grown up in a dressing-room environment and had a team mentality their whole life and they feel isolated, missing out on that. I totally get that. It's tough. You don't know what direction you're going, if a team's going to come in, if you're going to get the next wage packet. It's challenging mentally.' Worth bearing in mind the next time you want to yell at a player for a missed pass or mistimed tackle.

Coleman had invited me to join him in his office after the game, and I find him in a sparsely furnished portacabin at the back of the ground, sharing pizza with his staff. He's pleased with the way his team played in the first half, but disappointed the game tightened up after the interval. 'I can't fault the lads for their efforts. It's a setback, but we haven't become a bad team overnight.' I ask about his football philosophy, and he says it was influenced by the World Cup finals in South Africa when he was impressed by patterns of play in the Spain v Holland game. He came back full of enthusiasm for Spain's 4-3-2-1 setup, which he has evolved into 4-4-1-1 with emphasis on passing through the lines and no long balls. 'I think it's been a success so far,' he says. Not that it's made much difference to crowds coming through the gates. Today's official attendance of 1,321 is the lowest in all four leagues, less than a tenth of the League Two crowd at Notts County's clash with Lincoln City, but Stanley are still joint third and Kayden's goal took him to joint second-highest scorer in League Two.

Malcolm and I return to the Crown, where he is philosophical: 'We know our limitations and I think we're doing well to be where we are. To be realistic, League One is the best we can hope for and if we get a good cup run and get on the telly it'll be a bonus. About the only thing Accrington has got going for it is the football club. At least people know we exist, don't they?'

There's always next Saturday and he's looking forward to the coach trip to the Cotswolds: 'The Forest Green lads will make us welcome and it's a nice part of the world, even if the pies are vegetarian. There's no aggro, we're all in the same boat, aren't we? It's not like the Premier League.' With that we part and in view of my beer intake I wander off in search of a decent restaurant within walking distance. I don't find one and end up with a Chinese takeaway. Accrington has its limits.

Maybe one day its team will be in League One with a new stand, electricity to spare and a training ground of its own. And the dressing rooms might even be tarted up. 'If we get a good cup run we'll do up the changing rooms, that's the script,' Holt said. At least then Fulham might use the showers if they come calling again on cup business. The last time they turned up at Accrington with Roy Hodgson they took one look at the dressing rooms and asked if their hosts would mind very much if they changed and showered in their country house hotel out of town. 'They were very polite about it,' club secretary Mark Turner recalls. 'We didn't mind a bit and we all shook hands. Happy days.'

When Tony Pulis brought his expensively assembled West Brom for a League Cup tie more recently, he wasn't fazed by the facilities. 'Do the lads good,' he said. 'Remind them where they came from.'

Good advice, that.

Queen's Park

They play football for the right reasons

Founded:	1867
Ground:	Hampden Park
Average attendance:	687
Honours:	Scottish Cup winners ten times 1874–1893 Division Two champions 1923 'B' Division champions 1956 Third Division champions 2000 League Two play-off winners 2007, 2016

I ONCE had a brief illusion of a career in football. I was 17 and playing at right-half for an amateur team in Govan, the gritty Glasgow neighbourhood of Alex Ferguson where men made ships and ships made men. It was a rough-and-tumble game in those days, played by sons of shipyard workers and policemen who were not known for shirking tackles, and occasionally matches would degenerate into a kind of kung fu with football.

Grass pitches were few and far between for the likes of us, so most weeks we went home after games with smears of black ash or red blaze embedded in cuts and scrapes. Sliding tackles were a calculated risk.

One day our coach came up to me at half-time in a typically bruising match and said, 'Ye see that wee man in the bunnet ower there? He's a youth scout frae Partick Thistle an' he's watching you.' My heart leaped. I was playing well, and stardom beckoned. As I trotted back to the pitch, I was in high spirits. Until two big guys stopped me in my tracks. One announced, 'Ye're gie'in oor winger a hard time sonny' and the other rejoined, 'Up tae you, wee man. If ye want tae walk home ye'll lay aff 'im.' This was no idle threat. This was Glasgow in the 1960s, when hard stares were preludes to mayhem. The city's shipbuilding lifeblood was ebbing away and sudden, casual violence was endemic in neighbourhoods like Govan. Teenage boys learned to be fast on their feet or with their fists to survive.

I could still try to impress the Thistle scout and take my chances, but I'd more likely end up in hospital. So I let the winger fly by me, the scout lost interest, and boyhood dreams of winning the cup for Motherwell faded forever. So it goes.

A few weeks later I hung up my boots and swapped them for running shoes, and followed my dad into amateur athletics, where losers tended to congratulate winners instead of threatening to break their legs. The Corinthian code of playing the game for the game's sake and respecting the opposition appealed to me, and I found athletes were sporting gentlemen compared with the hard men of Glaswegian amateur football. It was a revelation after I won a half mile when a rival cheerily slapped me on the back and we walked off the track with our arms around each other.

At the time I was only vaguely aware that the same amateur code and ethics were being upheld by the oldest and one of the most distinguished association football clubs in Scotland. Pity nobody offered me a trial with them.

It is a raw November night in Glasgow, when most sane folk are curled up on a sofa with a coffee or a dram. Sean Burns was up at 5.30am for his shift as an electrician at a power station 35 miles away; on his way home he stopped to do a 'homer' repair for a friend's aunt, and now he's having a kickabout on a training pitch with a few mates. In a couple of days he will lead them on to the hallowed turf of Hampden Park, Scotland's national football stadium, for a League One match. This is the world of the captain of Queen's Park, for generations an institution and inspiration as the only amateur team competing in senior football in Britain.

There are probably more pointless things to do in Glasgow than support this merry band of part-timers, but there can't be many. In a football-daft city dominated by the mighty twin bastions of Ibrox and Parkhead, following a makeshift team of electricians and plumbers is up there with Don Quixote's campaign against windmills. So how do they survive in a fiercely competitive professional world, and why should anyone care? The answer lies in a mix of history, tradition and a commitment to the amateur code worthy of *Chariots of Fire*. It is hard to underestimate the influence Queen's Park has had on world football. When the club was founded by a group of track and field athletes in 1867, the game was played by anything up to 20-a-side with kick-and-rush tactics that were a recipe for mayhem – basically one man would dribble with the ball and his team-mates would batter anybody who got in his way. Sanity prevailed with the introduction of 11-man teams, then Queen's Park changed the game forever by introducing a revolutionary tactic known as 'combination play' – essentially passing the ball. This startling innovation bamboozled opponents, led to ten Scottish Cup victories in the late 1800s, two FA Cup finals (which they lost to Blackburn Rovers) and a series of crushing defeats of England by Scottish teams made up mainly of Queen's Park players.

The author of the club's 50th anniversary history in 1917 noted that the combination of dribbling and passing had raised the Scottish game to the level of a fine art. 'Dribbling was a characteristic of English play, and it was not until very much later that the Southerners came to see that the principles laid down in the Queen's Park method of transference of the ball, accompanied by strong backing up, were those which got the most out of a team.' This bright idea was employed to devastating effect in home internationals. In 1881 England suffered their heaviest defeat on home soil when Andrew Watson of Queen's, the world's first black international footballer, captained Scotland to a 6-1 victory at the Oval, and the following year Scotland thumped England 5-1 in Glasgow. About this time Queen's graciously accepted invitations to help the English up their game by playing friendlies in Manchester and Liverpool, where they were dubbed the 'Scotch Professors', and the club acquired its nickname, 'The Spiders', for weaving intricate webs of passing play. The innovative amateurs also dreamed up other revolutionary concepts such as solid crossbars, free kicks and half-time.

This season the club is celebrating their 150th anniversary, and recognition of their pioneering contributions to the game have arrived in a congratulatory letter from FIFA president Giovanni Infantino, noting that Queen's was 'instrumental in introducing the passing game as practised across the globe'.

The halcyon days of their pre-eminence in amateur football drew to a close with the advent of professionalism, but through thick and thin, and mostly thin, the club has so far remained true to the Corinthian spirit enshrined in its motto *Ludere Causa Ludendi* – 'To Play for the Sake of Playing'.

You might ask why. In eight senior Scottish and English leagues of 134 teams, why be the only one that refuses to pay players, and offers only travelling expenses and a pair of boots? For answers I start by meeting Christine Wright, club secretary and general manager, as well as child welfare officer and safety officer on matchdays, at Queen's training ground next to Hampden stadium. She used to be a bingo club manager who knew little about football and cared less until she saw an advertisement for her present job. A decade later, she is as dyed in the black and white wool of Queen's colours as the most ardent fan.

'It's everything we stand for,' she says of amateur status. 'It's the heart of the club and its uniqueness. From the moral point of view, it's important to us that nobody gets rich from the club, and that we're here for the betterment of football in Scotland. There is a sense of community, of belonging, and because we have such a small support everybody knows each other.' In the absence of Russian oligarchs and oil-rich sheikhs, the club is a non-profit limited company with an annual turnover at the time of writing of £750,000, owned collectively by 200 members, governed by an elected committee, and run largely by part-time volunteers. The perennial shirt sponsor is the soft drinks company Irn Bru, which is as Scottish as it gets. Reflecting its amateur athletic roots, it has a head coach instead of a manager, and he is one of only half a dozen full-time employees. Happily, Queen's can afford this set-up because for generations it has owned Hampden, once the world's biggest and noisiest football stadium, a life-saving vestige of its 19th-century golden era that has staged some of the most memorable internationals and cup finals in the annals of the game. More importantly for Queen's, a 20-year lease of the stadium to the Scottish Football Association (SFA) has ensured their financial survival when they struggle to fill a few hundred of the 52,000 seats for home games. This has kept them afloat in the turbulent waters of the Scottish Leagues One and Two, where they have bobbed up and down without any serious prospects or pretensions of climbing higher.

Having reached the dizzy heights of League One through the play-offs in 2016, they finished a creditable sixth the following year, but now in early November they're rock bottom with eight points from 12 games. This is accepted philosophically by a small band of loyal supporters who are stoics worthy of the discourses of Marcus Aurelius.

One of them is Andy McGlennan. 'Give Andy a call,' a friend told me. 'He's your man for anything you need to know about Queen's.' So I do and we meet on a midweek morning in the Langside Café, an old-fashioned eatery near Hampden that has been in the same Italian-Scots family since the 1920s. On a cold winter day it's like a warm hug, serving filled rolls, pies and spaghetti to customers squeezed around diminutive tables on red leatherette bench seats. In bulky winter jackets they look like giants in a doll's house, Glaswegians in Lilliput.

The owner seems to know half his patrons by name and encourages lively repartee that tends to get everyone involved. While I'm waiting for Andy, the café debating society is discussing train spotters and kindred spirits obsessed with buses. 'They prefer to call themselves bus enthusiasts,' one sage comments. 'I don't know where they get the time.' And so on.

Andy is a sprightly character in his early 70s who looks younger and fitter than his years, as befits a former player who has devoted much of his life to coaching youth squads, before becoming director of the club's youth programme. When he joined the club as a player, most of his team-mates came from middle-class backgrounds, and the city's football breeding grounds of tough housing estates and satellite towns were largely ignored. 'We have a duty to the community and I had to address the problem,' he says.

So he began recruiting boys for under-12 and under-13 teams from estates like Castlemilk on the south side of the city, where grass pitches were as rare as streets without broken glass.

One of his earliest discoveries was Aiden McGeady, a wing wizard who went on to win a string of league titles and cups with Celtic and play for the Republic of Ireland. 'As a 12-year-old he was exceptional, two-footed, I'd never seen anyone like him at that age.' It was no surprise when he was snapped up by Celtic Boys' Club, a sign of changing times.

'The game and the players have changed. In the old days the first team was largely graduates and professionals, and you kept players forever because they had careers outside football. Nowadays boys are lucky to find jobs, and if they get an opportunity to move they're gone.'

Inevitably the Spiders lose some of their best players to the professional ranks every close season, which partly explains their current position at the foot of the table. Earlier, club secretary Christine admitted that recruiting and holding on to players for an amateur club is hard. 'I sympathise with boys who move to Junior clubs for £100 or £200 a week, that's a lot of money for them. We try to look after our boys as best we can, but I think the loyalty days are coming to an end.

'We used to have boys staying with us for their whole careers because they loved the club, and when their playing days were over they became members and helped to keep us going. It concerns me that this is fading away.'

There is no prospect whatever of Queen's supporters like Keith McAllister, 60, fading away until they take him away in a wooden box, or more likely scatter his ashes around his beloved Hampden.

Keith is in the audience for a 150th anniversary talk by a club director in the Edwardian baroque splendour of the Mitchell Library, one of the finest buildings of its kind in Europe. Afterwards we repair around the corner to a real ale oasis, the Bon Accord, and over pints of Belhaven Best he treats me to an eloquent dissertation on the compulsion, passion and merits of following a wee club unlikely ever to win anything.

He went to his first game at Queen's with his brother at seven, started running the supporters' bus as a teenager, and hasn't missed a game, home or away, since 1979 – and that was only because his work as an accountant took him to London. 'I don't go to weddings on Saturdays during the football season, and I get a wee bit of grief for that,' he admits. 'I've asked my daughter not to get married on a Saturday, and she understands because she loves football too.'

It suddenly strikes me that the word 'fan' could be short for 'fanatic'. Funny I'd never thought of it before, but Keith is a classic example.

He's still running the bus to away games, as well as the supporters' association, social events and the club shop. 'It's a passion,' he admits. 'You have to have passion, especially when things are not going well as they are now. But even a bad day at the football is better than a good day at the office.'

Hyperbole notwithstanding, he makes a good case for his club and its enduring contribution to football.

'There's something special about Queen's. We're the finest football club in the world. We've given so much to the game, I don't think any club can dispute that, and I feel we don't get the credit we deserve.

'I've been told we're an anachronism in modern football as the game moves into the global sphere – that's a load of pish. The big clubs in England drag their players to god-forsaken places just to sell shirts. Football is moving the wrong way. At the highest level it's run for Sky TV, so people can sit in pubs seven nights a week to watch games. Sure, some of the top players are wonderful athletes, but you still get dreadful, boring games.'

It's all in stark contrast with the ethos of his club, he says: 'We are the antithesis of modern football, and not as treasured as we should be. We epitomise what the game should be about, the game for the game's sake. But it's all big business now. Football's lost its soul, certainly in the UK. Guys who turn out for Queen's Park show as much if not more commitment than players being paid £150,000 a week and still playing poor games.'

Keith recalls an example of the Spiders defending an amateur tradition of wearing their shirts outside their shorts at an exhibition match in Texas in the late 1970s, which he naturally attended: 'Strictly speaking, it's not allowed, according to a FIFA directive, but that's the amateur way, and the referee said he wouldn't start the game until their shirts were in their shorts. When the players refused he threatened to abandon the game, so finally one of our officials went up and told him the shirts were staying where they were, and if he wanted to abandon the game it was up to him to explain to the crowd why. The game went ahead with shirts worn in the amateur way.'

Next day I'm lucky to be offered a cancellation ticket to a black-tie Queen's anniversary dinner at Hampden. The keynote speaker is a familiar character who joined the club as a 16-year-old toolmaker in the late 1950s and scored on his debut. In gravel hard Glaswegian tones, he recalls a freezing New Year's Day game at Dumbarton when they had to clear snow from the pitch, and the coach handed round a bottle of whisky before kick-off to warm up. Years later he returned to the club to be interviewed for the manager's job and failed to get it. So Sir Alex Ferguson, for it was he, went on to win a few trinkets for Aberdeen and Manchester Utd.

This prompts the following speaker to suggest the board should have been sacked for missing the chance of Queen's winning the Champions League. Sir Alex beams at this. The Govan maestro is good value for his supper, expounding on the strategies of a successful career, and the importance of giving young players a chance and schooling them for the rigours of a highly competitive game. 'The key to successful management is recognising people and their value, because it's a people's game,' he says. 'What made Man Utd was the spirit of young players. When you give them a chance they very rarely let you down.' His recruitment policy was simple: 'Get the confidence of the mothers, they always do what's right for the boy.' Ferguson was not noted for mollycoddling his young charges, and he insists coaches are not tough enough on young players nowadays. 'They need a hard upbringing to prepare for the challenges of the modern game. There are lots of statistics on performance, but there are no mathematics for character and attitude.' Words of wisdom which bring him to the Spiders and their development of young players untainted by professionalism. To warm applause, he declares, 'Queen's Park are a symbol in the sense they play football for the right reasons.' Pity they never gave him the manager's job.

I find myself at the same table as the finance director of Clyde FC, who fills me in on the trials and tribulations of keeping a wee club afloat in the choppy waters of League Two. 'It's a real struggle, there's no money in the lower leagues. We have a stadium capacity of 8,000 and average crowds of just over 400. Sky isn't interested in Scottish football, and TV and sponsorship brings in barely £20 million a year. By the time it reaches us we're left with 0.1 per cent, hardly anything.' He says it means there is less and less chance of anyone other than Rangers seriously challenging Celtic, currently reigning supreme with huge gates and revenue from European competitions. 'The game in Scotland is nearing a crisis. If it goes on like this it will just be a boring procession of a couple of clubs winning everything.'

Glasgow has changed dramatically since I was a boy. The mean streets of crumbling tenements are gone, along with the shipyards, and a new vitality has transformed the city into a cultural powerhouse of music, creative arts, design and innovative cuisine light years away from greasy fish suppers as battered as some of the people who ate them.

The city still has its rough edges, but it has a big, friendly, socialist heart that cares for its own and anyone who takes Glaswegians for what they are, for all their faults. If ever I find myself in serious trouble, there is nowhere I'd rather be. I suppose its basic humanity was always there, I just couldn't see it through the grit and grime of hard times and the violence of aimless, angry youths. Now they're studying engineering again, and computer sciences, playing in bands and serving cocktails in hip bars. Yet Glaswegians take a perverse pride in their tough reputation, and they still smile at the apocryphal story of a hard man buried beneath a headstone bearing the inscription: 'Whit're you lookin' at?'

Queen's Park, like its home city, has a deeply ingrained sense of social responsibility and does its bit to transform and enrich lives. The football might not be much to get excited about, but as a social club it is peerless. The gathering place for young and old, and lost souls in between, is its campus known as Lesser Hampden in the shadow of the main stadium that has training and social facilities many professional clubs would envy. All-weather synthetic grass pitches beneath floodlights, a warm-up track used by Usain Bolt and his hapless rivals during the 2014 Commonwealth Games, and a modern pavilion housing club offices, fitness suite, members' lounge and a café/bar/bistro for social occasions are as good as it gets for lower league clubs.

The pavilion serves as a drop-in sports and social club for legions of boys playing in under age 'mini-Spiders' teams, their peers in youth and senior squads, a ladies' team, over-35s playing 14-a-side, dozens of pensioners treated to tea and scones and minibus outings, and a 'football fans in training' project for men and mostly women who want to lose weight through exercise and better diets.

One of the few trophies in the boardroom is a silver plate inscribed 'Mental Health and Wellbeing National League

Winners 2014'. This was won by a team of men recovering from illness, notably alcohol and drug abuse, who come to Lesser Hampden once a week for training under a former Queen's head coach and play once a month in a national league. This is a club that cares for people, whether they support the team or not, and its pavilion is a community centre any council would be proud of.

The man in charge of social projects is George Watson, one of Queen's few full-time employees, who heads teams of volunteers. He used to sell records for a living, but says he gets more fun and satisfaction from helping others cope with life.

'We don't tell the elderly folk what we're doing until they arrive, whether it's a quiz or a trip to Loch Lomond, and it's good to see them smile. Next month we're going to the panto. Lots of them have made pals, and it grows like a mushroom, some start going to games and take wives and grandsons to the keep fit classes.'

Currently there are a couple of dozen men enlisted in the 'Tackling Recovery' programme for those with drink and drug issues. 'Some of these poor guys stay at home most of the time, they don't engage with people. It's slow progress, but consistency is good for them, coming every week. When you see them picking up and getting a new lease of life it gives you a lift. This is a nice place to be.'

On the football side, it's also a nice place for visiting teams. Queen's are bottom of the league and headlines of match reports on the club website tell a sorry tale: *'Hallowe'en Horror Show from Spiders'; 'Missed chances prove costly'; 'Raith hit Queen's for 5'; 'Queen's need a wee break'*. They're unlikely to get a break next Saturday when Arbroath come calling, eager for points to lift them from fifth into a play-off place.

To prepare for the challenge, Queen's squad of plumbers, electricians, construction workers and fitness coaches have two weekly 90-minute training sessions after they knock off work. It is Thursday night, and head coach Gus MacPherson has just arrived for the final session. While waiting for him, I watch under-age teams going through their paces under floodlights on the smart green pitches of Lesser Hampden, wee boys playing short, passing, one-touch possession football. They are fast and skilful, ten-year-old fledgling stars emulating the tika-taka football of the Nou Camp in Glasgow. I think back to the hard-edged days of my youth on black ash pitches and sigh.

MacPherson is an affable, plain-speaking character who played full-back for Rangers, was a member of Kilmarnock's cup-winning team in 1997, and as manager led St Mirren to the First Division title in 2005/06. Appointed head coach at Queen's in 2014, he took them to promotion through the play-offs the following season, and against all the odds has kept them there. So far.

He admits his job is challenging. 'We are limited in the type of players we can bring in, and we have to accept we'll lose some in the close season. But we have an excellent youth set-up that can compete with the best (the under-17s drew 2-2 with Celtic the previous night) and it's fantastic we can get decent lads to come in and play for the right reasons.

'No matter what age level they're playing at, we insist they take pride in their performances. We tell them to aspire to the highest level they can and try to instil good habits on and off the park. This is a great place to work, because there are demands but no pressure.'

Life is a lot tougher in League One, and he reckons surviving in it so far has been a major achievement. 'The higher you go the greater the speed and power of players. In League Two we played a lot of good football and got plaudits for it, and we still try to play in an open way, but the game at this level is more physically challenging.'

Losing bad goals through individual mistakes hasn't helped confidence, but like any gaffer on a bad run he believes a couple of wins will lift his team. 'The supporters just want to see players taking pride in wearing the shirt and giving their best, and that's what we demand. It's a wonderful football experience being part of this club. Just now the players only think about the next game, but in years to come I hope they'll look back and appreciate the experience they had. I'm thoroughly enjoying being here, I can think of a lot worse places to be.'

So can his captain Sean Burns, who comes into the boardroom for a chat after training. An ex-pro with St Mirren, a transfer to Airdrie didn't work out and he was happy to be invited to train at Queen's. Two hundred appearances and 22 goals later, he's enjoying the experience. 'You're treated very well here, like a player at a full-time club, you get anything you need. I feel a wee bit privileged, especially playing at the national stadium every other week.' Having played in professional ranks, lining up against them as an amateur doesn't faze him. 'My mentality is that I've played at a high level and I can compete with them. It feels good when you're getting the better of guys earning £300 a week, there's always a bit of banter.'

At 25 he's committed to a career as an electrician but continues to drive himself hard in training to play at the highest level he can. 'It's been drummed into me since I was a kid that you train the way you're going to play. You have to give 100 per cent or you're wasting your time, and you never know who's watching and might take a chance on you.'

Luke Donnelly, a midfielder and striker, is another recruit rescued from a faltering professional career. Two seasons ago he was playing for Celtic's first team in pre-season friendlies against Real Sociedad and Dukla Prague, but after picking up injuries he was released when his contract was up. 'Anywhere from Celtic in Scotland is a step down, but sometimes you have to take a step backward to go forward,' he says philosophically. 'And this is a great club, it's very well run and welcoming.' He's just finished an 11-hour shift with overtime in a printing works, but you'd never know watching him haring after loose balls in training.

Should Sean and his team-mates be in any doubt what is required when wearing a Queen's shirt, they are forcefully reminded by a quotation from Sir Alex writ large in a staircase in the pavilion: 'If you play for Queen's Park you have to fight every game you play.' This is in the DNA of a Govan hard man who insists that in his Queen's playing days the so-called middle-class lads lining up with him were as hard as nails. Coming from him, that's high praise.

While the players are going through final drills, Alan Rhodes is in a back room folding freshly laundered shirts. As part-time kit man and lifelong supporter, he laughs at any suggestion of following a bigger club. 'Why would you? You see their buses coming from all over the country and they must pass half a dozen grounds to get to Ibrox or Parkhead. They expect to win every game and the only time you hear from them is when they're losing. If we get into the fourth round of the cup we're all jumping around like idiots.'

That's usually as far as Queen's get. 'We have more bad days than good days,' he admits. 'So you savour the good ones because you know you're going to come back down again sometime. But you can't fault the players for effort and commitment, they give absolutely everything in training and get buttons for it, just to get a game on Saturday.'

So it's all about tradition, loyalty, commitment – and something else equally important. A familiar refrain is that the Spiders offer a refuge from sectarian strife in the west of Scotland fuelled by Rangers–Celtic rivalry.

Andy McGlennan recalls his parents discouraging him from becoming involved in it: 'Once some pals got tickets for an Old Firm game on New Year's Day and I went against my parents' wishes. I was 16 years old, and do you know what happened? Celtic won 5-1 and I should have been happy, but it was my epiphany. The atmosphere was poisonous and I vowed I'd never go to another Old Firm game.' Instead he was drawn to Queen's Park: 'The neutrality of the club took me over.'

Archie Neilson is a kindred spirit. We meet after the anniversary talk in the Mitchell Library, where he has been browsing a display of club memorabilia, including memoirs entitled *The Game for the Game's Sake*, and *The Men with Educated Feet*.

A former postman and now a cleaner at Glasgow University, he followed in his father's footsteps by becoming a Queen's supporter a few years ago. 'I was brought up in a predominantly Catholic family, but I was disillusioned by the sectarian thing. I hated the atmosphere at Old Firm games. You try to ignore it, to pretend it's just a few nutcases, but you are identified with them. It's against everything I believe in and it drove me away from football.'

Eventually he 'just turned up' for a game at Hampden one day with his young brother and enjoyed the experience:

'You get a bit of banter like anywhere else, but I've never heard any sectarianism.' The fact that Queen's are unlikely to win anything is accepted rationally. 'You see it for what it is. You're not going to see Messi or Ronaldo, they're not pampered professionals, they're guys who work just like me. They're dedicated, you can see they're playing for the love of the game, not for money. The results aren't always the best, but win or lose I get a real buzz out of it.'

In keeping with its gentlemanly image, Queen's home is situated on high ground in Mount Florida, a respectable area of Victorian sandstone tenements on the south side of the city, vestiges of a prosperous past of trade and heavy industry that elevated it to second city of the British Empire. It is still a relatively genteel middle-class neighbourhood, where the local chippie does chilli and garlic squid, and halloumi and spinach rolls. Deep fried Mars bars have never been on the menu.

Nearby stands a large park that shares the club's name, an oasis of woodland and wild grasslands laid out in 1858 by Sir Joseph Paxton, architect of the Crystal Palace, and dedicated to the memory of Mary, Queen of Scots. The park is on the site of the fateful Battle of Langside on 13 May 1568, when her forces were defeated by troops loyal to her half-brother James Stuart and she fled to England, where she ended up in the Tower of London and had her head removed 19 years later.

A circle of large stones at the highest point of the park is believed to have been a military position during the battle, and is now a fine viewpoint with panoramas of the city and surrounding hills as far as Ben Lomond. The park is a tranquil haven, popular with mums pushing prams, dogs exploring mysterious bushes and children playing around a nature pond that attracts mute swans, moorhens and mallards. There is a boating pond, a poetry rose garden and a reptile house with exotic creatures that include bearded dragons, hissing cockroaches and giant wasps. And here's one for a pub quiz – the park is home to Wellcroft Bowling Club, founded in 1835, whose proud boast is that it drafted the rules of the modern game.

Barely a mile away, Hampden Park has also seen memorable battles in its day. When it opened on its present site in 1903 it was the biggest football stadium in the world, until the Maraçana was completed in Rio in 1950. It was also the noisiest, producing the famous 'Hampden roar' by massed ranks of Scots baying for defeat of the Auld Enemy, England. The story goes that it was first recorded during a game in 1929 when Scotland were reduced to ten men by an injury to Alex Jackson, who was taken to Victoria Infirmary a mile away. When Scotland equalised in the last minute direct from a free kick, Jackson knew about it because the roar rattled the hospital windows.

It was one of these battles with England in 1937 that attracted a crowd of 149,415, which remains the record official attendance at a football match in Britain. And Queen's were not far behind – a few years earlier 95,722 turned up for a Scottish Cup first-round match against Rangers. In those days monumental twin castellated gates reinforced an impression of Fortress Hampden, and on big matchdays it was like a gladiatorial arena.

Arguably the most dazzling European Cup Final was staged at Hampden in 1960 when the Real Madrid of Puskás, Gento and di Stéfano overwhelmed Eintracht Frankfurt 7-3 in a breathtaking display of sublime skill and teamwork. This was the beautiful game at its apogee. One man who had a close-up view of the epic encounter was Jim Hastie, son of a Queen's captain, who later played for the team himself before joining its committee and eventually the board of directors. When the Madrid maestros came to town Hastie lied about his age to be a ball boy at the match (he was under the permissible age of ten) and was behind the goal in which Puskas scored his fourth.

'They were like ballet dancers, the way they played and strutted about,' he recalls. 'They changed the game. Who'd have thought 134,000 Scots fans would have stayed half an hour after the game to applaud a losing German team 15 years after the war ended?'

I count myself lucky to have experienced the old stadium years later, before its stands and terracing disappeared in a major redevelopment in 2000 that reduced its capacity to barely a third of what it used to be. As a trainee sports (i.e. football) reporter, I used to climb a rickety wooden staircase in the main stand and walk along an enclosed corridor to a huge press box comprising a double bank of wooden seats in a glass-walled eyrie perched on the roof that seemed to defy gravity. Even before a match started you could hear and actually feel the rumble of the crowd as you came along the wooden corridor, and the view from the dizzying height was breathtaking. This was the Everest of football press boxes.

Sadly I was also there to report on its demolition, and recall sitting quietly in the old dressing rooms conjuring images of Puskas, and local heroes like Denis Law and Kenny Dalglish proudly donning the blue shirts of Scotland before emerging to the Hampden roar.

The stadium is not what it was – it has lost its iconic grandeur – but it remains the home of Scottish football, with a museum attesting to past glories. I am shown around by Colin Lobban, front of house manager, who takes me first to the dressing rooms. They're pretty much modern versions of the old ones with wooden lockers, non-slip rubber floors and adjoining rooms for staff and treatments. Nothing fancy, but they have the air of an inner sanctum in the bowels of the stadium, and Colin says, 'It gives them a bit of peace and quiet amid the general hubbub, and not too much can get damaged by angry managers.'

Visitors can hear echoes of a muted Hampden roar in the new stadium on guided tours of the museum, recorded during a World Cup qualifier in 2009 against Iceland. The collection is a treasure trove of old-style jerseys like rugby shirts, international caps, original turnstiles and general nostalgia. Video screens relay images from classic matches to appropriate soundtracks, so Scotland scores great goals to Rod Stewart belting out 'Can't Stop Me Now', Old Firm clashes are replayed to the martial strains of Wagner, and Real Madrid stars waltz past defenders to operatic arias. Watching Law and Dalglish banging in goals against England, a museum guide says ruefully, 'They were the good old days. When you see the quality of the players we had then, we should have done better.'

A section devoted to Junior clubs with romantic names like Shotts Bon Accord and Lugar Boswell Thistle has a large portrait of a half-back who played for Bonnyrigg Rose and was offered a trial by East Fife. In the end James Bond, *aka* Sean Connery, carved out a successful career elsewhere.

The prize exhibit is the SFA Challenge Cup, better known as the Scottish Cup, the oldest national football trophy in the world. It is a masterpiece of 19th-century silversmith art, a magnificent double-handed cup crafted in solid silver for the princely sum of £56, which included a set of medals. It is now priceless, which is why it leaves its fortified glass case for only an hour or so every year to be presented to the winning team. 'Then we hold our breath while it goes around the track,' Colin says. Meanwhile an exact replica is being engraved, which the winners keep for a year.

I'm enjoying the nostalgia of yesteryear and linger over scenes from a cup final between Aberdeen and Celtic in 1937 that end with a vast tidal wave of men wearing cloth caps, collars and ties, swarming out of the stadium and forming endless queues for tramcars. The attendance that day was 147,365.

There is even a section of the familiar old press box with phone booths relaying commentaries from the 1960s. I listen to them, and it's like being taken back to another life vaguely remembered from youth. On leaving I half expect to see tramcars rattling through the streets.

Outside, metaphorical dark clouds are gathering over the stadium. The SFA has announced it is contemplating quitting Hampden when its lease expires in 2020, citing the cost of renting and maintaining the stadium. Rangers, Celtic and the Scottish Rugby Union are quick to cash in by offering their stadia in Glasgow and Edinburgh, battle lines are drawn and passionate arguments rage back and forth. The Scottish football correspondent of *The Times* fires a withering salvo in support of Hampden as the home of Scottish football for more than 120 years: 'In the extensive history of stupid, knuckle-headed and just plain wrong decisions taken in Scottish football, leaving Hampden for Murrayfield (the rugby stadium) could be immediately inked in as the permanent chart No 1.' The consequences for Queen's would be dire, and as matchday approaches anxiety shrouds the club pavilion.

The prospect of a tight contest against Arbroath lifts spirits, and the café-bar starts to fill up at noon, with a Queen's supporters' team kicking off a match against St Johnstone supporters on the training pitch. Usually they'd be playing against the visiting fans' team, but Arbroath don't have one.

Among interested spectators is Moira Ellsworth, a Queen's supporter and foot soldier of Scotland's loyal 'Tartan Army'. Her husband is a Rangers man and her two sons support Celtic, and one of them is playing today for QP supporters. 'Let's say it's good fun in our house when Celtic and Rangers are playing. I think it's how it should be,' she says. 'Live and let live, you should be able to support who you want without getting involved in religious bigotry.' She remembers going to the Nou Camp for a Barcelona–Chelsea game and seeing a Spanish family of eight spanning three generations sitting in front of her. 'It was lovely to see, a real family atmosphere at the football,' and she wishes there was more of it in Scotland, which is why she follows Queen's. 'It's very friendly and civilized, you see different generations from the same families. And there's a sense of honour and tradition in this club, people play for the badge.'

By two o'clock the place is packed, largely with visiting supporters savouring Queen's Park ale, hotdogs and toasted paninis, an appreciable step up from customary football fare of lukewarm Bovril and greasy pies. Arbroath fan Allan Getty, a student teacher, has travelled from the east coast with his grannie Mary and they're enjoying themselves. 'Some clubs you go to the supporters aren't what you'd call friendly, but you feel welcome at Queen's,' Allan says. 'We all just have a laugh.'

Today the BBC Sports website is quoting the SFA chief executive as saying there is a realistic chance that the last internationals to be staged at Hampden could be group matches at the Euro 2020 finals. Mary is sorry to hear it. 'These poor souls won't be able to keep this beautiful stadium going, it's very sad.' Not on attendances of a few hundred, they won't. By the time the match kicks off the sweeping oval banks of a stadium built to hold more than 50,000 fans are virtually deserted, with only a bare scattering of 764 in the main south stand. A small knot of Arbroath supporters are doing their best to create a mini Hampden roar, but their voices echo around the empty tribunes like ghosts of a long-departed Tartan Army. I feel sorry for a handful of stewards with nothing to do except try to keep warm on a bitterly cold day. In front of me a row of Queen's men are discussing the hot topic of the day, the prospect and inherent dangers of cup finals being switched to the huge Murrayfield rugby stadium in Edinburgh: 'The only time they'll come close to fillin' it is for Rangers and Celtic, and can ye imagine a' them comin' an' goin' at the one time tae the one station at Haymarket? It'll be mayhem, a battlefield.'

Meanwhile a gutsy contest is warming up on the pitch as Arbroath press high and don't allow Queen's time on the ball to play their passing game. Gentlemanly reserve prevails in the home crowd with a chorus of 'oh dear me', with the strongest expletive directed at a player caught offside: 'Ye made a right arse o' that.' During a lull in the action, a man asks his neighbour, 'When did we last score?' and his pal has to think about it. I once heard the same query at a Motherwell match that elicited the response, 'Don't ask me, I'm only 20.' Arbroath look quick on the break and sharp up front, and in 18 minutes a slick passing move slices through the Queen's defence and ends with their striker, with his back to goal, spinning and thrashing home from 20 yards. The remainder of the half is stalemate, with Queen's holding their own at the back, but rarely putting the visitors under pressure, and as the ref blows for half-time the row in front of me is philosophical: 'Ach well, we're no' the best team but we're no' the worst.'

Interestingly, Queen's are not wearing their usual black and white hooped shirts. This anniversary season they're wearing replicas of the blue shirts of Scotland worn at the world's first international football match that took place against England in Glasgow in November 1872, when the Scots team was composed entirely of Queen's players. For the record the result at the West of Scotland cricket ground before more than 4,000 spectators was 0-0, which their descendants would probably accept happily today.

Jim Hastie has given me a ticket with access to the Millennium Lounge, a directors' and VIP area overlooking the pitch, for half-time snacks and hot drinks. The blazers are deep in conversation about the future of Hampden rather than today's match, and you can hardly blame them. It's a big place to look after with no rent coming in. Jim is an avuncular kind of chap who believes his club has a civic responsibility to young players in its charge. 'Families and communities know that not all kids in this football-daft city can play for Rangers or Celtic, and they can't all become David Beckhams. We pick up kids who are depressed after being dropped by big clubs and we teach them good playing habits, how to work as a team. That's the great thing about football, it should be a vehicle for creating good modern citizens.'

A classic case is a left-back by the name of Andy Robertson, who was told by Celtic at the age of 16 that he was too weak. After Queen's rescued his career he went on to play for Dundee United and Hull City, and as I write he is a rock and wing marauder in the Liverpool defence and captain of Scotland. His old amateur club could do with him today.

I linger in the warmth of the lounge at the restart, watching the action through plate glass windows with a sandwich in one hand and a cuppa in the other. At Motherwell matches I'd never dream of deserting my usual perch in a cold, draughty stand for VIP comforts, but on a cold winter's day in a neutral venue there's something to be said for them. Eventually I wander out in time to see Arbroath sealing the points when a loose ball in the box is fired into the roof of the net. Queen's rally and there's no shortage of effort, but sadly veteran Arbroath keeper Rab Douglas, ex-Celtic and Leicester City, doesn't have a save to make.

It's a familiar tale this season as the amateurs struggle to compete in a faster, more physical game in League One, but voices drifting out the turnstiles are stubbornly optimistic: 'We've been very ordinary, we just need a wee bit of luck … ye never know, we might turn it on next week.'

The enduring charm of wee clubs was summed up in part by Keith McAllister in nostalgic programme notes recalling past and present attractions at Scotland's minor grounds: 'The railway carriage that used to be the pie stall at Dumbarton … the covered terracing at Raith that rattled whenever a train passed by … the twee wee grandstand at

Brechin with a towering church spire in the distance, one of Scotland's most picturesque footballing venues ...' Evidently this is the place for memorable steak and black pudding pies and a fine pub next door. 'Take away the howling gales and stop restricting the punters nipping across the road for a pint at half-time and you have the perfect football venue.' Never mind the dodgy football lads, it's worth braving North Sea gales for the pies. The bad news is that Queen's look as if they are heading back to a familiar home in League Two, so Brechin pies will be off the menu for a while. But no matter where they play, I look forward to following the fortunes of this friendly, welcoming bunch of amateurs on its Quixotic adventures. Bring on the windmills.

* * *

This is where this chapter ended when first drafted, but as it was being prepared for publication momentous changes shook Hampden Park. The SFA finally decided it could no longer afford to rent the stadium and pay for its upkeep, and negotiated to buy it for £5 million with the help of a couple of Scots business tycoons. So Queen's will soldier on in the more modest surroundings of Lesser Hampden, but deprived of SFA rent its future would be bleak if it continued to lose its best home-grown talent to professional clubs for free every season. In November 2019, a majority of its members voted with heavy hearts to end more than 150 years as amateurs, allowing the club to offer paid, part-time contracts to first-team players and earn financial returns when they move on.

Faced with mounting competition from Highland and Lowland League teams eager to take their place through promotion to the professional ranks, it was felt they had no choice. 'It was head against heart,' president Gerry Crawley announced. 'The heart of a lot of the membership would be we really don't want to do this, but we have to do it.' So Corinthian ideals of the 19th century give way to fiscal demands of the modern game, but Queen's teams will still take the field wearing their distinctive club crest *Ludere Causa Ludendi*. It is a badge of honour of a sporting tradition that will never be matched.

Berwick Rangers

All that excitement and passion on the terraces, that's what football's all about, not sitting in front of a TV

Founded:	1884
Ground:	Shielfield Park
Average attendance:	453
Honours:	Scottish Division Two Champions 1979
	Scottish Division Three Championss 2007

THERE IS only one team in England that has had the balls to play in the senior Scottish leagues. Not content with that, Berwick Rangers had the audacity to humble their mighty namesakes from Glasgow by bundling them out of the Scottish Cup in 1967, in what *The Scotsman* hailed as 'the most ludicrous, the weirdest, the most astonishing result ever returned in Scottish football'.

It was probably the border town's biggest shock since the Duke of Gloucester turned up in 1482 at the behest of his brother Edward IV with 20,000 men armed with 2,000 sheaves of arrows and demanded the surrender of the Scottish garrison, which sensibly agreed and went home.

The English seizure of Berwick upon Tweed has faded into the mists of time, but the greatest day in the history of its football club has not. Mementoes of the historic event adorn the staircase of its modest clubhouse in framed strips worn on the day, and a photograph of local hero Sammy Reid firing in the only goal of the game in the 32nd minute. He didn't have much time to celebrate his new-found fame, as he had to be back at work as a gear cutter in an engineering yard on Sunday to make up time he had been given off in the week for training.

Not much has changed in the ranks of a part-time team managed by an estate agent and made up of tradesmen, labourers, a farmer's son and an abattoir worker. One former player was a prison officer. If the lights go out they call the chairman, who used to have an electrical business. His wife is the cleaning lady, she's on the door on matchdays, and she sells club raffle tickets. The previous manager was a qualified roofer who came in handy for repairs to the main stand that used to belong to Bradford City. It was bought in 1955 for the princely sum of £400, dismantled, driven north and reassembled by supporters and officials. Chairman Len Ayre is right on the mark when he says, 'This is a hands-on club, we have to be.'

On a good day they'll get a crowd of 500 for home games at a ground overshadowed by grain silos, and this season's main shirt sponsor was drawn from a hat in a lottery of local businesses. The others were given advertising hoardings and hospitality packages, and to balance the books the ground is leased as a speedway track in summer. As Plato observed, necessity is the mother of invention.

So we're not talking about Barcelona here. This is a club that has been defying economic and geographical odds against it since playing its first matches on a ground donated by a local fish merchant, where legend has it the goalposts were fir trees. From the start it couldn't make up its mind which side of the nearby border to play on, switching more than once between North Northumberland and Scottish Border leagues before eventually settling on the tartan side in 1905. The reasoning was, and remains, that potential opposition was generally closer in the Scottish lowlands, making it easier and cheaper to get to. Half a century later it was admitted to the senior Scottish Football League, where it has been hopping about the two lowest divisions ever since. Unsurprisingly, their nickname is 'The Borderers'.

Berwick Rangers were one of the first names on my UK tour teamsheet, partly because of its curious position straddling two historically antagonistic countries, and partly because I like the town.

Berwick is a gem of a place, as evinced by its changing hands 13 times in two centuries of intermittent warfare between the 'Auld Enemies'. In the Middle Ages it had the misfortune of being a thriving seaport in a strategic location and Scotland's wealthiest Royal Burgh, which inevitably incited England to capture it.

The border is less contentious these days. It lies a couple of miles north of Berwick in a lay-by on the A1 to Edinburgh. There are a couple of Scottish flags and a sign saying Welcome to Scotland in English and Gaelic on one side of the road, and English flags and a snack van on the other, and that's it. Two hundred years of murderous mayhem and they decide to call it quits in a lay-by. So it goes.

At least Elizabeth I bequeathed the town impressive fortifications, a ring of massive walls and ramparts that constitute the most complete bastioned town defences in northern Europe. They have kept out invaders for five centuries, even Asda and Lidl, who are banished to suburbs outside the walls. This allows quirky independent shops to thrive in streets called markets, and in lanes leading through narrow archways to views of old stone bridges spanning the river.

The Royal Border Bridge is the biggest and highest of the river crossings, a masterpiece of Victorian engineering and stonemasonry opened by Queen Victoria in 1850, its ranks of uniform, graceful arches carrying the main East Coast railway more than 100 feet above the Tweed. This is where Berwick begins to resemble a toy town.

From a distance the bridge and Virgin trains sweeping across it look like a model train set, and snub-nosed fishing boats chugging out to sea beneath it could have sailed from a child's bath. The illusion persists in the old town, a model fort protecting life-sized dolls' houses in solid Georgian residences with big windows.

The trick is in the perspective. Berwick is a mini-town of manageable proportions snuggling behind ancient battlements that keep the outside world at bay. The people with their mongrel mix of Northumberland and Lothian accents are easy-going and friendly, and the place soon becomes familiar, making visitors feel at home when they're away.

It is probably the ideal home for a mixed-breed football club that is technically English but effectively Scottish, recruits most of its players from Scotland and its directors from England, and draws support from an Anglo-Scots alliance of fans who would normally chant expressive slogans at each other at internationals. They play in Northumberland but train near Edinburgh, because that's where the first team mostly comes from.

To start finding out what holds it all together, I call Bill Purvis, membership secretary of the Berwick Supporters

Trust. A retired bank manager, he lives in a Scots village a few miles from Berwick and suggests we meet in Morrison's café on the outskirts of town. 'Easy to find and they make good coffee,' he says.

We find each other beyond the checkouts and early Christmas decorations, and settle in with flat whites as a sleet-bearing wind whipping in from the North Sea rattles the windows. Welcome to Berwick in November.

Bill is a hearty, bluff character inured to decades of perilous escapades of the club he has supported since his dad took him to his first match at the age of nine. 'At times I've wondered if I was going to have a club the next day,' he admits.

He reminisces on dark days in the early 90s when it went literally to the dogs, having to rent the stadium for greyhound racing to survive – and then being locked out of the ground by the greyhound promoter for failing to pay bills. 'We played games anywhere they'd have us for a while.' In fact other clubs rallied to help out, and Berwick played their last five 'home' games of the 1991/92 season in Edinburgh, Coatbridge, Alloa, Methil and Stenhousemuir. It is a minor miracle they averted bankruptcy and relegation.

The brightest day in Bill's football lifetime was, inevitably, the cup tie that saw wee Rangers beat big Rangers. 'Nobody saw that coming, but after we scored in the first half the longer the game went on the more likely it seemed. Big Rangers played into our hands by lobbing balls into the box, where we had a 6ft 4in centre-half and a keeper who wasn't afraid to come off his line, so it was meat and drink to them.' He pauses, and adds with satisfaction, 'The atmosphere was tremendous, but towards the end the Glasgow fans were pretty quiet.'

Then there was the time George Best graced Shielfield Park when he came with Hibs for a cup tie in the 1970s. It was near the end of his career when he was on a downward slide, but Bill recalls he still illuminated the ground with instinctive skills. 'Berwick stuck a man on him for most of the game, but he still launched beautiful passes. He was thinking faster than the Hibs players, sending the ball to where they should have been and they were just standing watching it.'

Bill tells me the Supporters Trust was formed in 2003 as an offshoot of the Supporters Association, with the aim of having a greater say in how their fundraising contributions were spent. 'We felt the club was being run into the ground by certain individuals, and there was too much going on behind the scenes. We felt nothing was happening, and we needed to change.'

The club is now effectively owned by the two associations that together hold the biggest block of shares and are represented on the board. Chairman Len Ayre recently declared the club had a healthy bank balance, after receiving more than £40,000 from the supporters' groups in the past year, but Bill says keeping it that way is a constant struggle.

'Everybody's got to work together to raise money to keep the club going, simple as that. Every year there's a massive deficit and it's up to us to fill that hole. What you hope for a club like Berwick is a decent cup run and maybe some TV money. I'd like to see us go up a league, but realistically I don't think we can aim any higher.'

The club escaped relegation last season by the skin of its teeth, with a 2-1 win over Edinburgh City in a final day cliffhanger, and Bill reckons if they had lost it would have been their swansong.

'If we go down it would be to the Scottish Lowland League, and once you're there it's not so easy to get out. If we drop out of this division I think that will be the end of it. We have to stay in it to survive.'

Before we leave, he offers an honest assessment of the team's current form, following a 5-1 drubbing at Elgin City the previous weekend. 'They're shite at the moment. None of them would get into Berwick teams of the past, they'd be lucky to get into the reserves.' But he'll be going to the home game against Stirling Albion next Saturday, of course. 'We live in hope,' he says.

Only diehard fans of small-town clubs understand the logic, or rather lack of it, in turning out in all weathers to watch lower league exponents of the beautiful game striving with more graft than craft for mid-table safety.

One of them is Colin Pike, former office holder in both Berwick supporters' groups, who works part-time for a local youth project helping youngsters with social problems to get their lives back on track. Drink, drugs and chaotic families are the usual suspects.

'We try to be human,' he says, and testimonies to their work are chalked on a board in the entrance to the project offices. One says, 'I wouldn't be where I am today without their help and guidance,' and another says, 'If it weren't for the staff here I would more than likely be locked up or lying in a ditch.'

Compared with dealing with such human dramas, supporting Berwick Rangers is a breeze.

'There is absolutely no glamour in supporting Berwick,' Colin admits cheerfully. 'You go to grounds that are pretty basic with crowds rarely over three figures, and the chances of ever winning anything are pretty remote. It's just loyalty to your team. There's no choice.'

The upside, as he sees it, is the freedom to buy a ticket on matchdays and stand or sit where he likes. 'I'm glad to support a team at this level. I don't have to call an automated service to buy a ticket for a game weeks later, I just turn up and pay at the gate. Most grounds I like to stand on the terracing and walk around. If I don't like the guy next to me I can move, if you buy a season ticket you can end up next to an arsehole for the season.'

It's a fair point, and one appreciated by legions of kindred spirits who prefer to huddle and move around old-fashioned terracing in bulky jackets and woolly hats and address pertinent remarks at the ref and opposition.

Colin reckons they're better off than supporters of Premier League teams who don't have the same intimacy with the people who run them. Like many small clubs, Berwick relies on its supporters for survival, fostering close relations between directors, players and supporters who are often on first-name terms.

'If your team is in the Premier League, whether in England or Scotland, you're getting a rough deal these days. You're regarded by those in charge as just a number, or at best a customer. A lot of people running big clubs don't understand this. We're all customers of various things like supermarkets, but they don't have that special feeling you have inside you for your football club.'

Like most fans he enjoys watching big games on TV, but fears that unremitting broadcasting is diminishing 'real' football. 'They talk about live football in pubs but it's not live football, you only get that at a ground. You have kids supporting teams they've never seen because they're on TV a couple of days a week. I've heard it said make sure your child doesn't grow up thinking football is a TV programme.'

If they do, much of the responsibility will lie with the FA and the Premier League and their subservience to the demands and financial lures of broadcasters. Shortly after my chat with Colin, *The Times* reported that Richard Scudamore, executive chairman of the Premier League, had decided to offer broadcasters a package of eight '*Saturday Night Live*' matches with 7.45pm kick-offs. It pointed out this would effectively prevent many away fans from travelling on public transport, with last trains departing cities before final whistles. The FA, supposed guardians of the game, had already paved the way by moving the FA Cup Final kick-off to 5.30pm to suit television, rather than supporters of the competing clubs.

Henry Winter, the newspaper's chief football writer, observed that unsympathetic scheduling is a fixture of the TV age, and commented, 'The Premier League succumbing to Saturday night fever is a parable about modern English football. It is about the greed and myopia of a game focussing more on funds than fans. Who matters most? The fan in the stadium, supporting his or her team through thick and thin, or somebody in a bar in Bangkok? All are welcome, but the match-going life-blood of the game deserves protecting first.'

It is a view widely shared at grounds throughout the country, along with a growing sense of unease about a surfeit of televised games.

I have a few more interviews lined up before Berwick's home match on Saturday, but it's only Tuesday, so next morning I go for a walk. One of the town's more illustrious visitors, along with Robert the Bruce, was L.S. Lowry the 'matchstick men' painter of working-class towns in the industrial North West, who regularly escaped the grime and grit of his subjects to sketch and paint in the bracing sea air of Berwick.

Enterprising civic officials have created a 'Lowry Trail' linking prints of his work displayed in situ where he created them.

One of them stands near the apartment my wife Claire and I have rented for the week, overlooking a pier that runs half a mile out to sea, so that is where I begin.

The pier is actually a massive stone breakwater with a red and white lighthouse at the end of it, built to protect the Tweed estuary from dangerous winds and currents. On a cold November day the lighthouse is etched dramatically against lowering skies and gunmetal seas, a lonely sentinel of a safe haven that drew Lowry in 1942 to portray what he called 'a terrible sea'.

The pier is a dog-leg shape, and as I turn the corner halfway along I lose the protection of a wall and the wind hits me like a fist. I stagger on, as far from the unprotected edge as possible, and pass a couple of locals chatting away happily as if being in a howling wind tunnel is the most natural thing in the world. In Berwick they call this a lazy wind, because it cuts through you instead of going around you.

The framed print of Lowry's *The Sea* is fixed to the wall of the lighthouse. It is one of his 'empty' seascapes that capture the mystery and infinity of oceans, with the black, white and blue-grey tints evoking the desolation of the North Sea in winter. He depicted a calm sea, but all around me cascades of white horses are flying and crashing towards the shore in a tumult of spray.

As an old man Lowry wrote, 'It's all there. It's all in the sea. The Battle of Life is there. And fate. And the inevitability of it all.' What would happen, he often wondered, if the tide didn't turn and came on and on? Perhaps if we continue burning fossil fuels we'll find out one day. As I turn back, a couple of matchstick figures with a dog appear in the distance walking towards me. They could have stepped from a Lowry painting.

On the landward side of the pier is a rarity. Lowry claimed that his work was unremittingly gloomy: 'Poverty and gloom. Never a joyous picture of mine you'll see. Always gloom. I never do a jolly picture.' In fact he did at least one, and a print of it is displayed where he painted children playing happily around a beach shelter. Today it is exactly as he portrayed it, minus the children.

The ramparts around Berwick are more than two miles long, and you can walk all around them, with views of the grey town below on one side and the sea and countryside on the other. Lowry was keen on football, and from the fortress he sketched a match being played below in a grassy expanse that was originally a moat, using short vertical strokes to depict the players and the crowd. There is no record of him having attended a Berwick Rangers match, which is a shame. If the club had ever acquired a Lowry painting of one of their matches it could have solved their financial problems for generations. The Lowry Trail extends over the river to an erstwhile fishing village and a seaside resort that are administratively part of the town. This is where Rangers' ground lies, but more of this later.

My wife, meanwhile. is off on explorations of her own with an aunt who has come up from Leeds. Claire is researching a magazine article on the Northumberland Coastal Path and returns with ruddy cheeks and glowing accounts of bracing walks to Bamburgh Castle and the Holy Isle. So on one side Berwick is blessed with a dramatic, unspoiled coastline and on another the bucolic countryside of a river that inspired the poetry of Sir Walter Scott. Not a bad place to kick a ball around.

Michael Smyth has had an eventful life. Before becoming chairman of the Berwick Supporters Trust, he spent years roaming the globe as a geography teacher and ended up refereeing football matches on the Atlantic island of St Helena.

This was of particular interest to me as I had been to the island years before on a travel writing assignment, and Michael is the only other person I know who has set foot on one of the most remote human settlements on Earth. At the time of writing, Napoleon's last place of exile has become less lonely, having acquired a scarily windy airport with flight connections to South Africa. Previously the only means of getting there was on the Royal Mail Ship *St Helena*, a mixed cargo/passenger vessel sailing from Cape Town and the UK, which was an adventure in itself.

Entertainment on the ship was of the home-grown variety, from pub quizzes to deck quoits and cricket matches on the sun deck that required a plentiful supply of balls. I recall an officers' performance of *The Pirates of Penzance* in which the purser's trousers fell down and the first mate's brassiere went a bit wonky, but the chief engineer saved the day with an enthusiastic rendition of 'Oh, there is not one maiden breast'. The production was unlikely to make the West End, but in the middle of the South Atlantic it merited a rousing ovation from an admittedly captive audience.

I meet Michael in the more familiar surroundings of a traditional English pub. The Pilot Inn is a warm, cosy place on a bitter winter's day with open fireplaces and real ales on hand pumps, where the Supporters Trust has its meetings.

Over pints of Fireglow spiced winter ale, we swap tales of an island until recently lost in space and time, and of Michael's brief career as a football referee. 'There were eight teams in two leagues and they were short of referees, and I had been seconded to a PE department, so they asked if I could help out. I had never refereed a football match so they gave me a book of FA rules and told me not to worry if I made a mistake, because players make mistakes all the time. People forget that. I have a lot of sympathy for referees now.'

He was fortunate in that flare-ups on the field were rare, since most of the players were friends and neighbours. 'I wasn't much of a ref,' he admits, 'but I was reliable and I can put on my CV honestly that I've refereed at national league level.'

Michael was nine when an uncle took him to his first Berwick game, a 2-2 draw with Stranraer, and he's been supporting them ever since, except during stints overseas in St Helena, Romania, Albania, Egypt and Kuwait. When I ask why, he says, 'It's my home-town team. Quite honestly if somebody gave me a ticket for Old Trafford I'd give it away, I'm not really interested.'

He'd rather have a ticket for the Supporters Club weekly draw – £1 for three numbers corresponding to teams playing that day, and the highest and lowest scores win cash prizes. It brings in £355 a week, barely loose change to Premier League clubs but important to Berwick's survival. 'We made big losses the last couple of seasons, and we've been knocked out of all the cups already, so this is going to be another tough one. If we go into the red, you wonder how deep we can go.'

It's only November and the squad inherited by the new manager appointed in August has been bundled out of the

Scottish Cup, the Betfred (League Cup) and the Irn Bru (Challenge Cup). Next up is high-flying Stirling Albion, lying second in the league, then away to table toppers Montrose. Tough games.

On the way to the pub I met a bus driver who believed the team lacked support because it had only one local player. It was a common complaint, he said.

'Theoretically it sounds great to have a team from the town,' Michael says. 'But we have a small population and most of the lads are happy to play with mates in local leagues, and don't have ambitions to go higher. The other reason is that we haven't had a training pitch in Berwick for years, and these are working lads with full-time jobs. To be honest, the East of Scotland league is probably the top level for them.'

Christmas is approaching, so on my way back through town I treat myself to a pack of mince pies and ask the cashier if she's from Berwick. She is, and has an English accent, so I presume she considers herself English? 'I suppose so, but a lot of us just call ourselves Borderers,' she says.

This is a local variation of sitting on the fence you might call sitting on the Tweed. It is probably wise, given centuries of riotous mayhem that has flowed back and forth across this fluid border. From the 14th to the 17th centuries it was a battleground of lawless Scots and English families known as Border Reivers (raiders) whose primary occupations were cattle rustling, arson, pillaging and murder. No social stigma was attached to this behaviour, it was simply an accepted way of life for skilled horsemen and guerrilla soldiers practised in the fine arts of kidnapping and extortion. The story goes that the wife of one notorious Reiver indicated her larder was empty by serving her husband his spurs on his plate for dinner, with the clear injunction that it was time to mount up and go reiving. The outlaws would happily join in battles between Scots and English armies but would swear allegiance to one side or the other only when it suited them and their families.

In a sense, Berwick Rangers continues this venerable tradition by taking the field on both sides of the border, with a club crest bearing the lion rampant of Scotland and a lion couchant of England.

I receive a call from John Bell, vice-chairman of the club and the Supporters Trust representative on its board, who has heard I'm in town. This takes me back to the Berwick Youth Project which he manages, and which gives him an insight into the economic difficulties facing his football team.

'For all it's a beautiful place, Berwick has the second lowest average salary in England and Wales,' he says. 'There isn't high unemployment, there's enough work to go around, but local business are not paying big wages and most people are on the minimum. So people are very discerning about how they spend their money. If they can afford a Sky subscription they don't want to pay more to stand around in the cold to watch a game.'

His complaint that most of the money that comes into the Scottish game through TV and sponsorship goes to the Premier League is a familiar refrain. By the time it trickles down to League Two its clubs are left with 2 per cent of the total, which works out at 0.2 per cent each.

'We start every year with a budget we know will fall short, with a wage bill of around £120,000 for the first team, and unless we get a good cup run or a game against the Old Firm we're going to be in the shite basically. Over ten years we've spent £1 million on players to achieve nothing. We've still got a team on the park, but that's about it.'

Overall, he paints a gloomy picture of limited resources and an ageing population of fans who literally die off each season, or drift away because they don't want to stand in the cold anymore. 'It's easy to get young kids in with special offers, the challenge is keeping them when they're older and we start asking them for a bit more money. The problem is that live TV matches, computer games and online betting become their contact points to football.'

Clubs have to make income outside football, he says, and he often visits small teams in Europe to see how they develop multi-sports facilities, sharing them with athletics and tennis clubs. 'We've had a few improvements at Shielfield, but it's crumbling a wee bit round the edges and it's a bit of a shite field to be honest. We have to do better.' He suggests a good start would be a quality artificial pitch that could bring in a bit of money by renting it to other sports clubs in the area, a scheme that has been discussed for years without fruition.

He's also investigating the possibility of a new stadium with two all-weather pitches and a running track on a 20-acre site near Shielfield, and the town council has pledged £5,000 towards initial planning costs. 'At the moment it's just an idea on a piece of paper that needs to win a Euromillions lottery, but in the long term it's the way forward.'

He says there is a perception that the powers that be regard lower league clubs as a bit of a nuisance, that they don't really matter. But of course they do, to hundreds of footballers and thousands of fans who follow them, and John makes a pertinent point: 'We've all become aware recently of mental health problems arising from players not having contracts renewed and worrying about moving home and supporting families. These are serious issues. We provide opportunities to relieve the pressure through part-time football. It's a good career choice for players who find they can't compete at the top level, where they can continue playing with like-minded lads and win medals, and still earn a good living from a regular job.'

It is midweek and there's unlikely to be anyone at the stadium, so John calls another club stalwart to arrange a guided tour next day.

Shielfield Park lies across the river in Tweedmouth, a former salmon fishing village swallowed up by the suburban overflow of Berwick and its town council. It's a fairly nondescript place with a dock that exports barley and fertiliser, and a decent fish and chip shop. There are no 'football traffic' road signs to the home of Berwick Rangers, which lies off a B road to Coldstream, past a retirement home and a row of terraced houses. A small sign, blink and you'll miss it, points down a lane to open grassy ground where locals walk their dogs and Rangers play behind an enclosure of metal and stone walls dominated by giant silver silos of malting barley. On weekdays the place has a vaguely abandoned air and the predominant sound is a repetitive mechanical clunking from the silos complex.

The clubhouse is a modest two-storey brick building opposite a 'Black & Gold' bar and function suite, neither of which the club owns. The stadium was sold to Northumberland County Council years ago and leased to the Supporters Association, and the bar and lounge went to a local builder. Most days the only car outside belongs to the groundsman, the club's only full-time employee.

Today he has company. I am greeted by a sprightly character in his late 70s who is too young in mind and body to consider retiring after a lifetime of service to the club. Ian Oliver joined Rangers as a centre-forward in the late 1950s and stayed on as kit man and occasional physio while working in a knitwear factory. He's been with the club in one capacity or another for 40 years, travelled with it to every senior ground in Scotland except one (Inverness Caledonian Thistle), and has seen 18 managers come and go.

Football is in the Oliver blood apparently. His son Neil began his career at Berwick, moved to Blackburn and ended up playing for Falkirk in a Scottish Cup Final against Kilmarnock in 1997. He scored but it was ruled offside and Falkirk lost. 'I've watched it lots of times on video and it was never offside,' Ian insists. Now Neil is back at Berwick, coaching the under-20s squad.

It doesn't take Ian long to show me around. The main building houses changing rooms, lounges, a boardroom and a directors' hospitality suite, all best described as compact and unpretentious. Ian admits the changing rooms are 'a wee bit small', and says a new problem is female match officials. 'We don't have separate facilities, we just have to wait for the ladies to change first.'

There are lots of cups and silver plates in the boardroom, none of them for any historic achievements. The biggest trophy is for the club's Player of the Year, and there is a literary award – for Scottish League Two Programme of the Month. The prize exhibits are the framed black and gold strips of Berwick and royal blue of Glasgow Rangers worn on that fateful day in 1967, along with a poster listing ticket prices for the game at 3/6d for the ground, 5/- for the stand and 1/6d for OAPs and juveniles. They were probably the best few shillings Berwick fans spent in their lives.

The old cast-off Bradford City stand provides cover for about 1,300 seats overlooking a speedway track that spits dirt in summer, beneath the snarling wheels of the Berwick Bandits, and the football pitch with a noticeable slope that looks in reasonable shape this early in the season. On the far side is terracing open to wind, weather and home and away fans alike, partially sheltered by an iron shed known as the Docket, which is dialect in the North East for a pigeon loft. The club shop is a shack by the toilets that opens on matchdays, beside a catering van. So hot pies, partial shelter from driving rain and new scarves and bobble hats are all available on Saturdays to brave bands of Borderers.

Ian is in his element here, a dyed-in-border-wool football man with a fund of memories and anecdotes of life among the grassroots of the game. 'I wish I'd kept a diary,' he says. 'With all the daft things that have happened I could have written a bestseller.'

He recalls a game at Stenhousemuir when he was the physio and attended to an injured midfielder, who played on. 'That was an easy tenner,' one of the coaching staff commented. 'Whit's that aboot a tenner?' one of the subs wanted to know. 'I told him that if I got an injured player going again I got a tenner, but if he had to come off I got nothing.' In the second half the sub was called into action and collapsed in a heap five minutes later. When Ian ran on and asked him what was the matter, the lad said, 'There's nowt wrong wi' me but that's a fiver each.'

Then there was the time the engine of their bus caught fire on the way to Montrose, and they hitched rides and caught taxis to the ground only to find the match had been called off because of the weather. Happily Kilmarnock were playing at nearby Arbroath, and their manager (ex-Berwick) obligingly sent their team bus to collect Berwick's players to watch the game while waiting for a replacement bus to arrive. 'When we turned up in Arbroath in the Kilmarnock bus in our Berwick tracksuits the supporters were a wee bit mystified,' Ian recalls.

Times have changed, and not always for the better in his view. 'I think the quality of football in Scotland has deteriorated. When I was a laddie we played every night wherever we could kick a ball, even if it was just an old tennis ball, that was what produced the likes of Denis Law and Jim Baxter.' They used to call them 'Tanner ba' players, men and boys who played in factory yards, back streets and school playgrounds every chance they got with balls that cost sixpence. On your own there was always keepie-uppie or headers against a wall until it was too dark to see. 'You don't see owt like that any more, there are too many other distractions, and how they get it back now I don't know.' His local hero was Dave Smith, Berwick player-manager in the late 70s, an ex-Glasgow Rangers left-half who took the club from rock bottom of the lowest league to promotion two seasons later: 'He was the best player I've seen playing for us. He never tackled a man in his life, he just stood there and took the ball off him.'

Both of Ian's sons played amateur football in their early teens, and one Saturday the local chip shop owner said he was sorry to hear that one of them had suffered a broken leg. 'He didn't say which boy, so I said "which one?" "I think it was the left one," he said. I couldn't believe it.' Another one for Ian's book of memoirs.

It is Thursday and I'd hoped to go along to the team's twice-weekly evening training session, but it's taking place as always on the synthetic pitch of Haddington Juniors, 50 miles away in the outskirts of Edinburgh. It's a cold, dark night with a threat of rain, no time to be driving up and down an unlit road to stand around for hours in a biting wind, so I opt for an evening with Oscar Wilde. *A Woman Of No Importance* is being broadcast live from a London theatre in The Maltings, Berwick's excellent little arts centre, and I settle happily into a red velour seat in a warm auditorium and wish the hardy lads of Berwick FC well in their outdoor endeavours.

It's a disappointing performance by actors more intent on bawling their lines than quietly delivering the *bons mots* of Wilde's waspish humour. I leave at the interval and return to the apartment to find lowly Fylde FC giving Wigan a hard time in a televised cup match and earning a replay. So all's well that ends well for another wee club.

Next day I arrange to meet the only Berwick player who lives anywhere near the town. Central-defender Jonny Fairbairn, 27, lives and occasionally works on his dad's arable farm in the hamlet of Millfield, about 20 miles inland from Berwick in the shadow of the Cheviot Hills. It's a pleasant drive on quiet roads through rural Northumberland, a land of rolling pastures and dry-stone walls where traffic pootles along at the speed of tractors and hay lorries. In winter lone, bare trees are works of nature's art etched on skylines of fields lying fallow. It is like driving through an open-air gallery of landscape paintings.

The Fairbairn family business produces wheat, barley, oats and oil seed rape, and Jonny's fitness training gets a boost during harvest season. The rest of the time his main focus is on holding down a place in Rangers' first team and coaching a new generation to succeed him.

We meet in the family kitchen, with fresh coffee on the stove and a combine harvester parked outside. 'I'm one of the lucky ones,' he says. 'Working on the farm with Dad has been a massive help for me, it takes a lot of the pressure off part-time football. I'm not pulling up trees financially but I'm not really concerned at this stage in my career. I've got a lot to thank Mum and Dad for.'

Jonny took an unusual route to Scottish football via four years with a university team in Mississippi that recruited him through an agent he met at a careers day at Hampden Park, the Glasgow home of Queen's Park. His appetite for the game had been sharpened by a year with St Johnstone's youth squad when he trained with the first team under Owen Coyle and then Derek McInnes, two of Scotland's leading managers.

In an ideal world he'd be playing in the Premier League by now, but in the meantime he's happy turning out for a team pretty much on his doorstep and running a youth academy he started at a local college. He began coaching with a UEFA B licence, and says, 'I just want to play and coach at the highest levels I can and make a living out of it. I like looking at the game in an analytical way, and I'm probably a better coach than I've ever been as a player.'

This is good news for teenage lads at the Berwick branch of Northumberland College, who train with Jonny twice a week and play against other college teams in the likes of Newcastle, Sunderland and Hartlepool. It is also good news for Berwick's under-20s squad that has begun to reap the benefits by signing two of Jonny's protégés.

It's a great grassroots experience, he says, although possibly not for his mum who washes the boys' strips. 'It's my number-one priority to look for promising players, bring them on and give the lads a chance to break into senior football. It's a massive step for them to be given a platform and get noticed.'

For this he is paid peanuts, if anything. I have just read that a Manchester City player is negotiating a contract worth a reported £200,000 a week, and I find myself wondering how many nights he spends coaching at a local college.

Jonny's next generation of would-be stars is hampered by lack of training facilities. On good days they use a public park next to Shielfield, but more often winter weather sends them to five-a-side synthetic pitches at a leisure centre. 'Berwick is crying out for a full-size 3G pitch, it's really hampering the town in terms of developing football. There are lots of teams in the area, but when it comes to this time of year they really struggle for training and playing facilities.'

His own training sessions involve driving 200 miles a week to and from Haddington, but it seems to be no big deal for something he enjoys. He drives up and down twice a week with the only other Englishman in the team, Chris McDonald, who comes from near Jarrow and has an impenetrable Geordie accent that his team-mates are only beginning to understand. Jonny says they are enjoying training under their new manager, which is raising spirits as well as fitness and skills. 'The sessions are really good. Simple, high-intensity drills make a massive difference to the mood and morale of players. If you're a footballer you don't mind working hard if it's structured and competitive, you enjoy it. If you have a good training session you walk away in good spirits, but if guys are just going through the motions it can create negative energy and you feel low. A good session is when everybody is demanding the same standards, it builds team spirit, and when you're biting into tackles in training it becomes second nature. Last night a lot of the lads stayed for a while, and everybody was talking in high spirits. It's such a good sign, there's big team spirit there.'

When they take the field tomorrow they'll be hoping their buoyant mood produces goals and raucous support from the fans. Jonny is frank about the impact of home support or abuse on players. 'The speedway track at Shielfield is a disadvantage because it disconnects us from the supporters. At Annan the fans are right on top of you and if they score first the fans' support builds up and it's a battle to stay in the game because they can bulldoze you. Some stadiums have that atmosphere that can intimidate away teams. I wouldn't say Shielfield is like that. It's fine when the fans are behind you when you're two or three up, but it's when you're losing you really need their support. If they get on top of you, players become anxious and scared of making mistakes.' And when a team loses confidence it's easy to go on a losing run. 'With only ten teams the league is so tight. A few good results can mean a good season, and a few bad results can make it horrendous.'

Jonny is an articulate, thoughtful footballer who likes to analyse games, and for much of last season he was Berwick's captain. He was dropped for the last game, the 5-1 drubbing at Elgin, and will learn tonight whether he has won his place back tomorrow.

'The gaffer phones you on Friday night and lets you know whether you're in or out of the team, and chats to you about it. It's the best you can hope for. You can't say he's not being honest or going about it the wrong way. You know exactly where you stand with him, so there's no negativity in the dressing room. Even if you're not playing you still feel part of it, and still want to be part of it even if you've been dropped. It comes down to respect.'

Jonny is wearing his club tracksuit, and we step outside to take photos of him posing beside the combine harvester. I wish him good luck for tomorrow, and genuinely hope he gets a game.

I have arranged to call manager Robbie Horn tonight, as he has to rush away after the match. I'm tempted to ask if Jonny will be playing, but I guess this would be a breach of team etiquette and start by inquiring about his career. Like Jonny, he played centre-half for Berwick and was captain in the League Three-winning season 2006/07, before moving to Hearts full time for five years, then on to Forfar as part-time player-manager for six seasons. He returned to Berwick as assistant manager for a couple of years, then took the reins at Bonnyrigg Rose, a Junior side near Edinburgh. I ask what brought him back for a third spell at Berwick. 'I wanted a crack at managing in senior football, and this was probably the only chance I'd get. It's difficult for a young manager to break into the senior ranks. I was no world beater as a player, but I was a wholehearted centre-half.'

Horn is under no illusions about the task facing him, with the team he inherited barely holding its own in the lower half of the table. 'Results have been disappointing to say the least. We've had to make do with what we've got, and we've lost cheap goals, but I can't fault the team for their efforts. The first priority is to make us safe, and I'll be assessing the squad before the January transfer window.

It's pretty clear we're missing goalscorers and I'll have to do a bit of wheeling and dealing. It's not an overnight fix, that's for sure.'

His long-term plan is to rebuild in the summer, cherry picking from junior teams, picking up players released by senior clubs, and looking for loan signings. It's a familiar scenario for lower league managers with ambitions bigger than bank balances. Horn has been impressed by three or four lads in the youth development squad who look good enough to step up, and he'd love to recruit more players locally, but reckons there are few with the attitude and dedication to succeed. Meanwhile, he's trying to adapt a 4-3-3 system that produced a strong side at Bonnyrigg. 'I want us to get the ball down and play the right way at a tempo other teams can't live with, but our current players are not quite up to it, so it's getting the balance right with a 3-5-2 set-up not to concede goals.' At least, like Jonny, he's enjoying the training sessions. 'I love training and the banter with the players and other coaches. It's like a drug. I can't give it up.' The portents for tomorrow seem good, with an ambitious manager and players on a high.

Saturday dawns reluctantly over the North Sea coast beneath grey wintry skies, but there's no sign of rain and the lazy wind has died. It's a good day for a match. The town is bustling with weekend street markets and Christmas shoppers, and I'm at the shops early to ensure a traditional matchday lunch of pie and beans. Aficionados of meat pies at Scots football grounds swear the finest are at Kilmarnock, but the specimen I buy at a farmer's street stall in Berwick is worthy of any connoisseur.

By two o'clock the field opposite Shielfield is beginning to fill with cars, and the Black & Gold lounge bar is buzzing with both sets of fans. I join a table of Berwick men and get into conversation with Ian Beresford, an accountant, and Alan Bell, an engineer. Both are originally from Yorkshire but moved to Berwick when they were boys and have been supporting Rangers off and on ever since.

'What sealed it for me was a cup game against Elgin in 2003 when we went two down and came back to win 3-2,' Ian says. 'All that excitement and passion on the terraces, that's what football's all about, not sitting in front of a TV.' He recalls freezing at a midweek game against Montrose when he could have been at home watching Chelsea v Barcelona: 'I suppose I kind of revel in the hardship. I've switched back to real football, and I think there's a movement back to it. Satellite TV is overdoing it a bit with games just about every night.'

Alan is a kindred spirit. He was 11 when his big sister took him to his first game against Stranraer: 'We got plugged 3-0, but I was hooked. It's just loyalty to my home-town team, simple as that. The club means everything to me, it's my main hobby.' He is a man of many talents is Alan, a bit of a historian, scribe and photographer who has written a book on Rangers' first 30 years and takes action photographs for matchday programmes. He was once offered a hospitality package for Newcastle v Man City worth £400 but declined it. 'We were playing Montrose at home, and I'd rather come here and freeze me nuts off.'

There is no rational explanation for this behaviour, and none is offered. It goes much deeper than logic, into the realms of unfathomable human nature and passion for standing in the rain with equally benighted souls urging a bunch of mud-spattered local heroes to get stuck into the opposition. Ian's take on the vicissitudes of supporting a team with prospects of not much more than survival is classic stoicism. 'You're not in it for the glory. Big clubs expect to win and when they don't it's a disaster. With us every win's a bonus and you get a right good feeling. You take it week to week and we get ups and downs, but I'm in it for the ride. It's not just about 90 minutes on the pitch, it's pints with your mates before the game and standing and shouting on open terracing, not sitting taking pictures of overpaid stars with your phone.'

Given Berwick's erratic form and Stirling's flying start to the season, they'll be happy with a draw today and are looking forward to 'a bit of banter' with opposition fans. 'There's camaraderie in the lower leagues,' Ian says, 'there's no great divide between us and we're not penned up in the ground.'

Nor in the bar, which has attracted roughly equal groups of fans and I wander over to a table of men festooned in the red and white of Stirling Albion. One of them has fond memories of Shielfield, which he knows well. Cammy Stuart was 18 when he made his debut here as centre-half for Stirling in 1970, and coming back is always special. 'It's grand comin' here, we aye enjoy it, even if it's in England. An' ye know the best thing aboot it? It hasnae changed in a' these years.' The rapid pace of change in the modern world can be unsettling for older generations, and when things stay the same it is comforting. Shielfield may be worn out and past its sell-by date, but Cammy enjoys being here because he can look at a familiar pitch and in his mind's eye see himself playing on it in another lifetime.

It's five minutes to kick-off so I stroll across to the ground where secretary Dennis McCleary has arranged press accreditation for me. He also hands me a team sheet, and I'm pleased to see Jonny Fairbairn's name in the starting XI. I'll be entering through the tunnel so I have to wait until the players and match officials emerge from the dressing rooms, and we chat about Dennis's career at Shielfield. His dad manned the turnstiles, he began as stadium announcer, and now he wears two hats as football secretary and co-promoter of the speedway team. He admits the place is run down and expensive to maintain, and says, 'A new stadium is the way forward, there's no doubt about that, though I doubt it will happen in my lifetime.'

A clatter of boots interrupts our conversation and a minute later I'm following the teams down the tunnel, fondly imagining I'm on the Berwick bench. Instead I take a seat in the half-empty stand, as Stirling launch a couple of early probing attacks. At least half the crowd of around 400 is on the terracing around the Ducket on the far side, so I stroll around the back of a goalmouth and join little clusters of woollen bobbin hats, red and white for Stirling and black and gold for Berwick. The spirits roused by Robbie Horn's training regime are apparent in high-tempo, fluent passing as Rangers swarm down the sloping pitch with the wind at their backs, and in seven minutes a speculative shot comes back off a line of defenders, and midfielder Michael McKenna volleys coolly home from the edge of the box. Cue roars of delight and surprise from the Berwick bobbins.

I find myself standing beside Ian Beresford, and Colin Pike spots us and comes over. Berwick are playing with confidence, but Ian is a realist by experience: 'This is Berwick, we can't take a win for granted. If we go three up we can begin to relax.' As if to prove the point, Stirling spring an offside trap and keeper Robby McCrorie pulls off an outstanding double save. The young keeper, a Scottish under-19 international on loan from Glasgow Rangers, is destined for a busy afternoon and it's no surprise when he's named man of the match. The game settles into an even contest waged mainly in the middle of the park, and Jonny is putting in a solid performance in the back three.

At half-time the catering van does a roaring trade in pies, fish, haggis and chips, and I buy a tea mug in the club shop to add to my 2017/18 tour collection. The second half has just kicked off when our attention is drawn to the sky. A glorious sunset is unfolding, a celestial chiaroscuro of encroaching night and the dying embers of the day, setting the heavens ablaze with glowing crimson and golden clouds. It is more dramatic than anything happening on the pitch, and Colin's phone buzzes with a message. A Stirling supporter has tweeted an image captioned 'Sunset at Shielfield'. It is hardly the poetry of Sir Walter Scott, but the appreciation of the beauty of nature is the same and we all share it.

In the absence of diverting action on the pitch, Colin reminisces about stars of yesterday who have graced it more memorably. Gary Lineker turned out for Leicester in Berwick's centenary game in the 1980s, Alex Ferguson played here for Falkirk, and George Best drew a big crowd when he appeared with Hibs. 'A bit of wall collapsed trackside because of the pressure of fans, but I guess Best wasn't aware he was here. He was on a downward track by then.'

Back on the park Stirling are pressing high for an equaliser, leaving gaps at the back being exploited by Berwick's pacey wide men. The game is livening up, swinging from end to end with flowing football and tasty tackles flying in between, eliciting choice language from the terracing directed at opposition players and match officials. 'There's two teams on the pitch, ours and the referee's,' Ian proclaims. Up goes a chant of 'Come on Stirling', that triggers a fruity response from the home fans, and lively verbal repartee. Ian and Colin are loving it. 'We enjoy the banter,' Ian says, urging on his team with cries of 'Go on Berwick, get into them.'

Rangers are unlucky not to double their lead when a header crashes off the bar, and Stirling's assistant coach is sent to the stands as tempers and frustration mount in the final minutes, then finally the whistle goes, to the joy and relief of home fans. The Supporters Trust website later declares it the best game seen at Shielfield so far this season, and few of the Berwick faithful would disagree. With five changes from the side humped by Elgin, the team played with their tails up and deserved their win.

In post-match comments, the manager is fulsome in his praise: 'I asked for a reaction from last week and to a man we were outstanding. The back three were immense. We rode our luck a wee bit in the first half, but the supporters can see the players gave everything. Now we're looking up the table at the play-off spots.'

I have arranged to meet chairman Len Ayre in the sponsors' lounge, which is open to all comers after the match. A lively gathering of club officials, players and fans is warming up with pints and laughter, and I spot Jonny in a corner in earnest conversation and we exchange thumbs-up signs. Ayre appears, wearing a suit and a broad smile. This has been a good afternoon, and he leads me into a quiet side room for a chat.

Berwick born and bred and a lifelong Rangers supporter, he has been on the board for almost ten years, and when he retired from a successful electrical business a couple of years ago he wondered what he was going to do with his time. The answer was to take over as chairman and bring his wife along to do the cleaning and sell lottery tickets. 'It's a very hands-on club, we have to be,' he says.

With money tight, he says his focus is on developing youth squads and helping supporters to raise funds. 'There's not a lot of sponsorship around, and with no cup runs our backs are to the wall. We've got teams from eight years old, and they're the future for this club. We have to bring young lads through, I see that as the way forward, but it'll take a few years.'

On Shielfield, he says plans had been well advanced for a new stadium with 3G playing and training fields, but then politics intervened. According to him a previous Labour Northumberland County Council had been planning to allocate £3 million for the project, but when the Conservatives came in the money went south for a multi-storey car park in Hexham.

So it's back to raffles, functions and race nights to keep the club going. 'I'd like to involve supporters more in social events and fundraising. They are the lifeblood of the club, without them there wouldn't be Berwick Rangers.' It is a deserved testimonial to the hardy bands of Borderers who ensure the humblers of mighty Glasgow Rangers survive to fight another day.

As I leave the darkening stadium I muse that maybe one day they will have a synthetic pitch where they can train in all weathers, maybe Jonny's academy will produce promising local youngsters to play on it, and maybe families and friends will come to support them.

Maybe.

On leaving the town next day, I pop into the Youth Trust to say cheerio to John and Colin. They're out, but their office manager Deborah is glad to see me. 'You must be a good omen, they haven't played like that for a long time. You must come back,' she says.

Invitation accepted.

Cambridge United

The club is the people and the people are the club

Founded:	1912
Ground:	Abbey Stadium
Average attendance:	4,523
Honours:	Third Division champions 1990/91
	FA Trophy 2013/14

WHEN YOU think of Cambridge, football is probably the last thing that comes to mind. This is an ancient pantheon of academia, a world renowned seat of learning for eight centuries that has produced a master race of scientists, philosophers and statesmen that has changed the world and our perception of it. From its hallowed colleges have emerged the likes of Charles Darwin, Stephen Hawking and Iris Murdoch. At the last count Trinity College alone had produced 33 Nobel laureates, more than most countries. But footballers?

Life is full of surprises. It turns out Cambridge University produced, unofficially, the world's first association football club, after drafting a playing code that formed the basis of the first FA rules in 1846. A few years earlier George Corrie, Master of Jesus College, observed an interesting spectacle while enjoying a stroll by a green common with a colleague: 'In walking with Willis we passed by Parker's Piece and there saw some 40 gownsmen playing at football. The novelty and liveliness of the scene were amusing.'

The 'Cambridge Rules' were fairly simple, aimed at taking some of the rough and tumble out of a sport in which the biggest, toughest and most ruthless usually won. The emphasis of the new code was on skill rather than brute force, forbidding catching the ball and wild lunging tackles known as 'hacking'. In 1863, E.C. Morley, the FA honorary secretary, declared: 'They embrace the true principles of the game with the greatest simplicity.'

For good measure, Cambridge University Association Football Club, founded in 1856 and still going strong, went on to provide almost 50 England internationals in the early 20th century, and has since been declared by the National Football Museum to be the world's oldest club.

By the time the Football League was founded in 1888, the university team had developed a game we would find familiar today. A researcher at the University of London concluded, 'Curiously, the side that was generally credited with transforming the tactics of association football and almost single-handedly inventing the modern game was not a professional team but the Cambridge University XI of 1882. Contemporaries described Cambridge as being the first "combination" team in which each player was allotted an area of the field and played as part of a team in a game that was based upon passing.'

Officials of Queen's Park FC in Glasgow might take issue with this, as the Scottish team that humped England 6-1 at the Oval in 1881 was composed entirely of Queen's men reported to be playing 'combination' football. But apparently we have the university men to thank for introducing the 'pyramid' system of two defenders, three midfielders and five forwards that some of us remember fondly from our youth. Those were the days of attacking football by flying wingers, crafty inside-forwards, and towering centre-halves who took no prisoners.

The professional club that followed in the footsteps of the university pioneers has no claims to fame, unless you count survival from administration and an FA Trophy, but it has a decent social club, a staunch support, and arguably the best groundsman in the country who tells good stories.

All of them are to be found at the Abbey Stadium, a tidy little ground a couple of miles from the city centre that has been there since 1932, and looks like it. There have been various proposals to build a new community stadium elsewhere, but nobody wanted it in their backyard, so the current plan is to redevelop the Abbey.

The next visitors in a few days are high-flying Mansfield Town, tipped by the bookies as pre-season favourites to win the league. One defeat in 19 games has taken them into the play-off places, a point from automatic promotion, and into the third round of the FA Cup with the prospect of a home tie against Manchester City if they can overcome Cardiff in a replay. Cambridge are unbeaten in four games and bobbing around mid-table, but the consensus is they will be doing well to get a point.

It is a cold, misty January day and banks of floodlights among the highest and oldest in the league are lost in the gloom when a taxi drops me outside a car park by a Cambridge United sign. It's only a side entrance for a portacabin ticket office and a supporters' social club, and a workman directs me to a puddle-strewn gravel lane that leads eventually to the stadium, where Dave Matthew-Jones is waiting for me.

Dave is a lean, sprightly figure with a shock of steel grey hair and a paintbrush in his hand, who is the fans' elected director. He's been varnishing doors, one of many odd jobs that keep him busy at the club since he retired from BT. 'The old place takes a bit of looking after,' he admits. This is clearly an understatement. The entrance to the offices in the main stand is closed off because a storm blew tiles off the roof and damaged down pipes. Happy days in League Two.

We repair to the Abbey Arms, a black square box a few steps away that used to be a gym and now serves as a matchday bar. Dave has been supporting United since he arrived in Cambridge as a boy from Coventry, and has never seen any point in following a bigger club. 'How can Man City and Glasgow Rangers supporters used to winning leagues and trophies every season say a particular match was the best day of their life? In 2014 we won the FA Trophy at Wembley and a few months later went back and beat Gateshead to be promoted back into the league from the Conference. You're never going to do that again. It was incredible, you can't beat the feeling we had, you just can't beat it, and you'll never forget it as long as you live.'

Another of his proudest memories was their first match after coming out of administration. 'We had only three contracted players and our first game was against Hereford, and it was on TV. Just to have a team on the park was magical. We had a samba band, but I was asked to move it because one of the fans had a heart condition.'

He's had less to cheer about this season, but staying clear of relegation is an improvement on a turbulent past including selling the ground in a vain attempt to stave off administration, an 11th-hour rescue deal with HM Revenue and Customs, and nine years in the Conference.

'When I was young I thought Cambridge was a glamour club, but since we went into administration and sold the ground, my expectations have changed. To me it's about surviving.' One of the survival schemes during administration was bucket collections that brought cash pouring in. 'Supporters dug deep into their pockets, and one day we ended up going for an Indian after a friendly with West Ham with thousands of pounds in the boot of the car. It was a bit daft, really.'

The old Abbey has seen better days, but Dave thinks it's magic. It's a word he uses a lot in showing me around a ramshackle ground that has been patched up so often that sceptics say talk of redevelopment probably means another portacabin. Abbey Stadium is no Emirates, but it has character and it is rich in tradition and memories. Old-fashioned turnstiles lead to the Newmarket Road End, iron-roofed stronghold of the Amber Army whose star emblem is emblazoned on the back brick wall. Shirts bearing the names of United's greatest players, voted for in an internet poll, are painted on the other side of the wall near the old changing rooms that are now a tea bar.

Dave explains the layout of stands and terracing: 'You start as a youngster in the family section in the main stand, then you join the ranks of the Amber Army in the Newmarket Road End. With advancing years you move to the Habbin terraces where the older guys stand, and when your legs begin to give out it's back to the main stand. The last one is a wooden box or ashes on the pitch.' For loyal fans a lifetime of memories on an East Anglian field of dreams from cradle to grave.

There's nobody else around, we have the place to ourselves, and the banks of towering floodlights are still wreathed in cold mist. It's an atmospheric ground and in the silence it's easy to conjure the roar of crowds urging on heroes of the past. It's as if the ground has a presence, waiting quietly for the next kick-off, and Dave says, 'You stand here and you just feel it, don't you? I love our National Trust buildings, but to me football stadiums are special. Just magic.'

This one plays an important role beyond football in a city with a split personality. Here's a thing: beside the wealth and prestige of its colleges, and a booming hi-tech industry with revenues of over £12 billion, Cambridge has areas of multiple deprivation where poor kids struggle to pass exams and find decent jobs, notably the Abbey Ward around the stadium.

'To survive these days you've got to be more than a football club, we can't ignore the social side,' Dave says. 'Most clubs started as a factory team or a social club who did a lot for their communities, and we have to do the same.' He cites the example of Chesterfield in the early 2000s as a 'club within a hub' of a bicycle wheel, with spokes reaching out to its local community with projects for health and wellbeing, education and social responsibility.

He takes me back to the Abbey Arms to meet a young man hired by the club to build its community bicycle wheel. Ben Szreter is an economics graduate in his early 20s, and as CEO of the club's Community Trust it's his job to reach out to people who need help with mental health, loneliness and other social problems, using the power of sport and the football club brand. A separate charity with its own finances, the trust takes sports to primary schools, runs disability sports sessions, lays on afternoon teas for pensioners in the club's hospitality suite, and has a project in secondary schools to help teenagers cope with stress.

'They're all examples of how the club can use its social power to positively influence the community,' Ben says. 'We don't pretend to be clinical experts but we can break down the stigma over mental health. In a city like Cambridge, famous for its university and economically dynamic, there are genuine areas of deprivation.' He cites surveys that state that Abbey Ward is in the bottom 20 per cent in the UK index of multiple deprivation in terms of income, education levels and health, and that being born in different wards in Cambridge can mean almost ten years' difference in life expectancy. 'We sit at the heart of a community with issues of inequality that drive a lot of the work we do,' he says.

An enterprising project is a literacy programme for 9- to 11-year-olds who are visited by a journalist and footballers, then come to a match and write a report on it. 'Maybe they'll come back as supporters. The positive association of what we do can only benefit the football club, as long as we're seen to be doing it for the benefit of the community rather than just to fill seats.'

Ben clearly enjoys his role of Good Samaritan, though he'd probably shrink at the description, and it's obvious the club and its community are lucky to have him. 'It's massively rewarding to serve the community through the football club. It is highly important for a club of this size. If we're not here to serve the community and address its needs, you have to wonder what the football club is for.'

Like the club, Ben has grand designs for the future. 'There's a lot more we can do and would like to do, and improving the ground would help. A stadium that could provide space for a community hub where people felt they belonged every day of the week and not just on Saturday is what I'd like to see.'

A balding figure with a cheeky grin has been leaning on the bar listening to us with interest, and Dave introduces him as Ian Darling, the groundsman. A veteran of 40 years' service at the Abbey, he has won every award going including Groundsman of the Year for Divisions Two, Three and Four, and the Conference. I suspect that if ever Cambridge got into the Championship he'd win that too. He's also been presented with an 'Unsung Hero' award by the Institute of Groundsmen for raising thousands of pounds for cancer research and children with brain tumours. The man is clearly worth his weight in golden pitchforks.

'That green patch out there is my baby,' he says. 'You could say I'm addicted to soil.' As a youngster Ian had trials with Norwich and Peterborough, where he was told he had the skills but not the physique to be a footballer. He knew he could never work in an office, so he started as an apprentice greenkeeper and at 19 was invited for an interview at Cambridge.

'There was a reserve game going on and when the keeper cleared the ball landed in the centre circle and kicked up a huge cloud of dust like a herd of buffalo running through Africa. The pitch was totally compacted, and starved of oxygen and grassroots. It had been rolled to death. I didn't think I had a chance of getting the job, so I just told them what I thought anyway.'

He got the job. 'To say it was a challenge was an understatement. The mower didn't work and the aerator hadn't been used for decades. I said we needed new equipment and was told the club didn't have any money.

This was my introduction to professional football. So my dad helped me to mix 50 tons of soil with sand and a cement mixer and it took us a week of long, hard days to lay it.'

Training discipline was more free and easy in those days. The players introduced themselves to Ian by pushing him over, hanging him on a crossbar with his woolly jumper, and using him for target practice from the penalty spot. He has fond but painful memories of Chris Turner, a giant of a centre-half with a huge beard and moustache who called himself King of the Jungle. The first time Ian saw him he had scar stitches over an eyebrow, looked like a pirate, and behaved like one by pushing him over, dragging him for 70 yards and saying, 'I'm Chris Turner, you'll remember me.'

As a player, Turner was outstanding and became the manager, and engaged in running battles with Ian involving giant snowballs, taking bites out of each other's sandwiches, and cutting the toes off socks and wellingtons. 'It was relentless mate, there was never a dull moment. I should write a book about it all.'

Cambridge's fortunes have gradually improved over the years, but not by much. Finances have always been tight, and Ian reckons he's spent over £30,000 of his own money on grass seeds, fertilisers, weed killers and lorry loads of sand. 'The mowers and the sprayer are from my own business outside the Abbey. It's just the way it is, it's what I've had to do.' In the mid-80s the team didn't have enough players for two teams, so Ian made up the numbers in training with his assistants and a local copper.

His next unofficial role was in marketing. When the club came out of administration it had no shirt sponsor, no advertising, no nothing. Ian became known as 'Mr beg, steal and borrow', and within a few weeks he had sold every ground advertising board and persuaded a local skip hire and ready mix concrete company to sponsor the shirts.

But it's an ongoing struggle to dress the Abbey in finery on a shoestring budget. 'She's a tired old lady. We can change her clothes every season and tart her up a bit and do the best we can, but she really needs a major facelift. Maybe one day.'

In addition to being a turf maestro, Ian is a natural storyteller. There was the time in 1985 when the club's commercial manager rented the ground to a private girls' school for an end-of-term prom event, strictly girls only. At nine o'clock that night Ian's phone rang and it was a panicking teacher asking him to come to the ground and switch on the floodlights, because some of the girls were missing.

'So I went down, but our lights don't power up immediately, they come on slowly. There wasn't supposed to be boys there, but when the lights reached the main stand all you could see was bare arses on top of the girls. You've never seen so many knickers round ankles in your life.'

On a more dignified note, Ian has lost count of people whose ashes he has buried on the pitch. One in particular left a lasting impression. 'He was a lifelong supporter who requested that his ashes be buried beneath the penalty spot at the home end. It was pre-season, so I dug a hole where he wanted to be, got the club chaplain to say a few words for the family, and back-filled with sand. A few weeks later I was in the stand when I saw a bright green cross exactly where he'd been buried. I couldn't believe my eyes.'

It eventually dawned on him that the ashes must have spread along drains, and that there had been something in them that enhanced the grass. 'Or maybe he was just saying goodbye. I just left it and it grew out.' Another chap who had worked with Ian for a few years after he retired had a different site request. 'He said he wanted to be buried on the touchline at the exit of the players' tunnel, so when the visitors came out he could trip the bastards up. That was him all over.'

It strikes me that people like Dave, Ian and young Ben are the heart and soul of small clubs, and without them they'd struggle to survive. Glasgow's marketing people came up with a slogan a few years ago, *People Make Glasgow,* which could be adapted for football clubs like Cambridge.

My final interview of the day is with Ben Strang, head of football operations. He played centre-half for Charlton and for Scotland under-17s by virtue of Scottish parents, and when his playing days were over he coached at Ipswich's youth academy and is now in his second spell at Cambridge. His priority is to build a team of youngsters around a core of experienced players in the hope of reaching the play-offs, but the competition is intense. 'League Two is very transient, it's surprising how quickly you can go up or down. With three automatic promotions, four in play-offs and only two relegated to the Conference, it opens up a lot of ambitions.

'Given our resources and current facilities, League One is our ceiling. The Championship is becoming richer every year, the transfer fees and wages are so disproportionate to League One, and it's becoming increasingly difficult to compete in terms of finance and quality.'

Ben's ambition has always been to work at the top level in the Premier League, but being at Cambridge has made him rethink. 'Jobs in the Premier League often don't last long, the number of staff they have is mind-blowing, they have crazy workloads, and they can all change at short notice.

Everyone knows we don't have the best facilities here, but there's a feeling of camaraderie and belonging. You're more likely to go above and beyond what's required than just see it as a job.'

It's late in the day and the cold is seeping into the club and me, so I wander back to my hotel and sink into a hot bath with a beer, a bag of crisps and a book of memoirs by Cambridge supporters, *Cambridge 'Til I Die*. There are familiar tales of bus breakdowns en route to away games, crushing defeats, rare, unforgettable triumphs, and marriage proposals in the Abbey car park. The front cover shows massed ranks of U's fans at Wembley in a blizzard of black and amber flags and scarves. I didn't know there were so many people in the town.

There were just over 130,000 at the last count, which doesn't make Cambridge a metropolis. The historic heart of the town is a surprisingly small maze of medieval colleges and churches, lanes of quirky independent shops, decent restaurants and real ale pubs, and a glitzy shopping centre where even TK Maxx looks like a fancy department store. Tudor gateways gaze imperiously at designer wear boutiques and Gothic spires to the glory of God soar above hi-tech offices that worship Mammon.

It is a city of culture, and on a morning stroll I am drawn to church railings festooned with billboards for classical concerts, life-drawing classes, and a lecture on Dickens's *Great Expectations*. The concert calendar for the Lent Term of the first three months of the year lists 57 orchestras, choirs and musical societies, and the busker outside Boots is playing 'Greensleeves' on a harp.

A big attraction is the chapel of King's College of Our Lady and Saint Nicholas, a magnificent Tudor temple to education and religion founded in the 15th century by King Henry IV that took almost a century to build. This was due to untimely interruptions by the Wars of the Roses and Henry's murder in the Tower of London. So it goes in turbulent times.

With its grandiose limestone façade and soaring twin towers, it looks like a giant spaceship designed by Leonardo da Vinci about to take off for the heavens. Inside it is a time capsule beneath a sky-scraping vaulted ceiling, with light filtering softly through masterpieces of stained glass depicting biblical scenes and illuminating Rubens' *Adoration of the Magi*. The House of Tudor has left its 'Henry was here' mark with heraldic carvings of armorial devices, and in this timeless shrine to God and academia there is a sense that the Wars of the Roses could still be raging outside, and any moment young Henry could stride through the massive oak doors with his battle-weary knights.

For five centuries the chapel was a male-only preserve, with women being admitted only in the 1970s, but there are still none in its world famous choir of men and boys who sing like angels anyway. At first sight this cavernous, austere chapel of kings is intimidating, and I wonder if alumni of the college such as Rupert Brooke, Alan Turing and Salman Rushdie were overawed or inspired by its severe grandeur.

At least they were probably allowed to walk on the grass. An information leaflet informs visitors politely that only senior members of the college and their guests are permitted to tread on manicured lawns running down to the River Cam, so I dutifully stick to a curved path said to have been designed in the spirit of 19th-century romanticism.

Even on a cold, misty day in mid-January a few hardy souls swathed in scarves and woolly hats are being punted along the river in flat-bottomed punts. The boatmen lack the colourful costumes of their Venetian brethren, but they charge a lot less and the water is cleaner.

I never went to university, having left school at 17 to learn shorthand and typing for a career in journalism, inspired by my dad. He was a first-rate reporter and I couldn't imagine anything more exciting and romantic, although my early assignments in draughty football press boxes in Hamilton and Greenock were anything but.

Now in later life I enjoy the cultured ambience of venerable seats of learning like Cambridge and St Andrews, a testament to our civilization and aspirations we should treasure and be proud of.

On my way back to the Abbey I pass Parker's Piece, scene of the historic games that supposedly laid the foundations of modern football. It is a large, open green space bounded by trees and fine Georgian terraced houses, and it is overlooked by the Gothic rocket of the spire of the Church of Our Lady and the English Martyrs, which would have observed the pell-mell skirmishes of the early footballers.

A few years ago the city council proposed a two-metre-high statue in the form of a Subbuteo referee be erected on a plinth engraved with the Cambridge Rules to mark the 150th anniversary of the FA rules and Parker's Piece's association with it. The idea was rejected due to negative feedback and concerns over cost, which seems a shame. Cambridge is littered with serious monuments to the great and good, and putting a ref on a pedestal for posterity would have been fun.

The common is still popular for games and summer picnics, and even in mid-winter it's busy with pedestrians and cyclists. Cambridge claims with some justification to be the bicycle capital of Britain. There are bikes everywhere, thousands of them, and they are not the flying, earnest road warriors of London dicing with death in dense traffic, but proper dignified sit-up boneshakers with front baskets freewheeling purposefully along cycle lanes and dedicated pavements. At rush hour beware of flocks of Mary Poppins.

An electronic scoreboard at Parker's Piece logs the passage of bikes on a perimeter path and by mid-morning it had counted more than 1,200. George Bernard Shaw, a keen cyclist, is reputed to have said, 'Every time I see an adult on a bicycle, I no longer despair for the human race.' His faith in humanity must have soared in Cambridge.

Given the popularity of two-wheeled transport and pedestrian precincts, the town centre is relatively peaceful, a sanctuary of studied calm. Amid its ancient colleges the air seems suffused with quiet reflection instead of petrol fumes. Motorists are generally considerate of cyclists and pedestrians, and the local constabulary clearly takes any offences seriously. A front page report in the *Cambridge News* says police are appealing for witnesses after a motorist 'unbelievably' splashed a mum and her two children by driving through a puddle 20 feet long. According to the newspaper's crime reporter, the splash-and-run villain could face a fine of up to £5,000.

Maybe there is something in the air of Cambridge that makes people clever and talented. The galaxy of stars of science and the arts who have walked through the hallowed portals of its colleges is dazzling. In 1831 a tutor at Christ's College suggested to one of his promising students that he join HMS *Beagle* on a scientific survey of South American waters. The name of the bright young man was Charles Darwin.

All this creative genius seems to have rubbed off on locals who have grown up to be Sir Richard Attenborough, Douglas Adams and Pink Floyd frontman Syd Barrett, and I'm on my way to meet another gifted local man, who happens to be a footballer.

Luke Chadwick was a protégé of Alex Ferguson who made 25 appearances for Manchester United, including coming on for David Beckham in a Champions League quarter-final against Bayern Munich. This, you might imagine, is as good as it gets, but he seriously insists his biggest thrill was playing at the tail end of his career for Cambridge, the home-town club that he supported as a boy. Now he's back as head of development for the under-13 to under-16 squads, and he's loving it.

'People think it's strange,' he admits. 'But it's nice to be home again. When I was a little kid my dad brought me here, it blew my mind the live game atmosphere, and being close to the action was amazing.

'This is the team I've always supported and loved, and it was always my ambition to play for them. I got more of a buzz playing for the team I used to stand and watch than at Man Utd.'

His first match for Cambridge against Welling United with his wife and children watching was a surreal experience. 'It was a scrappy game but I'd never felt like that on a football field, it was a dream come true. Afterwards I was exhausted, more from the emotions than the effort.' They still talk about Luke's wild celebrations after scoring his first goal for the U's against Southport, and he remembers it vividly. 'It was at the Newmarket Road End, where I used to stand with the Amber Army. It was so emotional I thought I was going to cry.'

And there you have it, the pride and passion that brings a grown man close to tears when he steps on to a field of boyhood dreams and becomes a local hero. Maybe playing at the ramshackle old Abbey feels more personal than in the vast arena of Old Trafford, but that's only half the story. The rest is a mystery shrouded in the enigma of football mania.

It's a fair bet he's instilling the same dedication in United's under-age squads, which include his own two boys. 'I feel really proud seeing them pull on Cambridge shirts, they're Cambridge boys.' But he won't be pushing them, insisting it's more important that they enjoy themselves. 'Coaching is more structured now. The days when you just kicked a ball around with your mates produced mavericks like Gazza and George Best. Now we're building players that are technically gifted, but similar. The academies get kids in so young these days, I wonder is there too much direction, are we taking them away from finding their own way?

'I'm trying to educate parents not to push too hard, not to take freedom away from young players. It's important to remember they're children and they should be enjoying themselves. You've got to love the game to progress in it. To get youngsters playing with a smile on their face, that's the key. Just watch Messi, you can tell he's loving it.'

Cambridge's youngsters are clearly fortunate to have such an inspirational figure coaching them. Luke still enjoys his football, turning out for his village team, and he won't say so himself but Dave says he's still banging in the goals.

The senior and youth squads are training on college grounds in the south of the city, and a taxi drops me at the end of a tree-lined avenue of substantial villas where the playing fields open out in an idyllic rustic setting. As I stroll towards the players I ask a couple of suits where I might find the head coach. They are drug testers on official duty and are not helpful.

Fortunately Matt Walker, head of performance, walks over and introduces himself. I tell him what I'm about, and he's happy to chat. 'There are only two emotions at this level, joy and gloom,' he says. 'We're selling a dream.' In his former role as head of youth development he 'had to do crazy things' to raise funds, including walking from Torquay to Cambridge, the equivalent of 13 marathons in 13 days. Thoughtful and articulate, he is keenly aware of the psychological and emotional aspects of his job as well as the physical playing side. 'These boys are not going to be millionaires. At best they'll move around clubs and get a year or two security at a time, if that. But some won't even make that journey and we have to prepare them for that. At the end of the day players are custodians of the jersey, but the club remains through thick and thin.'

And there you have it. Dreams of football stardom come true for a few, but they fade into a sense of failure for many more and it's up to the likes of Matt to assure them there's more to life.

As training breaks up and the players troop towards an old-fashioned college clubhouse I introduce myself to head coach Shaun Derry, and he invites me upstairs to his office for a cuppa. Uninvited writers can do this at League Two clubs; they can't at Stamford Bridge or Old Trafford.

Derry talks about big changes he has seen in the game, notably in the youth ranks, during a playing career with half a dozen clubs. As a 16-year-old apprentice at Notts County he would spend three hours tidying the boot room, making tea and cleaning toilets before he got to kick a ball, and after training it was back to the ground to finish menial tasks and take home a couple of senior players' boots to clean them. 'I feel the young ones suffer now for not having this routine. They're still kids and it comes as a shock to learn about pressure and the value of three points when you're fighting to pay a mortgage and support a family.' And a harsh lesson from playing in the lower leagues is that there's usually no way back from failure. 'We're dealing with young people with hopes and dreams, and if they fall out at this level they'll no longer be professional footballers. At least if they're with a Premier League club they can drop to lower leagues, but if they don't make it at this level there's only non-league.'

At least Cambridge's young hopefuls are given the chance to prove themselves. 'We're not a big club that throws money at the first-team squad. You've got to accept that youngsters make the worst mistakes, but for them to develop you have to give them experience at the coal face. You've got to give them a chance.'

The other big change is the ever-widening gulf between the multi-millionaires of the Premier League and their poor relations struggling to survive in lower leagues. 'There needs to be a better balance of finances. Every week we hear of a League Two club in financial trouble, meanwhile Crystal Palace get more cash for staying in the Premier League than AC Milan get for winning Serie A. And since the 1990s there's been a massive drop in English players at the top level, because the Premier League has become a European league that happens to be played on our shores. To me it's a scandal.'

Meanwhile, his aim is to see out a three-year contract and leave the club in better shape than he found it, hopefully by delivering pleasing, enjoyable football that keeps them clear of the relegation zone. 'At the end of the day it's about survival for the club, and me. If I can see out my contract this summer I'll be happy. Not many do that.'

Derry has one local lad on his books who dropped down from a Premier League club seeking a second chance, midfielder Liam O'Neil. Eight years at West Brom ended with ankle injuries and lack of game time, and he's grateful to be back at his boyhood club to help them push for promotion.

'It's a great opportunity to come home and get games and fitness, and work my way back up again and play at a higher level,' he tells me after the training session. 'We've all got aspirations to get into the play-offs, if not what's the point? I'm not here to sit in mid-table. League Two football is more frantic and direct, but Cambridge is more like a family club in a community that pulls together to keep the club going. All clubs at this level need that.'

The taxi driver who takes me back to the town centre shares a football memory. When he was a boy he used to sneak into the Abbey by skipping over a stream from a public park and squirming through a hole in a dead tree. 'Security was different then,' he says.

I have time on my hands before an evening meeting of the United Supporters Community Trust, so I wander down the road to Antarctica. The Polar Research Museum is a few steps from my hotel and it has an exhibition on Ernest Shackleton, leader of arguably the most epic and heroic rescue mission in polar history. A few years ago I retraced the last few miles of his heroic journey by hiking over a glacier in South Georgia, and then stood by his grave in a magnificent icy wilderness. Such experiences linger long in the memory, and I enjoy browsing odd bits and pieces from his expeditions in the museum display cases, where his family motto catches my eye: *Fortitudine Vincimus* (By Endurance We Conquer). A good one for Cambridge United, I'd have thought.

Memories of the club's past are cherished by its community trust, a cheery bunch of middle-aged men and a younger woman who serves as treasurer. We meet in the Abbey Arms, and an important item on the agenda is online interviews with fans and former players, including an MP who helped save the club when it went into administration. 'As a politician, it's the only time I went to a football match and the crowd chanted my name,' he recalls.

An 80-year-old woman has a fond memory of Dion Dublin, a legendary centre-forward at the Abbey who signed from Norwich as a teenager and went on to Manchester Utd for £1 million. Racial abuse was rife in the game in those days, but Dublin got none of it at Cambridge. The woman interviewed by the trust says: 'I almost cried when Dublin played for us and didn't get any abuse.'

Another club legend tracked down for an interview is Jonny Haaz, who played for the Hungarian Air Force in the 1950s, often against the legendary Ferenc Puskas, who was with Budapest Honved, the army team. During the Hungarian uprising in 1956 Haaz sided with the students and because he had military training someone gave him a gun. He says he shot people, but never knew if he had killed anyone. After emigrating to the UK he worked in coal mines and played for colliery teams before signing for Cambridge in the mid-60s, where he was universally regarded as streets ahead of anyone seen at the Abbey. International star as he was, he ended up as a tyre fitter in Doncaster. Changed days on Planet Football.

Memories drift around the gloomy little bar, rekindling passion for a team that has seen better days, and there is talk of t-shirts to commemorate historic wins, and a 'retro shirt day' with fans turning up in old-fashioned club shirts and scarves. Back in the present, someone proposes setting up a Twitter account to reach younger fans, and Caroline the treasurer suggests mirrors in the toilets to encourage more women to come to games.

This is where I learn that the favourite song of Cambridge fans is a 1950 recording of 'I've Got a Lovely Bunch of Coconuts' by the Billy Cotton Band. It began a few years ago after a home win when it happened to be on top of a pile of 78rpm vinyl records played after the final whistle. The breezy lyrics were in tune with the fans' buoyant mood, and it quickly became the club's victory anthem. An attempt to replace it with Cliff Richard's 'Congratulations' was unpopular, so it's been coconuts ever since. If ever West Ham fans turn up for a cup game singing about blowing bubbles, it could be an entertaining afternoon.

They are a motley crew in the Cambridge Community Trust. Pat Morgan used to be a journalist on trade magazines until he turned his hand to writing books about Scottish islands, Abba and Vikings. He came to his first game in the 1960s and was spellbound even before he got to the ground. 'I got the bug just walking to the ground and seeing the crowd in front of me. I was hooked even before a ball was kicked, it was weird.' Even realities of life in the lower leagues failed to break the spell. 'The average supporter's life is mainly misery, but I'm immensely proud of the club and what it has achieved, and of the people from a deprived area who literally built the club from the ground up. The club is the people and the people are the club.'

For treasurer Caroline Crossley, United is more like family. After years of begging her dad to take her to a game he finally took her to Wembley when she was 11 for a Fourth Division play-off against Chesterfield, and United won. When they won the FA Trophy in 2014, the players and manager celebrated back at the Abbey, and Caroline was among them. 'You don't get that in the Premiership,' she says. 'I see the club as an extension of my family, it's in my blood. Insult the club and you insult my family.'

Scot Tom McGrane is a relative newcomer, a retired BT engineer from Port Glasgow who moved to Cambridge in the late 1980s. His first game was a 5-1 FA Cup win over Bristol City and he felt immediately at home in an atmosphere that reminded him of the passion of fans of Greenock Morton, his home-town club. 'There are two types of football supporters,' he informs me. 'The trophy hunters who need their teams to win cups and medals for their own gratification, then there are what I'd call real supporters who follow teams that don't have much chance of winning anything because that's just what they do. I don't like elitism. I like being with real people in football pubs.'

The Eagle in Benet Street is not a football pub. It's a good old-fashioned hostelry serving real ales and quality pub grub, whose regulars have included brainy scientists, World War Two airmen and a few ghosts. On a cold winter night it's like a warm communal blanket and I gratefully grab the last free table for a supper of fish and triple-cooked chips and a tasty pint of Beavertown Neck Oil.

The pub goes back a few years. Supposedly beer was being sold here in the 14th century for three gallons a penny, in the 17th century it was a coaching inn en route to London, and on 28 February 1953 two regulars walked in at lunchtime and announced they had discovered the secret of life. Francis Crick and James Watson of the nearby Cavendish Laboratory had just cracked the double-helix structure of DNA, meaning they had discovered how it carries genetic information. It was a pivotal moment in science, and a blue plaque by the door attests to the fact.

The inn is a cosy warren of dark wood panelling and big brick fireplaces, and its inner sanctum at the back is known as the RAF bar because it was the haunt of wartime flight crews who scorched their names and squadron numbers on the ceiling with cigarette lighters. Some of them look out cheerily from black and white group photographs, including the crew of the US bomber *Memphis Belle*, the first to complete a tour of 25 missions and get back in one piece. Gazing at them and their signatures on the ceiling, I drift back in time. Amid the general hubbub it's as if they are still alive, thronging a smoke-filled bar, and a rising wind outside becomes the steady drone of Lancasters and Flying Fortresses rattling the windows.

On leaving, I notice an upstairs window is wide open. This is supposedly for the benefit of a ghostly barmaid who died in a fire centuries ago when she couldn't open it. So the story goes anyway.

Matchday dawns brightly and I make the most of it with an early morning stroll to the world's brainiest village. Grantchester is an absurdly pretty hamlet a three-mile walk from Cambridge that has attracted poets, philosophers, TV crews, a song by Pink Floyd, and more resident Nobel laureates than anywhere else in the world.

It's not hard to see why. It's your quintessential rural English haven of sleepy thatched cottages, country lanes winding through woods and meadows to the lazy waters of the Cam, and a splendid medieval church whose congregation raises money for worthy causes in Africa. Throw in traditional pubs and an occasional horse clip-clopping down the high street and you have a place made to fly the flag of St George.

I am drawn to this rustic vestige of Ye Olde England by tales of an illustrious group of friends who enjoyed a sybaritic lifestyle here in the halcyon days before World War One. The poet Rupert Brooke was a leading light in the 'Granchester Group' which included the likes of Virginia Woolf, Bertrand Russell and John Maynard Keynes, who were all studying at Cambridge. Brooke took lodgings in the village, commuted to his studies by canoe, and spent much of his time working in a rose garden and living on honey, eggs and milk. 'I am in the Country in Arcadia,' he wrote to a girlfriend in 1909 in an account of a sybaritic lifestyle. '... I wander about bare foot and almost naked, surveying Nature with a calm eye. I do not pretend to understand Nature, but I get on very well with her, in a neighbourly way. I go on with my books, and she goes on with her hens and storms and things, and we're both very tolerant.' He also reportedly swam naked with Woolf in a pool named after Lord Byron, but possibly didn't mention this to his girlfriend.

It was an age of relaxed elegance, full of energy and optimism. The world had been relatively at peace for nearly a hundred years since Waterloo, but the mass slaughter of the Western Front was looming. Brooke sailed with a British Expeditionary Force in 1915, but on the way to Gallipoli he died of sepsis from an infected mosquito bite. At least he was spared the horrors that followed, a world away from his rustic Arcadia.

I enjoy striding along the banks of the Cam in the freshness of the morning as cows are beginning to stir in meadows, and dogs freed from leashes are rediscovering the joys of life. Time doesn't exactly stand still in Grantchester, it just doesn't seem to be in much of a hurry to go anywhere. The casual elegance of Cambridge academics in pre-war years survives in a wooden tea pavilion in an orchard where Brooke and his chums gathered when it rained. A century later it is a fine place to tuck into homemade scones with clotted cream, admire a meadow running down to the river, and muse on Brooke's poem about gliding along its calm waters beneath a tunnel of chestnut trees 'green as a dream and deep as death'. I have rarely enjoyed such a pleasant, tranquil prelude to a football match.

Other historical treasures are to be found in the United supporters' social club at the Abbey ground. They include a 1949 record of 'I've Got a Lovely Bunch of Coconuts', a collection of vintage first-team shirts and old leather footballs, and a pair of ladies' knickers embroidered with the slogan Up U's. The priceless heirlooms are displayed in a small museum which also features an acrylic painting on canvas by the artist Paine Proffitt, titled *Under the Gaslamps*. I have long admired Proffitt's work portraying footballers and their supporters in old-fashioned shirts and grounds. This one is of boys kicking a ball around a cobbled street lined with tenements, evoking memories of my childhood in Motherwell, and I am drawn into it and back in time. It is such reminiscences of football before the era of millionaire superstars that drew me to the likes of Accrington and Berwick, and now the home of the Amber Army.

Its ranks are filling the social club a couple of hours before kick-off, and I spot Dave who invites me to join a table with his pals Will Weston and Chris Vessey. Will's dad was a Cambridge supporter, so he followed suit. 'It's force of habit,' he says. 'It's what you do.' Having said that, he appreciates the family atmosphere of a small club. 'The chairman used to sit in the stand with fans at away games and you could have a chat with him. You couldn't go up to Abramovich and say how are you doing, could you? Half a dozen Russian bodyguards would hustle you away.

'We were in a pub in Barrow for a cup game once and the owner came in and put money behind the bar and said it's there until it's spent. So we spent it, and when we went to the ground to buy tickets they said we don't need your money, the manager's already paid for them.'

Chris recalls fans being invited back to the club for drinks with the players, manager and directors after they had won promotion from the Conference. 'You wouldn't get that even in Championship clubs, they'd all be driving off in their Mercedes with headphones on.'

It doesn't bother him that United is unlikely to win anything else, and he's happy with fleeting triumphs when they come along. 'When you support a shit team your five minutes of fame is all the more special. A 90th-minute winner at Hartlepool is as important to us as Chelsea beating Man U. In our league there's a mutual understanding among fans about why you keep turning up at games, even if you don't understand it yourself.' Chris is not optimistic about getting a result today, and Will is hoping for a draw at best. 'You can always dream,' he says.

With Mansfield pushing for promotion, and gearing up for a cup replay against Premier League Cardiff, they'll probably do well to get a point. The *Cambridge News* is reporting that Mansfield boss Steve Evans appears to be living up to his reputation as a man you either love or hate by declaring, 'The players who don't perform at Cambridge have Bob Hope's chance of playing against Cardiff.' Not a man to mince his words, our Steve. It is 1.30pm when the Mansfield team bus arrives, and there are no casual outfits among the players who emerge. All of them are dressed smartly in club blazers, shirts and ties, without a headphone in sight.

Other visitors today include the Samaritans. Dave says they were brought in at Christmas, which can be a difficult time for some people, and they've been coming back quite often. 'It sounds bad, but if you have a run of bad results they can be useful.' It helps to have a sense of humour. Dave pinned a Samaritans poster outside the boardroom saying, 'Are you having troubles? Call the Samaritans.'

An early arrival on the pitch is United's mascot Marvin the Moose. According to folklore he was born of a sense of humour on the away terracing at Grimsby in 1989 after a Cambridge fan flew back from holiday in Spain and drove straight to the match without going home to drop off his bags or have a shower. Taking his place on the terracing, he warned his fellow supporters, 'Don't stand near me, I smell like a moose.' This prompted the crowd around him to raise their hands to the side of their heads in imitation of antlers and bellow like a moose. This seemed like a great idea, and within weeks the entire Amber Army could be seen 'moosing' visiting goalkeepers to put them off. It was only a matter of time before Marvin turned up.

The Army's vanguard is flooding into its citadel in the Newmarket Road End as Dave hands out programmes and half-time draw tickets to vendors, and goes around the stadium posting up team lists. Striker Billy Waters, just signed on loan from Northampton Town, goes straight into the side along with Uche Ikpeazu, top scorer with nine goals this season.

In accordance with the tradition of watching your first games at the Abbey in the family section, I join Dave in the main stand as the teams emerge. 'We've got the pantomime characters here today,' Dave observes. 'This ref never gives us anything and [Mansfield boss] Evans over there, nobody likes him.'

Evans is quickly on his feet gesticulating angrily when Cambridge start brightly and force a corner, which leads to a powerful low drive shaving a post. A minute later the Mansfield defence is sliced open again and a speculative shot is turned around for another corner. It's good, fast, one-touch football, and Cambridge are quick to run at defenders. Both sides are snapping into tackles, nobody has much time on the ball, and the Amber Army is in full cry to a rousing drumbeat.

After a few minutes I walk around the back of the Mansfield goal to the disabled section in front of the Amber legions. You can do this at lower league grounds, where freedom of movement is considered a rite of passage. A steward stands aside to let me pass and comments, 'Some ref, innit?' I'm now level with the pitch and so close to it there's a feeling of being on it.

On to the Habbin terracing where middle-aged diehards gather sociably. Cambridge, in their familiar black and amber strips, are still pressing and the new striking partnership of Waters and Ikpeazu is looking lively, eliciting the fans' approval: 'We've got them rattled, they don't like what they're seeing ... we've just got to stay strong at the back.'

I'm enjoying the game and the atmosphere. Sitting in a stand, you observe a spectacle from a distance, but on a terracing at pitch level you feel part of the drama being played out a few feet away. You get your money's worth here.

United hold their own in a goalless first half, and troop off to applause and cries of 'well done lads'. They're a hardy lot, Cambridge supporters. The temperature has dropped, a freezing wind is whipping under an old iron roof, and instead of seeking shelter a few Habbin regulars spend half-time squatting and lying on the stone terracing. Snuggled up in thick coats and woolly hats, they look like a cheery bunch of homeless. But of course they're not, they're as much at home here as anywhere.

I seek out Dave and mention my next destination is Plymouth. 'You'll like Plymouth, nice people and a good club,' he says. 'They're passionate about football down there.' He's less enthusiastic about Forest Green Rovers, Cambridge's next opponents. 'I don't like the concept of the club. It has no tradition and not much of a support, and it only keeps going as long as the owner puts money into it. There's no feeling about it, to me it's just a franchise.'

The second half is a scrappy affair with both sides resorting to long balls. The best entertainment is from the Newmarket Road End, where the Amber brigades are belting out full-throated chanting and drumbeats with occasional war cries, like a Pictish army lining up for battle. In the end there are no goals and no 'Lovely Bunch of Coconuts', but the fans are happy with a point that stretches an unbeaten run to five games.

After the game I have a chat in the Abbey Bar with Eddie Clark, a local haulage and storage contractor and United vice-chairman.

Eddie is a straight-talking character with a lifelong passion for the game. 'I love grassroots football, it's the type of football we learned as youngsters on muddy grounds with leather balls,' he says. He went to his first match in the 1950s at age 11, when United were playing in the Eastern Counties League and the main stand was wooden, and now he's aiming for League One. 'You can never tell what happens in football, we'd love to aim high, but realistically League One is our aim for the next few years.'

One of his fondest memories was a cup tie at Old Trafford when the travelling Amber ranks swelled to 7,500. Cambridge gave a good account of themselves before losing 3-0, but their fans won the battle of the stands. 'We outshone them that evening, the Man U supporters were very quiet, probably stunned by our performance. We were singing "It's like a library," and "Has there been a fire drill?"

'I've loved it all, and overall the team has put in some decent performances with lots of honest endeavour, but no coconuts.'

Up in the announcer's box, the Billy Cotton record is still top of the pile, just in case.

Plymouth Argyle

This is the heart and soul of the game

Founded:	1886
Ground:	Home Park
Average attendance:	10,413
Honours:	Third Division (South) champions 1929/30, 1951/52 Third Division champions 1974/75, 1985/86 Second Division champions 2003/04

IF YOU live in Plymouth it probably helps if you like boats. The city's seafront is inundated by a maze of yachts, dinghies, ferries, freighters, warships and the occasional nuclear submarine. It's a permanent boat show with all the paraphernalia that goes with it in dockside chandlers, Jolly Tar pubs and memorials to local hero Sir Francis Drake, who sailed from here in 1588 to sink the Spanish Armada. The main dockyard at Devonport is not as big as it used to be, but it still claims to be the largest operational naval base in Western Europe. This is a sailors' heaven.

Unfortunately, all this maritime activity attracted the attention of the Luftwaffe in World War Two, which blitzed the docks 59 times and flattened much of the city in the process, including the clubhouse of the Royal

Western Yacht Club and the main grandstand of Plymouth Argyle FC. As bad luck would have it the old grandstand at Home Park was being used to store furniture rescued from bomb-damaged houses that included 100 pianos, which tells you about home entertainment in south Devon before Netflix, and all of them went up in flames under a storm of incendiary bombs. Happily the club survived and its beloved home rose from the ashes, only to face an even more serious challenge in recent years, but more of this later.

It is mid-January and Scotland is shivering in a mini ice age. My flight from Glasgow to Bristol is delayed while bulldozers scurry to find runways beneath a wilderness of snow, and trucks de-ice our aircraft.

The weather in the West Country isn't much better. The M5 is like a demented washing machine, swirling with torrential rain and truck spray, and under black skies with darkness falling Plymouth seems pretty bleak. I'm deeply grateful for a warm hotel room, a hot bath and enchiladas with refried beans in a restaurant playing cheery Mexican music. I tend to acquire a few home comforts on my travels, and on my way back to the hotel I pop into a Co-op for a packet of biscuits to have in bed with a cup of tea and *Match of the Day* on BBC iPlayer. Happy days.

In the morning I have arranged to meet Keith Bulley, chairman of Argyle Supporters Club, who comes to my hotel wearing a red jacket which is apparently like a red rag to bullish Argyle fans. 'I'd never wear it to a game because it's Exeter's colours,' he confides. 'I'd be talked about for the rest of my life.' Exeter are the big local rivals of Argyle's green and white brigades, and encounters between them require a large turnout of Devon and Cornwall constabulary. Keith has a pal who moved to enemy territory in Exeter and found the garage of his new home painted red, so he promptly painted it green. This was no mean feat as he suffers from severe Parkinson's disease, and he was duly declared Supporter of the Year at the supporters' club AGM.

There are two theories on how the club acquired its quirky name. One is that its founders used to meet in an Argyle Tavern, the other is that the biggest football fanatics in town at the time were Argyll and Southern Highlanders who had a barracks here. Keith reckons it was the latter. 'We used to hear the regimental sergeant major barking in the parade ground in the morning, we didn't need alarm clocks.' I am warned not to make the mistake of calling the club Plymouth – it is always referred to as Argyle, with accent on the first vowel. Anyone who gets it wrong is obviously a visitor or an Exeter fan.

These are happy days for Argyle, having picked up 18 points from their last eight games, and confidence is high as they prepare to meet table-topping Wigan Athletic on Saturday. But like most lower league clubs they've had their ups and downs.

A lifelong Argyle supporter, Keith was among 37,639 fans who watched in incredulous delight their team beating the mighty Santos of Brazil, including a certain Pele, 3-2 in a friendly in 1973. Fast forward to 2011 and the club was in freefall down the divisions, penniless and plunged into administration. The manager at the time, Peter Reid, paid heating bills from his own pocket, but it was the fans who kept the club afloat with fundraising until it was rescued by property developer James Brent, the current chairman, who sold the stadium to the town council to pay the bills.

'We were in a sorry state, it was very painful,' Keith recalls. 'But the fan base stayed loyal. Argyle is a community club and when it's in trouble we rally round. I know there's bigger clubs, but I'm a great believer in supporting your community. My wife is also a season-ticket holder and we've made a lot of friends through Argyle, as you do. James Brent is almost a friend, he's very approachable, there's no side to him.

'Another thing I like about the club is the players are friendly. They're not paid very much and they're not prima donnas, they go out to schools and watch local matches, they're not up their nose.'

The heart of this community is a stadium up past the railway station seating 16,000 fans with an iconic art deco entrance that somehow survived the war, and at time of writing its administrative offices are the kind you'd expect in a district league club. Officials from the chairman down and the club shop are housed in a warren of portacabins, destined to be demolished in a redevelopment involving a new grandstand, an ice rink and a multi-screen cinema. But for the time being the reception is a small room with a glass cabinet containing a single trophy, the South-West and Wales Youth Cup 1975/76. But there are other awards of excellence as a family club, including League Two Family Club for two seasons running. This is a team that is clearly better at winning public affection than matches. Making the point, a large framed photograph portraying massed ranks of fans waving green and white scarves and flags is captioned 'Argyle's 12th man'.

It takes hard work to recruit an army of supporters for a lower league team in the largest city in England never to have hosted top-flight football, and hats off to Argyle's Community Trust that reaches far and wide in the South

West with schools coaching and health, disability and social inclusion programmes. The initiative was launched in 1992 with two men and a dog and now employs 100 full-time and part-time staff operating from North Devon to Penzance with a budget of over £2 million. Mark Lovell, head of the trust, tells me later, 'We use the power of football to reach out to communities and groups not easy to reach. The biggest attraction is the badge, it's been there for 130 years.' When trust staff went to HM Prison at Exeter to look at a sports education programme, they were greeted with a rousing chorus of 'Argyle Green Army' chants. The trust is now coaching in 130 schools, and at every home game 150 youngsters are invited for coaching, a tour of the ground and tickets for the family section. At one match every season the noise level soars to a youthful crescendo when the entire Devon Junior League of about 2,000 kids is invited.

Martyn Starnes, the club CEO, is proud of what it has achieved in difficult times. He is about to go on holiday, but calls to say we can have a chat at the ground. 'I've worked in many different industries and football is by far the most difficult,' he says. 'It's a mad place to be. We budget to break even. The problem is the Premier League and Championship argue it's their games that attract TV revenues, which is true, but the disparities in payments to the top and lower leagues is creating a bigger financial gap between them, making movement more difficult. There has to be a reversal of the current trend or we'll end up with just a handful of clubs who can aim for a higher league and realistically hope to stay there.'

There is a strong case that teams like Argyle are worthy community causes that deserve more support from the Premier League, which currently makes annual 'solidarity' payments of £645,000 to League One teams and £430,000 to those in League Two. This at a time when its 20 elite clubs received between £100 million and £150 million each from broadcast and central commercial revenues, a total of almost £2.5 billion.

Argyle survives on a budget that is a tiny fraction of even some Championship teams, but money isn't everything. The youth squad is in the last 16 of the Youth Cup, having disposed of Manchester City in a previous round. The Man City youth academy has a budget of £28 million and Argyle's is £500,000. Despite having to walk a financial tightrope, Starnes is a happy man. 'I'm in the game because I love football. I can't envisage a career out of it. I'm passionate for the game and the people in it, with the exception of agents. Our fans are salt of the earth, they don't go on social media forums criticising the club, they just help and support us, they're brilliant.'

I head back to town and wander down to the Barbican district, a time capsule of wealthy Elizabethan merchants' houses with dozens of listed buildings and the largest concentration of cobbled streets in Britain. History lives and breathes here. Charles Dickens wandered these time-weathered lanes that witnessed the passage of Henry VIII's first wife Catherine of Aragon, and the native American icon Pocahontas when she was presented to English society in 1616 as an example of the 'civilised savage'.

Since then somebody has opened a seafood restaurant with picture windows overlooking a yacht haven, which is where I tuck into a lunch of cod in deliciously crunchy batter with chips and peas, and watch rain sweeping over a forest of yacht masts and disconsolate seagulls padding about the sodden quays.

The sea breathes life and a sense of freedom and adventure into cities. Even on a grey, drizzly day a prospect of sailing boats jostling in a chorus of clinking halyards and fishing boats coming and going make for a lively scene that raises the spirits. There's a real ancient mariner feel to Plymouth. The Barbican spills out on to Sutton Harbour where a stone arch stands above worn stone steps where the Pilgrim Fathers set off for the New World in 1620, and plaques along the adjacent wall commemorate colonial pioneers who sailed to New Zealand, Newfoundland and North Carolina. On a quiet, rainy day in winter, with only the seagulls for company, you can stand and stare at a restless gunmetal sea and in your mind's eye see the square-rigged *Mayflower* rounding a headland and sailing into the history books.

I spend the afternoon reading up on the team that wears an image of *Mayflower* as its club crest and rejoices in the nickname of the Pilgrims. Founded in 1886 as Argyle FC, it achieved international renown in 1924 on a South American tour when it beat Uruguay 4-0 and Argentina 1-0 in exhibition matches. The *Buenos Aires Standard* praised Argyle captain Moses Russell as 'one of the brainiest players ever seen on the football field'.

They were toiling in the old Division Three when Pele turned up with Santos for a friendly and astonished everyone, including themselves, by beating the Brazilian superstars. Keith recalls hearing later that the visitors had agreed on a fee, but when they were in the tunnel they had demanded more. 'We thought it was just a rumour, but it seems it was true. It felt even better beating them.'

The club holds the record for scoring the fastest five goals in English professional football, racking them up in 17 minutes in a 7-0 thrashing of Chesterfield in the 2003/04 season. This was followed by six years in the Championship, before a decline and fall ended in administration and rescue by James Brent's Akkeron Group. A past helter-skelter ride up and down the divisions under high-profile managers like Paul Sturrock, Tony Pulis and Peter Reid has settled somewhere in the middle, following promotion to League One last season. Their main sponsor is a Cornish company that makes pasties and sausage rolls.

The Barbican is quiet on a dark, wet winter night, rain glistening on cobblestones and lights glowing invitingly from pub windows. I head for the Crown and Anchor on the harbour side for food and the second half of a Chelsea v Norwich FA Cup tie. This is not a big event in Plymouth. There are only four other customers in the pub and none of them are watching the game, and in truth they're not missing much.

When I began this journey I wondered if I might not be welcome at some clubs, a freelance writer intruding in daily routines at the height of competitive league campaigns, but I needn't have worried. With the exception of the Blackpool management, under siege from rebellious fans, I was received with courtesy by officials, players and supporters happy to share memories and ambitions. At Plymouth, the chairman's personal assistant Anne Smith organised meetings with anyone I wished, from her boss to the tea lady, as well as a complimentary ticket for Saturday's big match. Argyle prides itself on being a family club, and I was instantly made welcome to be part of it.

It is an immutable law of football that youngsters reared in lower league academies move on and upwards, or out of the game, and the best that clubs can hope for from their brightest prospects is a couple of years in the first team and a good transfer fee. Kevin Hodges, director of Argyle's youth academy, is ruefully aware that some you win, some you lose.

'We're making decisions on boys at 18, whether they're ready for the first team. If not, we have to let them go because we don't have the resources to keep them any longer. It's not fair, most of them have been with us since they were nine, but there are costs involved in wages, travel and hire of training pitches. One of our lads was a quick-paced striker but erratic in front of goal so we let him go at 20 and he went off and scored 15 goals for Luton in his first season and moved on to Birmingham for £1.6 million, we just let him go too early.' Other graduates recently moved to Liverpool, Southampton and Brighton, all of them England under-17 and under-19 internationals, and brought in £500,000 in transfer fees.

Times have changed since Kevin, a pacey winger, played a record 620 games for Argyle. 'When I was a young boy I just wanted to be a footballer and spent a lot of time practising on my own. Now children have other options and distractions with computers and social media, there are so many other things going on in their lives. And kids who do show promise and passion for the game can find themselves under huge pressure to perform.

'Some parents live their lives through their children, they see big rewards in professional football and it puts pressure on the kids. We put an accent on discipline and time keeping, but it's important that boys aged nine and ten enjoy the game. We try to produce well-rounded individuals, so if it doesn't work out here as a footballer we help to offer them other options. In life we all have setbacks, things don't always go the way you want, the thing to do is maintain a positive attitude.'

We are at a local sports college watching one of his youth squads training on a 3G pitch, and Kevin calls over Cameron Sangster, an 18-year-old midfielder. A local lad from Newton Abbot, he joined Argyle as an under-nine and has just made his break into the first team when he came on as a sub against Oldham when they were 4-1 up. He is one of the lucky ones, encouraged by his family and coaches to enjoy football as long as it lasts and take life as it comes.

'Until I was 16 I just enjoyed playing, my parents didn't put any pressure on me, they just told me to focus on studying. It was only when I was offered an apprenticeship and I came into a more serious professional environment that I realised this could be the future. I know professional football comes with challenges, but it's what I've always wanted to do. Every time I play it gives me a buzz, nothing else gives me that excitement. When I'm playing I never think about anything else.'

The dream is to play for Arsenal, the team he supported as a boy, but he comes across as a level-headed youngster who will find another path if necessary, thanks to wise counsel.

The players who have made it into the first team are training on a pitch outside Home Park and Anne the chairman's secretary takes me to watch them. The drills are over and a practice match is in full flow, being played with speed and intensity. The lads seem to be enjoying themselves, like a bunch of pals getting stuck in during a Sunday scratch game on a council pitch.

'I love football at this level,' Anne says. 'It's not as tidy as the Premiership, it's more of a battle, but that's one of the most joyous things about football. A team at our level can study a Premiership team and try to play up to their level, but they can't play down at ours.'

The tackles are flying in, and a late challenge makes Anne wince. 'I'm struck every time I watch them how vulnerable they are. At the top level it's all about hype, whereas here it can be a bit of a slog, but there's still skill and talent. I'm in awe at what I see. Here it's not just about talent. I can see in matches what they've worked hard at in training. This is the heart and soul of the game.'

Back in the players' lounge, I meet a player I've long admired. Lionel Ainsworth, an attacking midfielder, spent four seasons at Motherwell before moving to Argyle on a free in the summer. He made 138 appearances for the Fir Park outfit, including in the Europa League, scoring 27 goals and assisting 29. 'It was the best four years in my career,' he says. 'SPL football is a high level, there are no bad teams up there, and playing in Europe with 'Well is as good as it gets.'

Lionel is a classic journeyman footballer from Nottingham, having played on contract or loan for a dozen clubs, and I ask him about the insecurities of his profession. 'When I was younger I was on my own and moving around didn't bother me. It was fine as long as I was getting a game. Now I'm older with a fiancée and a two-year-old daughter it's so much harder to get up and leave. It's tough, but it's what I do. This is football, it's the job we're in and it's not forever.'

His family is happy and settled in Plymouth where his daughter goes to nursery, but with little more than two years left on his contract he can't commit to buying a home. 'I'm 30 now and in my mind and body I'm far from the end,' but whatever happens he's prepared for the future. He has property in Watford and Huddersfield, and during his time in Scotland he took courses in tiling and plastering. His brother has a plasterer's business, so if he can plaster walls as well as he moves a football he'll be fine.

I'm invited to join the first team for a buffet lunch, during which manager Derek Adams is deep in conversation with his erstwhile counterpart at Torquay who has just been sacked, and had asked to watch the training session. I arrange to meet Derek for a chat tomorrow, and follow the players into a darkened room for a video analysis of Wigan, Saturday's opponents. They give you room to play, a coach tells them, they're not physical, and they don't press or get in your face. Their weakness is a nervous keeper.

One man with the keeper in his sights is Graham Carey, a midfielder from Dublin who scored 15 goals last season and has netted six so far this season. He played under Adams at Ross County and won the Scottish League Cup with St Mirren and a goal-of-the-season award for a 35-yard screamer against Hearts.

'The way we play down here is more calculated, you have more time on the ball,' he tells me. 'In Scotland it's hectic, end to end, but the standard is similar. I imagine we'd acquit ourselves well in the SPL.' He has known since he was a kid that he wanted to be a footballer, and at 16 left Ireland to sign for Celtic. 'If you love what you're doing you go anywhere to play football. We Irish travel well.' Now in his third season with Argyle, he has a partner with two children who are not yet at school, and in a couple of years balancing his career and family commitments will be tougher, he admits. But in the meantime Plymouth is a great place to be based, with its beaches and summers that seem to last longer. In a short and uncertain career, there are worse places to be.

Anne has arranged a tour of the ground with Trevor Richards, head of maintenance, which becomes a kind of time travel into the past with visions of the future. He's looking forward to renovations that will increase capacity and provide new facilities, but with mixed feelings. We are standing in the old Mayflower grandstand that has seen triumph and despair in more than half a century of fluctuating fortunes.

'There's a lot of character in this old bird, but she's weary and you can't get parts for her any more. Look at these wooden seats, it seems a shame to take them out and replace them with plastic. They're old and tired, but there's something special about them in my opinion, they don't build them like this anymore.' The problem is they're a fire risk, and maybe the club can auction them, he says.

In the visitors' dressing room, no better than you'd expect at a council playing field, Trevor lifts a veil on psychological shenanigans that lurk in lower leagues. It's basic and drab enough, but a few years ago a manager asked him to paint the ceiling black to make it seem lower so opposition players would feel claustrophobic. To his credit, Trevor refused: 'I said I wouldn't do it. It's not in my nature. Jurgen Klopp in there, really?' Anne tells me later it's all part of widespread gamesmanship, such as turning off heating and sabotaging electrical outlets.

My last meeting of the day is with the boss. James Brent's Akkeron Group has a portfolio of hotels, retail, entertainment and conference facilities, but he doesn't have his own office. A youthful, charismatic figure, he works from a modest open-plan space in the club's prefab complex,

Northern grit. The phoenix of the north flies over Lancashire again, higher than ever before. Photo: Kipax

Stanley manager John Coleman's fairy tale comes true with table-topping promotion to League One. Photo: Kipax

Queen's Park amateurs who shaped the modern game with Andrew Watson, the world's first black international footballer and Scotland captain.
Photo: Queen's Park FC

A lone spectator at Hampden Park appears through the murk of a grisly matchday. Most of the 581 crowd at Queen's Park v Elgin were in another stand.
Photo: Angela Catlin

England's Berwick Rangers and fans celebrate a victory in 1979 that sealed promotion to the Scottish First Division for the first time. Photo: Berwick Advertiser

Fans from Tyneside (NE28) fly the flag for Berwick (TD15) in a Scottish Cup tie at Shielfield Park. The excitement mounts. Photo: Alan Bell

Marvin the Cambridge Moose warms up for battle as the Amber Army takes up its posts in the Newmarket Road End. Photo: Simon King

Award-winning Cambridge groundsman and storyteller Ian Darling prepares the pitch for matchday. Photo: Gavin Bell

Past, present and future. Argyle's 1930s art deco turnstiles welcome a star of tomorrow before kick-off against Wigan. Photo: Gavin Bell

Great way to begin a Saturday. Beer and relentless jokes about the opposition flow at a Plymouth pre-match 'fansfest'. Photo: Bob Wright/Greens on Screen

We only sing when we're fishing. A shoal of blow-up Grimsby haddocks invade Wimbledon for an FA Cup fifth-round tie. Photo: Mariners Trust

Grimsby's Ancient Mariners display new strip for a cancer charity calendar. Luckily Blundell Park was empty at the time. Photo: Mark Cribb

Tangerine is the colour of revolution. Blackpool fans in full cry demand ousting of their club owner. Photo: Blackpool Gazette

'Do You Hear the People Sing' – Les Miserables *of Blackpool take to the streets in a mass protest. Photo: Blackpool Gazette*

Look out EFL, the 'little club on the hill' is coming. Forest Green chairman Dale Vince celebrates promotion to League Two.
Photo: Chris Gardner (alias Rambling Man)

Family support. Young recruits to Rovers' green army take the field. All the fun and excitement of grassroots football. Photo: PSI/Shane Healey

and the only office he has is in a hospital where he is part-time chairman of a large hospital trust. So he takes me to the boardroom in the Mayflower stand, a fairly sparse room with a conference table and bar, and a couple of league-winning trophies.

A few years ago Brent knew nothing about football and cared less. He was more interested in a big reconstruction project in Beirut, until one day the chief executive of Plymouth Council called with a request: the football club was in serious trouble, could he offer some advice. 'The first word that came to mind was danger,' he recalls. 'To get involved financially with a football club, especially one in trouble, seemed like madness. I told him "wouldn't you like me to advise on an airport project instead?"' As chairman of a quango advising on development projects in Plymouth, this was more his line of work.

Argyle was going into administration with debts of £20 million, and if a buyer couldn't be found it would go out of business. Brent reluctantly sent one of his associates to survey the ruins, and the conclusion was that it was basically a good club with a big catchment area that could be saved. Brent wasn't prepared to go any further until the administrator called to say they couldn't find a buyer and the club was going into liquidation. 'So we ended up buying it. It wasn't reckless, we'd done the sums and thought the club could be saved, but the first couple of years were tough. The staff hadn't been paid for nine months, mortgages were being foreclosed and cars repossessed. It was horrible, very messy.' On the field the team were faring no better, being reduced to mainly under-18 players. Having dropped into League Two, they had gained a single point from their opening nine games of the season. Neil Warnock was living in the area, and Brent asked for his advice. 'He said I'll give you two pieces of advice, don't get relegated to the Conference, and with one point out of 27 you've no chance in hell of avoiding it. We'd become serial losers on and off the field. Sponsors were reluctant to be associated with the brand that had let down so many people.'

Brent began the salvage operation by selling Home Park to Plymouth Council and renting it back, paying missing wages and millions of pounds in liabilities. 'Looking back we were in the trenches fighting a battle to survive. It was blinking tough.' Gradually he began to turn around the club's fortunes. In the last three years it has returned cash profits and bought back the stadium, and last season they gained promotion to League One.

In the process Brent has been infected by the football bug. Last season he missed two games, and when he talks with pride about 'my' football club you have the sense it is as a fan rather than major shareholder. 'I have no regrets, it has been a real privilege. When you invest in something voluntarily, it's a lot of fun. There's so much about a club like this, I take a lot of pride in it as a genuine community club.'

The man who once considered rebuilding Beirut admits he experienced a Damascene conversion on the road to Plymouth. 'Last year we took 9,000 fans to Merseyside for a cup tie and outsang 45,000 Liverpool fans from start to finish.' The fact that they lost is beside the point. 'Our playing standard is a long way from excellence, but we have aspirations and we have a really good manager.'

Unlike some owners, Brent is not involved in recruitment or team selections. 'If Derek wants to sign a player and he has the budget I say okay go ahead, I'm not going to meddle. I'm a great believer in recruiting senior people to do a job and let them get on with it. My job is to support our manager rather than interfere.'

But severe financial pressures remain. He reckons the average loss in the Championship last year was £10 million, and only one club made a profit. It's a horrible place to be, he says, but with new revenue streams through redevelopment Argyle could aim to be in it and stay for years.

'One of our supporters is in charge of a ball bearings factory. He tells me that our results directly affect production – if we win it goes up, draw it's the same, and lose it goes down. That tells you something about the power of football.'

If ever someone comes along who can take the club to the next level he says he'll step aside, but he's in no hurry to quit. 'I regard myself just as a custodian of a fine club, and I'll always be a supporter and so will my children. It's in the blood now.'

In the evening I'm invited to attend a meeting of supporters' club officials and meet a man who has seen the best and the worst of lower league football and its fans. Mike Arthur is a lifelong Argyle supporter, having followed the team for almost 70 years, and is now the supporters' club life president. But for half of that time he was a policeman, ending as a superintendent policing games at Plymouth, Torquay and Exeter City. He was kept busy. 'The 1980s were the worst for crowd trouble, there were idiots everywhere you went, even Torquay.' Now he's out of uniform and in among the fans, some of them familiar faces from the past. 'Since I retired I miss male company, and I get it through football. Lots of fans know me from my days as a policeman, even the hooligans.'

Like many of his generation, Mike is nostalgic for a time when football stars were forged in rough-and-tumble, back-street games rather than coaching academies.

'We lived across the bridge in Cornwall. We had an end-of-terrace house with a goal marked on the wall and you were always kicking a ball around. Everyone was poor but someone always had a ball. I hate to think the number of shoes my mum had to take to the cobblers.

'You didn't support big clubs in those days, nobody had money to travel and there was no *Match of the Day*. If you wanted to see a cup final you had to go to the cinema and watch Pathe News. Now I could go to Man Utd or Chelsea if I wanted to, but my wife and I still love Argyle because it's our club.'

Friday morning, the rain has eased off and the city is brightening, if not basking, in pale sunshine. I head for a stroll on the Hoe, an historic open space by limestone cliffs that has witnessed centuries of war dramas. An apocryphal story has Drake amusing himself with a game of bowls on the Hoe in 1588 while waiting for the tide to change before sailing off to blast the Spanish Armada out of the water. It is also the closest Napoleon came to England, but more of this later. More recent unwelcome visitors were German World War Two bombers that destroyed a 'grand pleasure pier' below with its dance hall and cafes, and the splendid residence of the Royal Western Yacht Club. It is unlikely this helped their war effort much.

An imposing row of Victorian terraces still gazes imperiously over the green sward and a massive 17th-century stone fortress reminiscent of the era when Britain's burgeoning naval power ruled the waves. If anywhere symbolises Britannia's past as a 'land of hope and glory' it is this bracing panorama facing the sea where foes were conquered and colonies acquired.

The Hoe has a deserted air in the early morning, with only a few dogs showing their owners the best places to wee and chase balls, and the lonely cries of gulls carrying in a light breeze. I am enjoying being here out of season without holiday crowds, savouring the quietness, solitude, and winter sunshine. The noise of the city is a distant rumble and there is a sense that this restless sea is at the core of its being and its history.

A parade ground is littered with memorials to war heroes, notably the great navigator Drake, resplendent in bronze doublet and knickerbockers with a sword at his side, gazing offshore where he ventured in 1577 to begin a circumnavigation of the world. On his return he announced he had taken possession of California and called it Nova Albion.

Britannia dominates a nearby monument to Drake's subsequent victory over the Spanish, bearing images of galleons being tossed in stormy seas and an inscription indicating Divine intervention: 'He blew with His winds and they were scattered.'

There is also a memorial to the Beatles' bottoms, a set of four copper moulds in the shape of the rear ends of the Fab Four who deposited them here for a photo-shoot in 1967 during filming of *Magical Mystery Tour.* It now provides a whimsical photo opportunity for Beatles fans, but not today because they are filled with rainwater.

The eastern end of the Hoe is dominated by the Royal Citadel, a star-shaped Elizabethan bastion that loomed over chaotic scenes in the summer of 1815 when HMS *Bellerophon* anchored below with an important passenger.

It was barely a month after Waterloo, and on board was Napoleon en route to exile and death on St Helena.

Word spread quickly, crowds came from as far as London, and hundreds hired boats and rowed close to the warship in the hope of catching sight of the defeated emperor. On 30 July it was claimed that 8,000 people were afloat around *Bellerophan*, and midshipman George Horne described the scene: 'The Sound was literally covered with boats, the weather was delightful; the ladies looked as gay as butterflies; bands of music in several of the boats played favourite French airs to attract, if possible, the emperor's attention that they might get a sight of him ...'

This behaviour did not meet with general approval. On 5 August, the *Plymouth and Dock Telegraph* reported, 'On Sunday we regret to say a large portion of the spectators not only took off their hats but cheered him, apparently with the view of soothing his fallen fortunes, and treating him with respect and consideration.' The only casualty of the maritime mayhem was a local stonemason who drowned when two boats collided.

It seems fitting Napoleon's only view of the country he tried to conquer was a mighty fortress built to keep the likes of him from our shores. It was the last time France and Britain fought each other, and a nearby memorial fashioned from granite from Dartmoor Prison, where thousands of French prisoners were held during the Napoleonic Wars, bears a plaque with a conciliatory tone: *May our hearts be open to friendship and our arms reach across the sea to unite our two nations.* This was before Brexit, of course.

I never cease to wonder at the telescoping of time and the accessibility of European history. In terms of the age of the planet we live on, the exploits of Drake and Napoleon are a mere heartbeat away. It is more than 20 years since Motherwell last won the Scottish Cup, but it seems like yesterday.

Plymouth may be rooted at the bottom of England with little prospect of Premier League football, but it has arguably the best pre-match hospitality and entertainment of any club in the country.

It is called Fansfest, essentially a giant beer and food tent with two hours of musicians, comedians and comperes that sells out every home game to 300 fans of Argyle and whoever they happen to be playing. It is the envy of every club in League One, and a few have asked the Argyle entrepreneurs to help organise similar events at their home matches, which they do by pitching marquees in the grounds of local pubs. And it's all run by volunteers with profits going to local schools for sports equipment, to scout groups for summer camps, to churches for Christmas clubs, and to one-parent families and asylum seekers for meals.

'This is a beast,' says Big G. 'For the last five seasons we've said this can't last, and every year the membership increases and creates camaraderie and friendships throughout the league.'

Big G is a painter and decorator and leading light of the Green Taverners, a group of supporters and sponsors created during the dark days of administration to raise funds for the club, and which then had the bright idea of providing entertainment on matchdays. He is a modest man who prefers not to be identified, but fans of Argyle and their opponents know him as a big guy with a big heart who once climbed Ben Nevis to raise funds for a school bus for the disabled. 'I think the club officials and players appreciate the value of what we do, and the fans love it,' he says.

The club has cause to be grateful for the Taverners' intervention in 2011 when they raised funds to pay staff and for away travel and food for the team. 'It was a crap time to be around this club,' G admits. 'We did everything we could to raise money, we were washing cars in car parks, it was never ending. But every week every member of staff who asked for it was given money to put food on the table.

'We paid for the team to fly with supporters to Newcastle for a Hartlepool game because we needed the points. People came and opened their wallets and purses to us because we were independent and never got involved in disputes on fans' forums. We're just here to help and have fun, that's it.'

With the club now on an even financial keel, the Taverners have turned their attention to supporting local community projects and are looking forward to bigger Fansfests in a new building. They began in a tent, then a solid floor and fireproof ceiling were added, and hopefully soon redevelopment will endow them with a 'Far Post Club' to stage matchday entertainment for 500 and other events.

It's all a far cry from when G came to his first games in the 1970s as a youngster with his granddad, a dockyard worker. 'It was great, everything about it, the football was good, the smell, the atmosphere, the singing, the Bovril at half-time, for a kid it was mesmerising.' When he was older he became part of a group that rarely missed a game, home and away, and not for the first time I hear about the camaraderie of a lower league club. 'It was the same old ritual, meet in a pub for breakfast and a beer, on to the game, then back to the pub to analyse it like *Match of the Day* pundits. There's a closeness among our supporters, they get to know each other and form friendships. I know

Man United fans who've been going to games for 35 years and say they barely nod to people in the crowd they vaguely recognise.'

Optimism in adversity is a prerequisite of supporting a team whose occasional wins come as a nice surprise, and Argyle fans have it in spades. 'We've always had a great fan base. I remember we went down 3-0 to Wycombe in the play-offs in 2016, and we got two back and all the fans lit their phone torches and sang Bob Marley's 'Don't worry about a thing. Cause every little thing gonna be all right.'

But G has cause to be worried about tomorrow's match against high-flying Wigan, and admits it. 'They're the best side in the league by far, they're playing good football and scoring goals for fun. I'll take a point now.'

I've been concentrating on taking notes and it's only later as I'm transcribing them that I'm struck by the measure of what the Taverners and the community trust are achieving. In an era when there is a sense of community spirit being lost in urban societies they are an inspiring example of people helping each other for fun and the satisfaction of supporting worthy causes. More power to the Fansfest beer pumps and entertainers' microphones, and tomorrow I'll be enjoying both because G's latest charitable gesture is to provide me with a ticket for the sold-out event.

One man who knows more than most about Argyle's bumpy ride in the lower leagues is Chris Erringon, chief football writer of the *Plymouth Herald*, whose wife manages the club ticket office. 'It's a family club, at its best when there's a close-knit family feel to it,' he tells me. 'Under Paul Sturrock everyone from the chairman to the tea lady felt part of the club, and after it came out of administration Derek Adams brought back inclusivity and a feel-good factor.'

Not everything's perfect, he says, but they have a good manager and players, a core support of 9,000 fans and financial stability off the pitch. 'The problem is there's a lot of expectation. It's one of the biggest things in the city after the dockyard, but it's never fulfilled its potential. It's a big city with a huge catchment area and no other senior club for miles, it should be able to get back into the Championship. But it's an even more difficult place to survive now, most teams have foreign owners pumping in big money.' But they can always dream, he says.

Derek Adams is a bit of an oddity in football management. A soft-spoken Scot from a religious background, he neither drinks nor swears and prefers being away from the media spotlight. As manager of his previous club Ross County he had to attend twice-weekly press conferences in front of BBC and Sky cameras and a dozen print journalists, and he admits he's happier chatting with Chris Errington and a handful of local reporters at Plymouth once a week.

It is Friday afternoon, he has done all he can to prepare his squad for tomorrow's battle with Wigan, and he invites me into his office, a sparsely furnished room in the prefab complex. Adams comes across as a realist, ambitious but well aware of the challenges of managing a team with aspirations greater than its resources. His approach is to take each game as it comes and aim for gradual progress.

'Trying to attract players isn't easy where we are,' he admits. 'With budgetary and geographical restrictions, realistically the aim is to consolidate in the division as high as we possibly can. You can't run before you can walk in this division, you have to do it in stages. He reckons the Championship is achievable in the long term, and refurbishment of the old stand should increase revenue and allow the club to sign players of a higher calibre. But at his back there is always pressure for results.

'As a football manager you need time, but do you get time? No, you lose a few games and everyone wants you out of the door. My chairman is very supportive, but the problem is the fans want results and you live every day as if it's your last in the job. I'm sometimes asked if I have a five-year plan. The truth is I don't have a plan for the next day.'

In his managerial career he has never had resources to speak of, and he concentrates on developing young players and selling them for a profit as building blocks of the club, and on fostering unity that strengthens a sense of purpose. 'As a football club we try to talk to everyone and make everyone equal. We need to be pulling in the same direction.'

Tomorrow it all comes down to 11 men on the field, and Adams knows it will be tough. Wigan are aiming to bounce back into the Championship at the first attempt, and away from home this season they've won nine and drawn one out of 12. In midweek they beat Premier League Bournemouth 3-0 in an FA Cup replay. 'They usually have a dribbler, a lot of pace, a target man and physical presence. It will be hard, but we're not bad at defending deep,' Adams says.

He has been polite throughout the interview, but measured and reserved in manner. He warms up and we have a friendly chat after we discover our parents lived in the same part of Glasgow, and I tell him one of my favourite memories was when he played for Motherwell and scored against Rangers in a Scottish Cup semi-final in 2003 (which we eventually lost 3-4). He smiles at that and I wish him well for tomorrow, and I mean it.

A social event is taking place in the players' lounge, where Josh and his pals are having tea and biscuits and playing memory games. Josh is a bright, young guy in an Argyle tracksuit and his pals are mostly elderly men, some of them with early dementia. It's a regular community get-together that sometimes goes on stadium tours and sometimes for walks in a public park. Their wives and carers are having a 'wellness café' upstairs in the boardroom, getting a break from them and having a good old chat about coping with life. Josh is an inspiring example of an aspiring young footballer who didn't quite make the grade and found another path in life helping others through his club.

A trainee since the age of 12, he was released six years later and went off to study in the US. He returned with a degree in sports and business management, and is now health and disability manager of Argyle's Community Trust. 'Once you get over the disappointment of not making it as a professional footballer, you take stock and realise there's more to life. My job is extremely rewarding, I'm very happy here.'

That's clear from his easy manner with the men in his charge, who have more than a passing interest in football. One of them is a star striker of Argyle's walking football team and says scoring a winning goal against Blackpool was 'Roy of the Rovers stuff'. You sense he still dreams of scoring for the first-team squad.

The Dolphin is a good old-fashioned pub in the Barbican that has been welcoming customers with good beer and cheer for a couple of centuries, notably the Tolpuddle Martyrs who found lodging there on the day they came back from exile in Australia in 1838. A more recent regular was a former showgirl married to a merchant seaman who loved watching folk having fun in the pub, and then painting them. Critics dismissed the work of Beryl Cook as shallow, but her vivid oils captured simple happiness, people took her to their hearts and she became Britain's most popular artist. It is almost impossible to look at one of her images of jolly ladies prancing around being silly without smiling.

The only fancy part of the pub is an art deco façade adorned with golden dolphins. Inside it's everything a welcoming, no frills hostelry should be, a small, low-ceilinged ale house with fine cask beers, hand crafted wooden benches on a flagstone floor, and a blissful absence of giant television screens.

Outside it's cold and dreary, but inside it's warm and lively and an old man wearing a red woolly hat is nursing a pint of Dartmoor Jail Ale by an open fire. It's late on Friday night, drink has been taken, and Beryl's characters are easy to spot. Couples and groups are thronging the bar in various stages of alcoholic haze, the noise level is rising with folk music belting out of a sound system, and somebody is offering the old man by the fire another pint. Mercifully, there are no male strippers or drag acts beloved by Beryl.

As I sit scribbling a few notes I feel much as she must have done, amused by the boozy bonhomie of down-to-earth folk enjoying themselves and each other. I imagine her sitting in a corner, surreptitiously sketching the revellers before going home to paint them. She was a heart-and-soul painter who recorded human frailties and absurdities, but above all joy.

'I'm mainly motivated to paint by people enjoying themselves,' she said in a television interview. 'If I saw something sad I wouldn't dream of painting that, it wouldn't mean anything to me. I love it when I see people enjoying themselves. I would quite like to be the one singing and dancing drunkenly in the middle of the crowd.'

In fact, she was extremely shy and hated being the centre of attention. She didn't turn up at any of her gallery openings and didn't even go to the palace to collect an MBE. 'I feel much better when I'm painting,' she admitted. In her last TV interview, a sprightly, silver-haired lady in her 80s, she modestly acknowledged the enduring popularity of her paintings: 'They still cheer people up and I'm awfully pleased about that.'

Beryl would have enjoyed watching two buxom women of a certain age on the far side of the bar applying make-up to each other and cackling with laughter. By the time I leave, one of them, with unruly blonde hair tumbling halfway down her back, has hitched up with a big man with a salt-and-pepper beard and romance is blossoming. He looks like a jovial lion king purring with the devotion of his mate.

When I walk back to my hotel the rain-soaked streets don't seem so dreary any more.

It's Saturday lunchtime and the Fansfest is packed, its rows of tables a sea of Argyle green with flashes of Wigan blue, and a local comedian is in full swing, taking the piss out of the visitors.

'I got a puncture in a place called Hindley Green, on the outskirts of Wigan. I pulled into the garage and said, "Have you got an air line?" He said "Bugger off, we've not even got a bus station" …

'… a word of advice for Wigan fans today. When you judge us southerners, please try and remember that we haven't had the benefit of your disadvantages …

'… people think it always rains in Wigan. Not true, though it's the only town in the country with a lifeboat drill on the bus routes. The B&B I was staying at was so damp the mice were strangled by an octopus ...' And so on, and even the Wigan fans are laughing.

Forget three-course meals with wine in executive boxes, this is the Rolls-Royce of pre-match entertainment with beer on tap and a warm-up act by a guitarist and singer who appeared on *Britain's Got Talent*. Next up are children singing a club song with fans joining in a rousing chorus, followed by the comic announcing he likes Wigan because you can go to the chippy in your slippers, and I'm having the best fun ever before a football match.

An appreciation of Fansfest came in an email recently from a Bury supporter, who wrote, 'Just wanted to say how fantastic the experience was in the Green Taverners Suite on Saturday. The best pre-match entertainment ever ... the hospitality extended to us was overwhelming, you are a credit to your city and your county. Plymouth Argyle are now officially my second club ... so when you play Noblot (anagram for Bolton) next season I'll be there cheering you along, with the scarf that I was presented with. Well done and well played.'

For train driver Miles Bidgood it's all part of the game. He's a third generation Argyle supporter who's been a regular at Home Park for the best part of half a century, and there's as much chance of him switching to a bigger club as a Celtic fan buying a Rangers season ticket. During a break in the stand-up routine he tells me, 'It wouldn't feel right, would it? Argyle's always been my team, I don't see how you could ever change that. Once it's in you, it's in you. I don't care which league we're in, I'm just happy to have a club.'

So is Anne Styles, an NHS clinical manager who sneaked off to her first game as a child when her mum thought she had gone shopping. 'I was so excited. To be at a live game was absolutely magical,' she says. She's been coming ever since, and last year missed only one home game when her daughter was unwell. 'Not everyone wants to come down here, but we like it. We've got the sea and moors, and Cornwall on our doorstep, what more could you ask for? And we're proud of Argyle, it's like another family.'

For the match, my allotted place in this close-knit family is in the Devonport End, one of three modern stands that sweep into each other in graceful curves. In sharp contrast, the old Mayflower stand is a throwback to the 1950s, its iron stanchions and sloping green roof a window into the past when the likes of Stanley Matthews trotted out in Blackpool colours to dazzle Argyle defenders. It has nostalgia written all over it. I find myself musing that it has a *Chariots of Fire* look to it, and I'm happy to have seen it before it is consigned to history.

Before kick-off it is announced that a guest today is Dave Regis, brother of football legend Cyrille, who has just died, and 12,000 people duly stand and accord a minute's warm applause to a black icon of the game beloved by supporters of West Brom, Coventry and England. The day before it was reported that one of the Argyle players, Ryan Edwards, had been diagnosed with cancer, and as the game starts the stadium rings to 'One Ryan Edwards, there's only one Ryan Edwards ...' The spontaneous collective support is heartwarming, invested as it is with the passion of football fans.

Then they warm to the task in hand, and when a Wigan player goes down under a meaty challenge he is greeted with, 'Soft northern bastard, you're just a soft northern bastard ...' Argyle have the best of the opening exchanges, and the green and white barmy army is in full voice to a crescendo of drumbeats with songs, taunts and observations on the referee's performance.

After 25 minutes, Argyle win a penalty, which Wigan's keeper prepares for by jumping up and down and prancing about on his line like a demented donkey. Irish international Graham Carey ignores him, sends him the wrong way and calmly slots into the bottom corner. Argyle's joy is short-lived as Wigan equalise virtually from the kick-off, and a young woman sitting next to me is philosophical: 'I'll be well happy with a draw.' There is a good sprinkling of women and young children in the Devonport End, filling it with excited fervour without aggression. My wife is expecting our first child, a daughter, and I'd be happy to bring her here for a match.

Argyle are holding their own against fancied opposition with fast-flowing, incisive football. Carey is a handful, running at defenders and firing in dangerous crosses, but on the stroke of half-time Wigan score from a suspiciously offside breakaway, prompting cries of, '2-1 to the referee.'

During the interval hopeful stars of the future are paraded around the ground, the under-nine youth development squads bearing trophies, as an announcer extols their exploits. I can only imagine their thrill at being given a standing ovation.

I chat with my neighbour who says she's from Newquay, '50 miles down a rubbish road', but Argyle's her local team. She came to her first match with a boyfriend at the age of 16 and was immediately smitten. 'It gets you inside, it grips you so you've got to keep coming. I like that I'm sitting among other season-ticket holders, we're just a big family really.'

She thinks it would be lovely if they got into the Premier League, but that it'll probably never happen. 'They're playing some nice football but they're not doing much with it' – a familiar Saturday lament up and down the country. She learns I'm Scots and our conversation digresses to her brother-in-law, whom she says spent years as the fireman and harbour master on the tiny Hebridean island of Muck, where his wife was the community teacher and nurse. 'He wanted to show his kids there is more to life than computer games.'

It doesn't take Wigan long after the restart to score again, and my neighbour says, 'That's why they're top, they take their chances.' Argyle press forward, but chances are few and missed, and the visitors take home another three points for their promotion challenge.

As darkness falls and a cold, blustery wind rises, the men in green and white are given a standing ovation for their efforts, and Wigan fans are sent on their way with cheery chants of 'Top the league, you're having a laugh,' and 'Accrington Stanley, they've won more than you ...'

Beaten, Argyle? Never. Just wait till next Saturday.

Grimsby Town

I've been going too long to stop. I wouldn't know what to do on a Saturday afternoon.

Founded:	1878
Ground:	Blundell Park
Average attendance:	4,658
Honours:	Division Two champions 1901/02
	Division Three North champions 1955/56
	Division Four champions 1971/72
	Division Three champions 1979/80
	Auto Windscreens Shield 1997/98

THE BLOW-UP fish were a big hit. Grimsby were preparing for a cup game against Wimbledon and a sports reporter on the local paper had the bright idea of creating a mascot to represent the town's fishing heritage. It was a paper trout, but they called it Harry Haddock.

He persuaded the management to buy 50 to test the water, they promptly sold the lot, and the company producing them couldn't keep up with demand. In the end 2,000 fish went to the game and Gary Lineker declared on *Match of the Day* that the club had put the fun back into football. That was 30 years ago, and they're still selling blow-up fish in the club shop. Harry has since become the world's most widely travelled haddock, having been pictured on tour with Town fans at NASA in Florida, below the iconic statue of Christ the Redeemer in Rio, and on the Great Wall of China.

The tale says much about the irrepressible spirit of fans who follow a struggling team in a town in the depths of post-industrial decline. As recently as the 1950s, the Lincolnshire port on the North Sea boasted the world's biggest fishing fleet, until Britain lost its cod wars with Iceland, and Grimsby lost its trawlers and a way of life that had sustained it for more than a century. The story goes that Grimsby was one of the last towns in Lincolnshire to form a football club, because so many men were fishing and not available to play regularly. Fishing was its lifeblood, and when it drained away in the 1970s the town almost died. At the time the football club wasn't faring much better, prompting a *Guardian* writer and Grimsby fan to write that the footballing knowledge of the club board could have been written on the dorsal fin of a small cod.

But Grimsby Town supporters still sing about their seafaring heritage. When opposition fans taunt them with 'You're not singing any more', they fire back: 'We only sing when we're fishing'. Known derisively as codheads, they have entered into the spirit of the banter by naming their fanzine *Cod Almighty*.

They haven't had much to sing about this season. It's late March and Town haven't won a game all year. The previous week they lost 4-0 at Coventry, stretching their winless run to 18 games, and now they are down among the fall guys of League Two, three points above the trapdoor into the bottomless pit of non-league football. They know all about the Conference, having fought for six years to get out of it just two seasons ago, and they are in no hurry to return. They are in a battle for survival with seven games left, including against the two teams below them. Stevenage lying 16th are next up on Good Friday, and a week later they face a potential decider against Chesterfield, three points below them with two games in hand. In three matches under a new manager they have scored two goals and conceded eight. These are grim times in Grimsby.

The name, incidentally, is said to derive from its founder rather than its character, a ninth-century Danish fisherman called Grim. The town does not immediately endear itself to visitors. Approaching it across the sleepy green flatlands of Lincolnshire, the rural landscape gives way to a complex of gaunt smokestacks, a petrified industrial forest, where a road sign welcomes you grandly to 'Great Grimsby', twinned with Bremerhaven.

I check into my hotel with an unprepossessing entrance in a car park; it is late in the day and the receptionist points me in the direction of an Italian restaurant. The shopping area outside is deserted, it's like a ghost town, and I remark to a lone pedestrian how quiet the streets are. 'The town is dead,' he says bluntly. 'It all went with the fishing.'

On my way back to the hotel I stop to admire a striking bronze memorial depicting a trawlerman in wet-weather gear hauling in nets from a slanting deck. It is a vivid image, but as lifeless as the lost industry it portrays. The only signs of life now are a few teenagers in a garishly lit McDonald's, a homeless man kicking empty cans from his sleeping place for the night in a doorway, and a pile of dog shit outside a betting shop. Back in my room I am startled by loud, crazy growls and groans from the street outside my window, as if a pack of zombies are on the loose. I close the curtains and switch on the TV, anything will do.

And here's a thing: over the next few days I find that despite their hard lot and first appearances, Grimbarians, which is what they call themselves, are generally a cheery, friendly, down-to-earth lot.

I meet four of them next morning when they come to my hotel to explain their lifelong loyalty to their team. It is worth mentioning that the club's nickname is the Mariners, a reference to the town's seafaring heritage, and inevitably it has given rise to a loosely affiliated group calling itself the Ancient Mariners. Pete Cribb and Billy Callendar are members of this merry band of brothers of a certain age who play walking football, and roam far and wide over the North Sea in search of kindred spirits from Holland and Germany for international friendlies. Winning for them is of secondary importance to having a good time, which is just as well given the team they support. They have brought along a couple of pals, and we order coffee in the lounge and talk about the good old days when the boats used to come in and the Mariners dumped Liverpool and Spurs out of the League Cup.

In the early 1950s Bill Shankly took them to second in the old Third Division North, and with well-intentioned hyperbole he lauded the team as 'pound for pound, and class for class, the best football team I have seen in England since the war. In the league they were in they played football nobody else could play … you could not wish to see more entertaining football.'

A brief golden era in the early 70s saw them winning the Fourth Division under Lawrie McMenemy, who was duly accorded divine status. Pete recalls a vital 2-0 win at Stockport on Easter Monday, when thousands of Grimsby fans stayed to celebrate and wouldn't get back on the buses.

'The police couldn't move them on, so they called McMenemy out of the dressing room and said can you ask them to go home? So he went out and said, "Look lads, we've got to get home, we've got a big game on Saturday to clinch promotion, let's all get off home."

'One of our lads had broken his leg and was walking on crutches, but he turned to the police and said Lawrie McMenemy says it's time to go, so he chucked his crutches away and hobbled off into the sunset and the policeman said, "Bloody hell, he's not a football manager, he's a bloody Messiah." It was back page headlines in *The Sun*.'

During his 18-month reign at Grimsby, McMenemy, an ex-Coldstream Guard, introduced a novel motivational approach, Billy remembers. 'He used to take all the team down to the docks at five in the morning when the fishing was thriving and make them appreciate what the fans were doing for them, and that's how he became a god really.'

The Messiah manager quickly acquired a huge following, drawing 18,000 to Liverpool for an FA Cup game, so many they couldn't all get in the Grimsby end and a lot of them ended up in the Kop. 'In those days there weren't television, the fans were fanatical and the players would die for them,' Billy affirms. And for McMenemy, probably.

Then there were days of Wembley glory in 1998 when Grimsby went en masse to London to watch their team win the Auto Windscreens Shield (2-1 against Bournemouth), and went back a few weeks later to see them triumphing in the Second Division play-off final (1-0 against Northampton).

'It was a fabulous trip,' Pete says of cup final day. 'It wasn't just the football, it was the fact the whole town went to Wembley. There were so many buses they had to take different routes, or they'd have clogged the main road out. There were signs on the motorway saying last one out of Grimsby switch the lights off, and first one back put the kettle on.' For the record, the crowd of 62,432 was the biggest for a sporting event in England that weekend.

Changed days. Now they're lucky to get 3,500 at a league match and Pete feels sorry for a new manager who has just been brought in to try and save their season. There is exasperation and despair in the stands: 'He's been left with a load of duffers. They're journeymen footballers and all they want is another payday. They've no affinity to the club or the town, and they're not bothered if we get relegated or stay up because at the end of the season they're all going anyway and they'll get another year's contract somewhere else. They've no heart, there's no heart in the club at all.'

Billy bemoans a lack of home-grown talent in a team that used to thrive on scouting and developing local youngsters. Now there's only one, his grandson Harry Clifton, a midfielder who is being given a chance under the new manager. Pete agrees: 'We're crying out to have Harry in the team, the crowd's been wanting him in for months. He's got a good engine, full of energy. They all wear heart monitors and after his first game the manager called him out and said he was the only one who managed the same energy output as anybody in the Premiership, none of the others got anywhere near him.'

The root of the problem is a familiar one, a general decline in local amateur football. Their pal Len Davidson says that until a few years ago there were ten divisions in Sunday football in the Grimsby area. Now there are five, and from 135 teams they're down to 40. 'It's all over the country this is happening. It's a different generation, they'd rather play football on tablets. Somebody said they're going to have a world championship for thumb texting.'

It's hard to argue with him. It doesn't seem so long ago that you couldn't pass a Glasgow shipyard or factory or a school playground at lunchtime without seeing games of 'tanner ba' football with jackets for goalposts. But of course it is.

In Grimsby it's not just the trawlers that have gone, it's playing fields that the council no longer has the money to maintain, and Pete says, 'You don't see kids out playing football in the streets, them days have all gone.'

In recent years the town's fortunes have mirrored those of its football club, and the Ancient Mariners are nostalgic for better times in Christmases past. Billy came from a fishing family, and he remembers when the docks were a bustling town in itself and it took 20 minutes for a train of fish wagons to pass. At Christmas he says the fishermen were all home and you could walk right across the docks on their boats, it was so packed like sardines some couldn't get in.

'On Christmas Day the fishermen all went to the match with bottles of whisky and rum, and would pass them to the opposition fans. You all just mixed in the same stands and some of the crack that used to go from one lot to the other was just brilliant. It was so exciting, now when you go most of the time you're just condemning the manager.'

Pete chips in: 'In the 60s this used to be a happy town. I used to travel a lot, and you could go to any town and be glad to come back to Grimsby, it used to be such a nice place. But now there's nothing here really.'

It still has its football club, but Pete reckons Stevenage at home on Friday is a must-win game if they are to survive in the EFL. 'If we go down I don't think we'll come back up, we'll just go down the leagues.' But whatever happens there's no chance of him walking away from the team. 'I've been going too long to stop. I wouldn't know what to do on a Saturday afternoon.'

There's not much in Grimsby to cheer the spirit, but there is next door. The town merges seamlessly into the seaside resort of Cleethorpes, and on the main road between them it's not clear where one ends and the other begins. But gradually the difference is obvious in an air of relative prosperity with housing that doesn't look half derelict. Barely a mile from Grimsby's crumbling docks, its neighbour presents a cheery face to holidaymakers and day trippers with a breezy promenade by a seemingly endless Blue Flag beach lined with amusement arcades, cafes and ice-cream parlours, and a vintage pier adorned by 'the world's biggest fish and chip shop', whose takeaways were judged the best in Britain in a BBC competition. There is a boating lake and donkey rides on the beach in summer. Cleethorpes is a very different kettle of fish from Grimsby, thriving on a rich seasonal harvest of visitors who do like to be beside the seaside. I find it old-fashioned, cheesy and charming, reminiscent of cheeky seaside postcards of the 1960s, and even under grey March skies and drizzling rain the town has a lively, festive air.

I head for lunch at Papa's, the award-winning fish and chip shop on the pier ('nobody does it batter') and am pleasantly surprised to find it is a far cry from the usual northern chippie. It's an elegant old ballroom transformed into a glitzy 500-seat seafood restaurant and tearoom beneath glittering chandeliers, with smart staff and panoramic windows overlooking the beach. A timeless gem, and classic haddock and chips has never tasted better.

The reason I have come to Cleethorpes is an anomaly worthy of a pub quiz. Grimsby is the only senior club in Britain to play all of its home games away, because its ground is in Cleethorpes. To add to the confusion, Cleethorpes Town FC plays in the Evo-Stik League East Division against the likes of Pontefract Collieries in a tidy little stadium in Grimsby.

Grimsby's Blundell Park, named after an early benefactor, is only just outside the town, off the main Cleethorpes road. You can't see the sea from here but you can often feel the wind whipping off it. A few weeks before, a winter storm and high tides battered the nearby promenade with waves as high as a double decker bus. Given the weather it's a testament to the builders of the oldest stand in the EFL that it is still standing after more than a century. The original wooden main stand dates from 1901, and admittedly it is given to creaking in its old age, and according to local lore it's not always the wind.

'We've all heard noises, banging and doors closing,' the club's media officer Dale Ladson tells me. 'There are supposed to be spirits in the old boardroom, and a couple of years ago a bunch of ghostbusters got a fright and left in a hurry.'

Groundsman Mike Phillips is sceptical. 'It's an old stand, you hear a lot of creaking and banging in the wind, but it can be eerie when you're alone.' Having been at Blundell since he left school almost 30 years ago, he's seen a few changes. He remembers days when the team drew crowds of 13,000 for games against Barnsley, in an era when training was basically a kickabout then lighting up fags. 'Now it's cone city, all fast feet and backroom staff with physios and sports scientists and whatnot. But in those days if they got ten corners they'd score six goals. Now they're lucky if they get one.'

On the way back to my hotel I cruise down Freeman Street, once a legendary haunt of fishermen when the boats were in, a poor man's Champs Elysees of cheerful pubs thronged on matchdays. To have half a pint in every pub in the street was regarded as a supreme onshore challenge.

No more. It is a grim picture of urban decay, a street in its death throes, most of the pubs and shopping centres closed, boarded up and crumbling, mute witnesses to remorseless dereliction. Here be ghosts for real in an electoral ward ranked among the most deprived in Britain for education, employment and crime.

One of the few survivors is the Wellington Arms, where members of Worsley Cricket Club held a meeting in 1878 to form a football club to occupy winter evenings after the cricket season was finished. They called it Grimsby Pelham after a local landowner, and a year later changed the name to Grimsby Town. It is a basic two-room pub on a corner opposite a tattoo studio, and one of the snugs is a shrine to the Mariners with walls covered with images of past glories and heroes. I ask an old chap nursing a pint if he's a Town supporter. 'Wouldn't waste my time,' he says gruffly. 'They're a useless lot.'

It is not all doom and gloom in Grimsby. Almost, but not quite. A cluster of offshore wind farms provides hundreds of jobs and there are plans to develop a renewable energy industry. They don't catch fish any more but they process it in vast quantities, making it one of the biggest centres of the industry in Europe. This has prompted the local council to promote Grimsby as 'Europe's Food Town', which is misleading. It might have a good restaurant, but I didn't find it.

Next day I'm back at Blundell Park to complete a tour of the stadium and hear more about the resident spirits. Lisa Piggott, the tickets and events manager and lifelong Town supporter, takes me upstairs to the boardroom. 'We don't have many trophies,' she admits. The biggest is the People's Cup, a huge pineapple-shaped trophy won by the Ancient Mariners. The other prize exhibit is a rare piece of football memorabilia, a large metal plate inscribed Grimsby Town FC in shiny silver letters that adorned a railway locomotive in the 1960s. The National Railway Museum has a replica and would like the original, thought to be worth £20,000, but the club refuses to sell it. It's good to know there are treasured possessions in small football clubs that money can't buy.

The boardroom and neighbouring corridors are said to be the haunt of Charlie, an elderly caretaker from the same era whose restless spirit wanders around switching televisions and vacuum cleaners on and off. 'He's never hurt anyone, but he likes you to know he's there,' Lisa says. 'I've heard his grunts and groans and bangs, but he's just cleaning. Other people have heard footsteps when there was nobody there, and once a tree in a pot of cement fell over and set off the alarms. I suppose he was just being careless, but he's harmless. The ones on the other side are more sinister.'

By 'the other side' she means the Platinum Suite in the old main stand on the other side of the park that was the original boardroom, strictly for men only. After persistent reports of mysterious knocking and banging, the club began making a few bob for youth development by hosting 'ghost vigils' in the supposedly haunted room. Lisa was present at one on Halloween when ghostbusters turned up with infrared cameras. There were about 15 in the group and after a while they smelled cigar and pipe smoke, the women began to feel sick, and one of them swore she felt a cold slap on the face. At this point someone said, 'If you want us to leave make it known.' There was a single, loud knock at the door and the women used it to rush out, one of them in tears. Film from the infrared camera is said to have subsequently revealed a shadowy figure about seven feet tall, wearing a hat, flitting out of an adjacent kitchen. So goes the tale of the misogynist ghosts of Grimsby FC, where Lisa insists the old stand has a creepy presence. 'When it gets dark you feel the whole stand is looking at you, it's spooky.'

Fortunately it's mid-morning when assistant groundsman Derek Smith gives me a tour of 'the other side'. Sunlight is streaming through the corridors, hopefully banishing cigar-smoking spirits, but as we climb the stairs and he opens the door to the Platinum Suite I hear a distinct knock on another door behind me.

'Did you hear that?' I ask.

'Mmm,' Derek affirms.

He reaches behind me, opens the door, and it's a closet. I assume it was the wind, and then I realise there isn't any. I'm glad I don't have an infrared camera. There are no further manifestations of unearthly displeasure in the musty bastion of departed directors, and we leave them to their cigars. In a couple of days there will be a lot more noise in the old stand when Stevenage come calling, but Lisa is right. When the crowds have gone and darkness falls, I wouldn't want to be left alone with the creaks and groans and things that go bump in the night.

On the way out Derek fulminates against pressures of the modern game that prevent home-grown lads from breaking into first teams, and the ditching of senior players deemed surplus to requirements. 'A lot of young lads don't stand a chance of making it into first teams because managers are under pressure from chairmen and supporters to produce results. It's not like the old days, when you had your Beckhams and Giggs coming through, it doesn't happen now.'

An exception is Billy Callendar's grandson, Harry Clifton, being given a run-out by the new manager. 'The fans like him because he's one of our own, that's what it's about, isn't it?' But one day Clifton could be among squad members shown the door in a change of management, and Derek feels for them. 'At a flick of a switch they can offload you. These are men with families and mortgages, and wives who come to support them. It would stress anyone in a normal job. To me it's criminal.'

On to Cleethorpes promenade and Oliver's Eatery *aka* Jonny Donuts, an art deco café-restaurant famed for home-baked cakes and pies, for a weekly get-together of Ancient Mariners. Pete introduces me to half a dozen of his pals, men who have experienced the highs and lows of supporting Grimsby over lifetimes. They include the 'Man on a Hot Tin Roof'. Rick Todd, a retired taxi driver, is one of the adventurous figures photographed on the slanting roof of a Blundell stand on a memorable night in 1972 when Town beat Exeter 3-0 in the last game of the season to win the Fourth Division before 22,489 fans.

'We couldn't get a place on the terraces where we could see anything so we tried to get up the floodlights, and we were halfway up when the cops told us to get down. So we walked round the back of the stand and saw a way of getting on the roof and took it.' Given the state of repair and inclination of the roof, this was like climbing on to a rickety old Olympic ski jump and hoping for the best. Rick remembers his bootlaces came loose but he didn't dare lean forward to tie them in case he slipped down – and off – the roof. 'When the second goal went in we had to hold on because the whole stand was vibrating. When you look back now you wonder what the hell we were doing.' Fortunately it all ended well. 'When we got down the cops didn't arrest us, they just gave us a clip round the lug. It wasn't hooliganism, just high spirits.'

His pal Dave Walton was 14 at the time, five years younger than Rick, but the Exeter game ranks top of his football memories. Over the years he has also supported Manchester City, and was at the Etihad in 2012 when Aguero scored an injury-time winner against QPR to clinch the Premier League title. 'It was brilliant but it didn't come close to matching that night when we beat Exeter. Games like that stick with you for life.'

Before kick-off Lawrie McMenemy famously warned the Exeter manager, 'You've got no chance. The crowd will beat you tonight.' And so it proved. Years later an article in the fanzine *When Saturday Comes* said Exeter had surrendered to the will of a crowd intent on nothing less than sporting slaughter. The author recalled it as the greatest night of his life, one of many fond memories of the McMenemy epoch 'because he showed something that transcends mere sporting pinnacles. He demonstrated the role that football could play in a northern backwater; having a club to cherish and, quintessentially, one that belonged.'

I'm enjoying the Ancient Mariners' light-hearted gathering with its laughter and fond memories. The talk is not of the current parlous state of the team, but of great days out among a bunch of lads who have become lifetime friends. Last year they took a team to Holland for an international walking football tournament, festooned with sombreros as well as the inflatable fish.

The Mexican attire grew from an incident at Barnet a few years ago when a steward was struck by a blow-up fish. The perpetrator was taken to court, because of 'pain and distress' suffered by the steward, and was duly fined £800 for assault with an offensive weapon. Grimsby fans responded to this judicial nonsense next time they were at Barnet by substituting their fish with a Mexican mariachi band they had heard at a function in Grimsby, and naturally they all wore sombreros and ponchos. Pete has no idea where they got them all from as there weren't that many in the local shops, but he recalls, 'The band was fabulous, they went round the pitch at half-time.' So they took the big hats to Holland for a bit of fun, and had a job explaining what they had to do with a north-of-England fishing town.

One of the few places you can still see a trawler in Grimsby is on the Mariners club badge. Another is berthed outside a fishing heritage centre, a veteran of the 1950s heyday of the industry preserved as a monument to a seafaring community engaged in the most dangerous and arguably toughest peacetime occupation in Britain. The *Ross Tiger* was one of the last Grimsby trawlers to sail to the icy wastes of Greenland and Arctic Norway on three-week voyages from which many never returned. In the 1950s alone 32 ships were lost.

A few years ago more than 150 retired trawlermen attended a reunion at the heritage centre, and they included a deckhand on the *Ross Tiger* who survived being washed overboard in heavy seas. In a YouTube video of the event, he says, 'What saved me was they saw me among a bunch of seagulls. I'll never forget that day. I still think about it today.'

There is a dramatic tableau in the centre depicting men hauling in nets on a fish deck, battling freezing mist and spray that could sink ships with a build-up of ice. At fishing grounds skippers went without food and sleep for days on end, living on adrenalin because it was their job to find and catch the fish. Yet in the YouTube video an elderly former skipper says, 'I enjoyed it. I'd go back tomorrow if they'd let me.'

As a weekend sailor I am familiar with challenging conditions in relatively sheltered coastal waters, and I left the centre with renewed respect for deep-sea fishermen who braved far, far worse. The sea was their life as well as their livelihood, and no wonder the heart went out of their close-knit community when they were deprived of it.

Thursday morning, the day before the crunch match, and a readers' survey in the *Grimsby Telegraph* paints a gloomy picture. One writes, 'I honestly feel we will be in the Conference again next season. A freezing cold Tuesday night at Blundell Park against Boreham Wood or Champions League football and a beer sat at home? No contest for me if we are non-league. I never thought I would feel like this.' Another expresses a widely held sentiment: 'What really gets us locals is the lack of passion and commitment on the field.' During the week the newspaper's headlines have been spelling out the team's dire situation: *Stats make grim read after Mariners' slump – Town must pull their socks up – Seven games to save season.*

For light relief I head for a municipal football centre on the outskirts of town to play my first game for more years than I care to remember, having been invited to join the Ancient Mariners at one of their three-weekly walking football sessions. It is a bright, crisp day beneath blue skies as I take to the astroturf and promptly produce a string of wayward passes and mistimed tackles, but happily nobody seems to mind as the aim is to have a good time, and the result is beside the point.

But it is not, as I supposed, a walk in the park with this cheery bunch of Peter Pans. It's fast-paced, one-touch football below head height by men who clearly know how to play the game, and whose enthusiasm has not waned with physical condition. We play three 20-minute games of six-a-side, and I'm grateful when our volunteer ref blows for time on the last one. I'm not surprised that in Holland they won matches against the likes of Werder Bremen Old Boys.

Afterwards everyone gets together in the centre café and I meet Ken Thompson, a retired teacher who was on the Holland trip. 'It's just a bit of fun,' he says. 'Some of the English teams play to win, but for the Dutch and Germans it's just more of a social get-together and that suits us. Our philosophy is anyone who signs for us plays, it doesn't matter if we win.' This year they're heading back to Holland with two teams, including a man who plays with a walking stick.

In a quiet village a few miles down the road, the real Mariners are winding up their final training session, and I'm invited to join the manager's pre-match press conference.

While waiting for it to start, I have a chat with Billy Callendar's grandson, the promising local youngster Harry Clifton. He's a pleasant, fresh-faced lad and the first thing he says is he's proud to be wearing the club shirt. Football is in his family blood, with his father and grandfather both running amateur leagues. 'Grimsby used to rely on home-grown talent, but not many have come through in recent years, so when my family come and watch me it makes me feel proud,' he says. But his one-year deal expires at the end of the summer and he has no idea what will happen next.

'The situation we're in, I don't know. If we go down, if I feel it helps me to stay I will if I'm asked. There's always a bit extra when you play before fans you know. But it's a results game, if you don't perform you'll be out.' He admits confidence is low in the dressing room. 'We're trying to stay positive and never give in. The next three games will be real battles.'

Going into the press conference, I have a quick word with a reporter from the *Grimsby Telegraph*. 'If they don't get a result tomorrow they're done,' he says. 'The heart and soul have gone out of the team.'

The man entrusted with their league survival has had an unusual career, initially more to do with playing the stock market than football. After being released by Barnsley as a teenager, Michael Jolley went off to Cambridge University to gain an MA in economics and become a successful bond trader in London and New York. But football was his passion, it was always in the back of his mind to find a way back into it, so one day he quit the world of high finance for a modest income as part-time youth coach at Crystal Palace. It was a brave move that led to a string of coaching roles at Burnley, Notts Forest, Lincoln and Crewe, and eventually the manager's job at a Swedish First Division club before arriving at Grimsby. He was working in New York a mile from the Twin Towers on the day they fell and the dead included one of his friends, which puts the perceived disaster of non-league football in Grimsby into useful perspective.

Now he's facing the massed ranks of the media in his portacabin office in the form of the man from the *Telegraph*, a local radio and TV reporter, and me. It's a small space with no room to hide from awkward questions about dismal performances, and Jolley is honest but upbeat about their prospects. He is under no illusions about the challenge, but is clearly relishing it.

Afterwards he invites me to stay for a cuppa and I pose the obvious question – what made him give up a lucrative financial career for the parlous world of football management?

'It's in the blood, it's a passion, an obsession,' he says. 'I've loved the challenge of the game from day one, the tactical side and so on. Also it's an emotional game, you get good days and bad days and it's all about enjoying the good days when they come.' I have to agree, even watching Grimsby these days must be better than crunching endless numbers on a computer screen.

He said as much in a television interview on the day he was appointed: 'The way people phrase the question is "how did a trader end up as a football manager?" I'd flip it and say "how does somebody obsessed with football end up being a trader?", because that's the way it happened.'

His priority is to stay in the league, but if they are relegated he says he is keen to stay and work with a club run by good people with fantastic support. And youngsters like Harry will have their chance to break into the first team. 'Harry's performances have been one of the highlights of my three weeks here. He's really stepped up and shown that he can be a good player for us in the future. We have a few local lads who understand acutely what it means to play for Grimsby Town, and I'd like to have more of them in our team. The ideal would be a mix of experience and young, hungry local players.' He sounds like Alex Ferguson talking at Carrington.

Given the nature of the job, there is a high risk of being sacked and I wonder how Jolley copes with the insecurity. 'I'm pleased you've asked me that because it's one of the few chances I've had to say anything about it in an interview. My wife is really supportive. I think we've moved house ten times in seven years because of changes in my football career and that's tough for anybody, especially a spouse who wants to have her own life and settle down. It's been difficult, but I couldn't do what I'm doing without her support.'

On the broader question, he says you have to understand that insecurity is part of the industry and not fear it. 'I'm fully aware that as a football manager at some point it's likely that I'll be dismissed. That's the nature of the job. The big thing for me is keeping a sense of perspective, because if the worst thing that ever happens to me is that I lose my job as a football manager it isn't the end of the world and life goes on, and it can be a good life.'

I sense that under the circumstances, this level-headed born-again footballer may be the best the club could hope for, and wish him well for tomorrow. The match falls on his 41st birthday.

Good Friday, matchday. Over breakfast in my hotel I see a big guy wearing a black t-shirt with a slogan that seems appropriate for Grimsby Town: 'Born to lose, live to win.'

I have arranged to meet Terry Hall, chairman of the Town supporters' travel club, in a shopping centre coffee shop and he is easy to spot. He's the jolly character wearing a Mariners bobble hat. Born and bred in Grimsby, he's been going to games since he first went with his dad when he was six, and he'll still be going if they are relegated. 'It's in the blood,' he says simply. 'Football is my life.'

We chat about days when the club ran 11 coaches to a cup game at Liverpool, which they won 2-1, and he admits the travel club has lost a few members in the current free-fall. 'But the majority are older and we stick together, we enjoy the days out. One thing I will say about the Conference, when we go to away games the rival fans are good to chat to.'

He missed just one home game last season when he collapsed with low blood pressure and was rushed to hospital, and couldn't get out in time for kick-off. The last time he missed an away game was nine years ago, when he was on a Mediterranean cruise with his wife.

'How was it?' I ask, meaning the cruise.

'We lost 4-1 at Tranmere,' he says.

Since it's Good Friday I wander into Grimsby Minster, a magnificent medieval pile of Romanesque and Early English architecture that has been a spiritual sanctuary and a navigation mark for seafarers since the 13th century. Among its splendid stained-glass windows the town's fishing heritage is celebrated with images of trawlers, dockside scenes and the patron saints of mariners. In 1907 Bishop Edward King, in an address at Grimsby Town Hall, declared, 'There it stands in that grim immovable old way, right in the eye of the north-east wind, steady and firm and strong … there is in this church of yours here a certain mystery that comes from the excellence of proportion as well as strength, and which leads one's thoughts to something higher than you can visibly see.'

Today it is a cheerful, friendly place and coffee and biscuits are on offer. I am surprised by a small choir of children and their parents singing what sounds like a familiar football chant, but it turns out to be 'Lord of the Dance', a hymn with the lines:

I danced for the fishermen, for James and John;
They came with me and the dance went on …

The Fir Park faithful have adapted the chorus to, 'We are the Motherwell FC, we hate the Hearts and we hate Hibees [Hibs]…' This is not the most inventive of matchday arias. My personal favourite is an interpretation of 'La donna è mobile' from Verdi's opera *Rigoletto,* with which Derby County fans celebrated their Italian striker Fabrizio Ravanelli by singing: 'We've got Fabrizio, you've got fuck allio …'

Canon Andrew Dodd, preparing for the day's service, is rector of Great Grimsby and an occasional Town supporter. He confesses that more people talk to him when he's wearing his club scarf on matchdays than when he's wearing a dog collar. I ask if he's downhearted by the team's position. 'No, it's par for the course,' he says with a laugh.

I've long had an impression that football is a new quasi-religion, bringing congregations together in faith and devotion, singing hymns to the Holy Grail of league or cup glory. I put it to Canon Dodd and he agrees up to a point: 'I wouldn't stretch the analogy, but football is a collective act of engagement by people who gather in hope and expectation. I think it's interesting that in post-industrial societies like

Grimsby, football clubs are more accessible than big teams like Chelsea and Manchester United, giving people a sense of identity and belonging. This can only be positive.'

With this canonical blessing, I head for Blundell Park via the docks that once were crammed with a vast, jostling armada of 700 trawlers. Now they are silent and deserted, a decaying ghost town on a public holiday. I'm hoping to see the ice factory, one of the biggest in the world in its day and an architectural landmark that supplied crushed ice for preserving fish, but it is beyond a security barrier which is closed.

'There's not much going on in the docks these days,' the guard says. 'It's mostly to do with the wind farms.'

'Are there many trawlers left?'

'One or two.'

It turns out the ice factory is derelict anyway.

Dining options are limited around Blundell Park, so I end up in McDonald's. It's packed with fans and I find myself sharing the only free table with David Spittlehouse, an art dealer, and his wife Sue, a retired teacher. Originally from a nearby village, they are living near Cambridge but are still loyal season-ticket holders at Grimsby, though Dave admits things are not what they used to be: 'Lincoln City supporters say this is a dead-end town and it is now, but it never used to be. All this road used to be thriving little shops, and the docks were like a separate town with cafes, chandlers and rope-makers serving the fishermen. But the area and the club management are dying on their feet.'

Sue remembers when the team used to send players to her village school. 'They did lots for the community then.' Dave says, 'This is one of the worst teams we've ever had, and it could be terminal if we go down. I think we could become a part-time club.'

Yet they are stoics worthy of Marcus Aurelius, insisting they'll still be at games no matter which league Town are in. 'It's part of your growing up and how you feel about the area,' Sue says. 'It's more than football, it's about friendships that have been built up over generations supporting a club with close affiliations to the area. What other ground can you sit and watch ships sailing up and down the estuary?' Dave adds, 'It's not a jumped-up little club like Forest Green Rovers that was bought by a bloke that stuffed money into it. Town has history and tradition.'

As kick-off approaches the Supporters Trust bar in the main stand is packed with a lively, good-natured crowd, but the talk is all of the threat of relegation. I join a table of men discussing team news and jot down snatches of conversation: 'We've got no centre-back on the bench … the midfield doesn't create enough … they haven't won in 18 games, how the fuck are they going to win in the last seven? … if we go down where will we go for away games, they're all miles away.'

One guy calls up the Conference table on his phone and says, 'It's a tough league to get out of. Teams like Wrexham, Tranmere, Hartlepool, they've all been down for a long while.' I ask my neighbour if he thinks Town will stay up and what he'll do if they don't. 'I doubt it, we're not good enough, but you never know. If we go down I'll still come but I won't have a season ticket like now, I'll pick and choose matches.'

The day dawned bright and clear, but as the teams come out the sky darkens and a cold, grey mist sweeps in from the sea. It seems like an omen. I take a seat beside Pete Cribb in a stand named after an old fish market and he tells me young Harry Clifton is on the bench. 'Should be starting with him,' he says.

In theory Stevenage have little to play for, being safely ensconced in mid-table, but you wouldn't know it from the way they set about Grimsby, forcing a series of corners and last-ditch tackles. The Mariners slowly edge into the game and it becomes a frantic kick-and-rush affair with no time on the ball. In 19 minutes Town midfielder Siriki Dembele cuts inside from the left and unleashes a searing shot that looks destined for the top corner of the net until the Stevenage keeper gets his fingertips to it and tips it over for a corner. It becomes a pattern, with Town creating half-chances but not taking them, and at half-time Pete sums up the general frustration: 'Lots of effort but lack of ability, but we've known that all year.' His neighbour looks on the bright side: 'This is the first time in three games we've been level at half-time.' At this stage in the season Grimsby fans take any hopeful signs they can find.

The second half is much the same, but this time it's Stevenage who come closest with an effort that canons off the bar. Harry Clifton comes on and impresses with well-timed tackles and deft touches, confirming he is a prospect for the future, and Town press hard for a winner, but there is a sense they could play all day and not find the net. As time runs out there is a lone, despairing call from the stand: 'Twelve minutes to save the world.' They don't exactly save their league status, let alone the world, but they live to fight another day with a deserved point, and Pete says it's a hopeful sign.

As the crowd disperses I head into a portacabin that serves as a press room, grateful for its warmth and hot coffee, to hear the manager's thoughts on the performance.

Jolley is encouraged by what he saw. 'We created a few chances in the first half and defended well. It's the first clean sheet and best performance in the four games I've had so far. It's a point that could prove vital with six games left,' he says, and it's something to build on. 'It's important not to panic, I have faith and belief in these players.'

Faith and belief, the cornerstones of support for the Mariners and their brethren in perennial struggles in the lower reaches of the professional game. A few years ago a fine book of prose and poetry by Grimsby fans came out, *We Are Town,* a collection of nostalgic, euphoric and funny reminiscences of three decades of roller-coaster rides in the EFL.

The enduring loyalty of men and women who turn up week in, week out to support their local team more in hope than expectation is eloquently summed up in an introduction by Pat Bell, an editor of the Grimsby fanzine.

'Grimsby are extraordinary to us because they are ours. They were there when we grew up, there when we fell in love, and still there when our hearts were broken. It was often Town who did the heart-breaking ... Grimsby are extraordinary because we cannot imagine our lives without the Mariners ... this book is largely a celebration, but sometimes what we are celebrating is our powers of endurance ... a football club will always be a thing of passion.'

They should make a copy of this and pin it up in the Mariners dressing room.

Blackpool

There's still a few of us that love the club. I think we're all cut from the same piece of Blackpool rock.

Founded:	1887
Ground:	Bloomfield Road
Average attendance:	4,178
Honours:	Second Division champions 1929/30
	FA Cup winners 1953

EVERY YEAR people flock to Blackpool to live on benefits in cheap flats and die sitting in pubs staring at the sea. They seem to see the town as an end point.

I am informed of this cheerfully on my arrival by the owner of my guest house, who adds that the town has the lowest mortality rate in the UK. I take this to mean hardly anybody dies here, but what he means by lowest is the average age that people shuffle off their mortal coils. 'We have some of the worst health statistics in Britain,' he says.

He forgets to mention the town has the fourth-highest murder rate in the country, so if anyone gets bored waiting by the sea for heavenly choirs there may be a way out.

To make matters worse, the town's football club is in the grip of a civil war that has divided families, ended friendships and sparked lawsuits. The main protagonists are a convicted elderly rapist who owns it, a Latvian banker accused of money laundering who would like to, and thousands of angry fans boycotting games to force regime change. Under the circumstances the club motto *Progress* seems ironic.

At Grimsby a few months before I met Ken Thompson, a retired teacher from Blackpool living on the banks of the Humber who refuses to return for home games on principle but occasionally watches the Tangerines playing away. 'The club is losing money every week and the idea is to starve the owner of funds until he gives up,' he said. 'The problem is it could destroy the club, it could end up in administration, lose ten points and get relegated.' Happy days by the seaside.

Under leaden grey skies and drizzling rain, Blackpool is haunted by ghosts of summers past. It is early spring, and the amusement arcades, bingo halls and fish and chip shops haven't geared up for the holiday season. They seem sad and forlorn, as if hibernating and dreaming of halcyon days before cheap flights lured their customers to the sun and sangria of Lanzarote and the Costa Brava. The illuminations haven't been switched on yet.

The top of the iconic tower, England's seaside Eiffel, is lost in swirling clouds and its headless iron torso looms in the mist like a spectral illusion. Ranks of cheap hotels and guest houses along the deserted promenade are silent and watchful, as if waiting for guests who may never come, and wondering what to do next.

So much for first impressions of Blackpool on a rain-lashed day in April. I suppose there's more life to it when the skies clear and the donkeys are back on the beach, but I wonder. I guess its best days are long gone, for the moment like its football team.

The club's glory days were in the 1950s, the era of Stanley Matthews and Stan Mortensen thrilling packed crowds at Bloomfield Road, when it regularly finished in the top six in the old First Division and won a memorable 1953 FA Cup Final against Bolton after fighting back from 3-1 down to triumph 4-3. It became known as the 'Matthews Final', although it was Mortensen's hat-trick that sealed victory. A few months later both were back at Wembley along with two team-mates, playing for England against Hungary with rather less success. They lost 6-3.

Another Wembley visit in 2010 sparked delirious celebrations when the team captained by Charlie Adam beat Cardiff City 3-2 in the Championship play-off final to earn its first promotion to the Premier League. Two days later police estimated a crowd of 100,000 lined the route of a victory parade through Blackpool, and manager Ian Holloway told them, 'This is the most unbelievable moment of my life.'

A year later they were back in the Championship, and by the time I arrive they have been down to League Two and back up to League One, where despite the toxic atmosphere they are ending the season strongly with four wins that have lifted them to mid-table. Next up on Saturday is Shrewsbury, who are already assured of a place in the play-offs.

Everywhere I have been on this tour I have been well received by club staff and fans generously sparing time to chat about their lives in football and share reminiscences of triumphs and disasters. Blackpool is different.

I begin by calling Tim Fielding of the Blackpool Supporters' Trust (BST), an independent pressure group leading the campaign to rid the club of its controversial owner, to arrange a meeting. I ask if he can recommend someone I might speak to at the club, and he says, 'You'll be lucky to get anyone, a lot of them have left and those who are still there have a bunker mentality.'

This proves to be true. When I email the media manager to ask if he can arrange meetings with club officials, he replies tersely, 'The owners are not conducting interviews as things stand.' To be honest this is fine with me, so I ask if I can attend the manager's weekly press conference, as I have at every other team. 'We're not doing anything outside the manager's usual commitments with the local media to discuss Shrewsbury,' he says. The drawbridge is up and the gates are firmly closed at fortress Bloomfield.

Tim's office next to a comic store near the ground is open, however. Legal diplomas above his desk attest to his credentials as a solicitor, but are outnumbered by football memorabilia. The largest is a signed shirt worn by a member of the 1953 cup-winning team, and the screen saver on his desktop terminal is a Blackpool fans' forum. This is a man who would happily spend more time in a football stadium than a courtroom, but he can't because he is a flag carrier of a volunteer army in a prolonged war of attrition. Inevitably there have been casualties, notably himself.

A lifelong Tangerines supporter, not least of his sacrifices has been the excitement and companionship of matchdays. 'Other than the passion of watching a football match it was all about going for a pint with your mates and visiting towns you wouldn't otherwise visit, and living for the moment when you have that brilliant away win that's etched in your memory forever and a day. Though they were few and far between to be honest.'

'The season in the Premier League was a surreal experience', he says. 'People fell in love with Blackpool because they were so gung-ho about how they went about things, and it was great to hear people talking about us when previously they hadn't really bothered.

'But once the initial novelty wears off I don't think you get any more out of Premiership football.'

Victory at Liverpool is the only Premier League match that features in his top-five away games of all time. 'The others mean more to me, maybe because I was younger. The one etched on my memory was beating Darlington 4-0 on a Tuesday night in 1985, which effectively got us promoted from the old Division Four. I was 18 at the time and it was the first time I'd ever seen us have any success. A lot of Blackpool fans of my era will have that game in their top-five aways.'

Three years later the club was in dire financial trouble and was snapped up for £1 by Owen Oyston, an estate agent with interests in the media and cable networks, and a sideline as chief executive of the Miss World beauty pageant.

In 1996 he was convicted of raping a 16-year-old girl and sentenced to six years' imprisonment, serving three and a half years, during which his wife ran the club before handing over to their son Karl.

It was assumed Blackpool's brief elevation to the Premier League would produce a windfall that would secure its immediate financial future and badly needed investment in the stadium, and in training facilities that Holloway described as a 'hell hole'.

It was not to be. Early this season a High Court judge ruled the Oystons had 'illegitimately stripped' the club of £26.77 million, and ordered them to pay this amount and more that they owed to Latvian banker Valeri Belokon, a major shareholder.

Meanwhile, the team still trains on a couple of pitches near the airport with no showers or toilets, and players have to wee in the bushes. Holloway eventually refused to use it, saying, 'Every player the club has ever had hates it, and every player we have is frightened of it. It is a horrible environment to work in.' Which pretty much sums up the current toxic atmosphere of Bloomfield Road.

Tim recalls, 'The wheels started to come off when Holloway and the Oystons fell out and he left. They brought in Michael Appleton, but he walked out after a couple of months and went to Blackburn, saying there's no structure to the club, it's an absolute joke. I began to get a bit worried at this stage, along with a lot of people, and the fans' forums became very active.'

The stirrings of unrest flared into open revolt in 2014 when fans staged a coffin march around the stadium, symbolising the death of Blackpool FC. This was followed by a 'Not a Penny More' campaign in which fans boycotted home games, or attended but refused to spend money in the stadium. The Oystons hit back by suing fans who criticised them on internet forums, including Tim who had to pay £10,000 in damages plus legal costs. He got off lightly, as others had to settle for £30,000 and £40,000.

'We've had 16 fans sued, it's appalling. It's affected some people quite badly mentally, including myself at the time. The apologies started coming out, fans couldn't afford to take on millionaires in court and put their homes and families at risk, and I ended up having to pay them ten grand compensation plus a fortune in legal costs and a public apology.

'It could have been worse, I was petrified where I was going to end up because they had the wherewithal to keep going and drag me into the ground. They could have cleaned me out. One fan went bankrupt and another nearly did.'

The increasingly bitter feud descended into farce when protesters planned to lay flowers and messages around a statue of Stan Mortensen outside the ground on the anniversary of his cup final heroics. The club promptly removed it with an angle grinder. Eventually it was restored, but fans are still raging at perceived vandalism and the team is playing in a stadium three-quarters empty.

'But for all this trouble, we'd have about 7,000 fans for home games,' Tim reckons. 'Now the demographic of people going in is older people who think if they stop going they might not get to see the team again.

'The club is a shell, there's no commercial department because nobody will advertise with them. It's a sham of a football club, it's really weird, everything's wrong, the stands are empty. It's surreal, as if somebody is masquerading as Blackpool FC.'

By the time I arrive the civil war on Bloomfield Road has been raging for four years, and Tim admits his troops are becoming battle-weary. 'We're ready to go back to what we're good at, which is supporting our football team. It hurts to be outside and not be able to go in, it's the ultimate sacrifice you can make as a football fan.'

It is a gloomy scenario with no sign of resolution, and Tim's parting comment hangs in the air: 'We're not unique. We say every football club is only one bad owner away from the situation we find ourselves in.'

Oh well, there's always a pub with good beer by the sea. In the evening, at my landlord's suggestion, I repair to the Highlanders Bar, a traditional hostelry offering Wainwright Ale, healthy portions of lasagne and the first leg of a Liverpool v Roma Champions League semi-final at Anfield. It's a classic game of attacking football with scintillating skills, teamwork and goals and my spirits are restored. Klopp and the Kop are a perfect match, unlike Blackpool's owners and fans.

Next day dawns bright and breezy, with a chill wind snapping off a gunmetal Irish Sea. If the question of how Blackpool got its name ever comes up in a pub quiz, the uninspiring answer is a drainage channel running over a peat bog used to pour discoloured water into the sea here.

Money has been spent refurbishing the promenade and it looks cheerful in the sunshine, but the town behind it still looks shabby and careworn, as do many of its residents. The streets are full of ageing, unhealthy people fuelling a roaring trade in walking sticks, wheelchairs and mobility scooters, and the purveyors of fags are clearly making a mint.

In fact, Blackpool is a net importer of ill health, attracting the highest share of people in the country living on incapacity benefits, much of it due to depression, stress and anxiety. Local GPs call it SLS – 'Shit Life Syndrome'.

It could be worse, here's something you might not know. Documents have been found suggesting the town escaped heavy damage in World War Two because Hitler had earmarked it to remain a pleasure resort after his storm troopers had raised swastikas on the tower. Despite this, eight people were killed when German bombs fell near a railway station, but Blackpool had its revenge. It was from here that No. 303 Polish Fighter Squadron took to the skies and became the most successful Fighter Command unit in the Battle of Britain by shooting down 126 German aircraft in 42 days.

The tower, minus swastikas, has emerged from the mist, so I buy a ticket to go up it. I hadn't realised that the structure is anchored in a grandiose red stone building housing a circus, a wondrous ballroom and the inevitable fish and chips restaurant. On the first floor is an impressive solid silver model of the tower created in honour of Sir John Bickerstaffe, the Blackpool mayor who visited Paris, saw the Eiffel Tower, and decided his town should have one half the size. It took three years and 2,600 tons of steel and cast iron to construct what was proudly proclaimed the tallest building in the UK at 518 feet nine inches when it opened to great fanfare in 1894.

On production of my press card, one of the cheery guides allows me a peek into the ballroom. It is a vision of the past, as if I have stepped through a time warp. An afternoon tea dance is in full swing in a gloriously ornate great hall swirling with smartly dressed couples strutting their stuff in unison in a quickstep to the jolly strains of a Wurlitzer organ playing 'If you knew Susie like I knew Susie…' Above the stage, a legend is embossed in large gold letters: 'Bid me discourse, I will enchant thine ear'. The guide says, 'This was designed in the 1890s when Britain was quite poor. The idea is that a mill worker could come here and feel like a princess for the day.' Roll on the good old days in a gilded time capsule, I love it. I could almost hear the Polish fighter pilots roaring overhead.

A lift with wraparound picture windows glides me smoothly to the top of the tower, where I step gingerly on to a viewing platform. I occasionally suffer from vertigo and am relieved to find I am enclosed by glass walls, though a glass-floor section is a bit scary. It's not the Eiffel Tower and there are no Champs Elysees or Sacre Coeur, but it's an impressive panorama and on a clear day you can see the Isle of Man.

In every other direction massed ranks of terraced houses reach to the horizons of a densely populated city, a rabbit warren of brick and slate. Thousands of them are HMOs – houses of multiple occupation – defunct guest houses bought up by landlords to profit from housing benefit claimants who arrive from poor areas of the North West every year and head straight into cheap bedsits.

Later I read an interview with one of them lured by the bright lights and amusements, who says it isn't what he had hoped for but it's better than his old town where the shops all shut at 5pm and he would spend the rest of the night alone in his flat.

'At least in Blackpool I can walk out my door and go into the town and put 10p in the console machine, or go and sit on the beach. The other day I went and sat on the beach and had a couple of cans, just playing my music, watching the tide come back in. I enjoyed myself.'

Today the beaches are deserted, their piers reaching out to sea spookily like the spindly legs of gigantic insects. Blackpool is like the painted face of a clown, presenting a pantomime smile to the world that masks a deep inner sadness. Still fun for some, but for others it is a place where dreams die.

Later a friend of my landlord, a lifelong Tangerines fan, pops into the guest house and we have a chat. Mike Fradgley is beyond retirement age, but still works a couple of days a week for a catering company selling breakfast sausages and portions of butter, jams and marmalades. He says my landlord is one of the precious few still prepared to pay for high-quality Cumberland sausages.

'Blackpool isn't what it was, unfortunately it's very much a transient town. We've had an awful lot of people coming into the town thinking the grass is going to be greener, and sadly it isn't. When it gets to winter there's absolutely nothing here, so they tend to go on benefits. It's a struggle and that's why there's a lot of problems with alcohol and drugs.

'All the investment has been put into the promenade and it's really nice now, but they've left out parts behind that have a lot of social deprivation. It's sad to see.'

Mike reckons the changes have impacted on crowds at Bloomfield Road, with fewer native residents and incomers with less money to spend. But he still goes to matches home and away in spite of the fans' revolt, as he has done for more than half a century since the tail end of the Matthews era.

'We've had awful problems with the Oyston family, but I love the club and I don't feel I should desert them. I'm of the opinion that if you're from a particular place you should love and support your own football club. So I'd rather just carry on and support them as I have done for so many years.'

Home games are social occasions when he meets a bunch of his mates in The Albert in Lytham Road to chat about what they've been up to in the week, and who they think should play and who shouldn't.

'We just love the football and we love Blackpool, and we're all sandgronins.'

Sandgronins?

'It's what we call people born and bred in Blackpool.' He has no idea where the term comes from – and neither does Google – but he assumes it refers to the sands and growing up near them. It seems fair enough, given their team's nickname of the Seasiders.

Mike enjoyed their brief foray in the Premier League, especially the team's gung-ho approach with three up front that made them popular with fans of other clubs, but he's in no hurry to watch the big guns again.

'I've watched Blackpool since I was ten and I'll watch them until I can't get there. I'm a true Tangerine and I'll never watch anybody else. Manchester United, Liverpool, mean absolutely nothing to me whatsoever. If they were playing at Bloomfield Road I'd sooner travel to Gillingham and watch Blackpool playing there.'

Having said that, the game isn't what it was and he prefers the 2-3-5 days of all-out attack in the late 50s and early 60s when half-backs fed wingers and forwards and went in hard on the opposition.

'There were no restrictions on tackles then, while nowadays players tend to go down fairly easily and managers tell them to shout to influence referees. There's much more deliberate cheating going on now because there's much more money in the game and it makes people dishonest. Stanley Matthews used to jump on a bus to get to matches.'

It seems pretty much doom and gloom at Bloomfield Road, but Mike sees glimmers of hope for the town.

'A new conference centre and a four-star hotel are being built, and the Young Farmers are coming next weekend. Some of them misbehave a little bit, they come from rural areas and they're not used to drinking 24 hours a day, but it's good business for the town. The farmers are always welcome in Blackpool.' No doubt Mike's quality Cumberland sausages will aid their recovery from the high jinks.

So far, I have heard from both trenches in the phony war, and this evening I am meeting someone caught in the crossfire. Fiona Martin is chair of the official Blackpool Supporters' Association, which Tim Fielding says is somewhere in no-man's land. She suggests meeting in her local pub, which is showing a Bayern–Real Madrid Champions League semi-final later, so a good evening is in prospect.

A digital project manager, Fiona comes across as a level-headed, loyal supporter trying to hold the fan base together in tough times. Her members want a change of ownership as much as anyone else, but also want to continue going to games to support the team.

'As an association we're not well liked in other sections of the fan base. We're seen as being too close to the club and supportive of the regime, but I don't know anybody who is.

'Friendships have broken up. It's a bit of a civil war, but it's a war where everyone wants the same result in that everyone wants new owners and for the club to be successful on the pitch. But everyone has different ways of achieving it, and of expressing their views, so it's a civil war with everyone on the same side. The club won't recover until there are new owners, and the only people who don't recognise that are the current owners.'

They should, given the state of siege prevailing at Bloomfield Road according to Fiona. 'The club is understaffed, they're all running around and nobody can get anything done because they've got too many jobs.'

This probably explains why nobody answers the phone when I call, and I begin to have sympathy for the dismissive media guy when Fiona says he has about eight jobs.

The toxic atmosphere spreads to away games in the vicinity, which she has stopped going to. 'They're easy for big groups of young lads who are boycotting home games to get to, and I don't really like going to games where they're singing songs about people being rapists. When you go a bit further away it's not so bad. It is what it is.'

Fiona enjoyed the Premier League season, but like Mike she doesn't miss it. 'The Premiership has this mystique, an aura about it that it's special and important, that comes from its own branding and self-promotion. But if I was a fan of a constantly mid-table Premiership team I don't think I'd find it very exciting personally. Lower down the leagues there's a bit more to play for with less pressure.'

The team plunged back to earth from the dizzy heights of the Premier League with back-to-back relegations, and Fiona blames the Oystons for it getting a reputation for not being a good place to work as a footballer.

'It was dire on the pitch. You go into a game with the mindset that it's going to be miserable, we're going to lose. There are people choosing not to go as a protest and that's fine, that's their decision, but there are people I know who stopped going because they'd stopped enjoying it, they lost the love of the club really. It came at a time when everything was going on with the Oystons and the two just collided.'

Fiona has no difficulty separating the political turmoil from the football, but there is a personal price to pay for it. 'I don't have an interest in the politics of football, especially fan politics. I'm more interested in watching my teams win football matches, supporting the players, and I find it quite easy to separate what happens on the pitch to what happens off it. But it's caused big rifts in our family. Whether they'll ever properly heal I don't know.'

Thursday morning big news breaks in the sports pages of the *Blackpool Gazette* under the headline 'Turkish delight for the Tangerines?' It is reported that a Turkish group is in talks with Oyston's solicitors to buy the club, with a local restaurateur acting as intermediary. The same group is said to have shown interest in taking over Sunderland, but was put off by the club's debts.

It's all happening on the Fylde coast. Neighbouring Fleetwood Town has just announced it is appointing Joey Barton as coach from next season. Good timing for Joey, banned from football until June for breaching FA betting rules. In other news, the *Gazette* reports that RSPCA inspectors have rescued 19 donkeys, including Blackpool seaside donkeys, from a farm near Preston where a man and two women have been accused of abusing them.

Today I learn that my affable landlord Simon has been endowed with a title, Lord Guilderoy, and that his wife Rona rejoices in the name of Baroness Chief Whip Guilderoy. The honours were conferred upon their becoming members of the Monster Raving Loony Party, which happens to stage its annual party conference in Blackpool.

The main political parties have long since abandoned the town, citing lack of decent accommodation, but madcap delegates of the MRLP still turn up every year to ride in an open-top bus around pubs extolling policies that include making morris dancing an Olympic sport and dog food fluorescent so people can avoid their poo on pavements. 'If a smile was a vote we'd win by a landslide,' their leader Howling Laud Hope declared last time.

Disillusion with the main parties led my hosts to join this loony lot at the invitation of a couple of MRLP guests, Lord Toby Jug and Lady Jezebel Luxury Yacht. Framed certificates of insanity in the hall beside the toilets certify that they are as nutty as fruitcakes and thereby worthy of being politicians. Eat your heart out Basil Fawlty.

In the evening I am given a succinct appraisal of the Turkish delight story. 'Utter rubbish. A load of bollocks. Oyston is a delusional showman.'

Jeremy Smith is not a man to mince his words. Nor is he someone to pick a fight with. He cheerfully admits to having been a nutter in his youth, travelling to Blackpool away games with like-minded spirits more intent on battling rival fans and smashing up their grounds than watching football. He looks back fondly on those days, with no hint of regrets.

We meet in the bar of Blackpool Cricket Club, at the suggestion of Tim Fielding, who says Jeremy has a good story to tell about a brush with the Oystons.

His early memories of following Blackpool are equally interesting. 'Back in the 80s it was a bit rough, the football was secondary and it was more what was happening off it. We had a bit of notoriety about us and there were riots at Rochdale and Bury, it was just bedlam, pitch invasions and smashing grounds up. We were all just nutters in the 14 to 25 age group, we were the foot soldiers, it was bloody mental.

'Looking back, you think god ... but it happened, everyone were doing it and we stood and fought with the rest of them. I can't say I hurt anyone wilfully, it was just lads against lads, youthful boisterous behaviour. They were good times, looking back.'

Now a middle-aged family man with car showrooms, Jeremy has toned down his combative instincts, but not completely. Three years ago he took part in a demonstration against the Oystons at a live Sky Sports game against Cardiff, when it was planned to stage a walkout. It so happened the *Gazette* was carrying a front-page story about the owners under the headline 'We are not thieves', and Jeremy had the bright idea of scribbling out 'not' and holding the page up in the crowd. And as luck would have it, Sky Sports spotted it.

'I was just one fan among 12,000 that day, and of all of us the Sky cameras zoomed in on me, boom, ping. We walked out in the 53rd minute and no sooner had we got out of the ground than my phone went into meltdown with people saying you've been on TV. I thought I know what's going to happen now.'

Within a week he received a letter from the football club seeking damages for defamation of character. 'He'd done a few people for things they'd written, and everyone else had paid thousands and written letters of apology. It was just financial bullying and I thought there's no way I'm getting done for holding up a newspaper, I'm going to fight this.' So he did, all the way to the High Court in Manchester, where the libel action was withdrawn at the last minute and legal costs awarded against Oyston.

There was never any chance of Jeremy supporting any team other than Blackpool, as he lived from infancy in Bloomfield Road, about 300 yards from the ground, and was brought up improbably watching Premier League players. He remembers going to reserve games in the Central League on Tuesday nights in the 70s against the likes of Man Utd, and seeing stars from their first team who had been injured and were playing their way back to fitness. But his heroes played for Liverpool.

'When I was a kid Liverpool were fabulous, bloody hell, it was my second team. I watched great Liverpool sides in the 70s and 80s stuffed full of Scottish players,

Graeme Souness, Tommy Smith. When we played as kids everybody wanted to be as hard as Tommy Smith. There was no airy-fairy football back then, it was whoever was the strongest, and Tommy Smith was the strongest, you wanted to be like him.' It comes as no surprise to learn that Jeremy's 14-year-old son is called Tommy.

He recalls approvingly that in his youth Blackpool had their fair share of Scottish players not given to shirking tackles. 'We had Steven Crainey, ex-Celtic lad, we got him from Leeds. He was a proper down to earth, lovely Glaswegian lad, hard as bloody nails, put his leg or head anywhere, and as humble as you'd want to meet.'

We get on, Jeremy and I, although I'm glad his days as a nutcase are over, and I am invited to join him and his wife for dinner in a local restaurant.

'Did you know this man was a hooligan in his youth?' his wife Dana asks with a smile. There is no hint of disapproval from the woman who stands by her man in the prolonged conflict with his club's owners.

'It's great that there's this passion and power going on behind the scenes,' she says. 'I think it's fantastic, it's been going on for so long but the passion doesn't leave them.'

Jeremy sums up: 'It's only through Oyston's suing of fans that's brought us to where we are. Some people have said I was the straw that broke the camel's back, I kicked the doors in by winning the court case.' In the style of Tommy Smith.

Next day there's no word on any Turkish buy-out, and latest news in the *Gazette* is a club statement claiming that agreement has been reached with an investment group, and a deal will be finalised in the next week. It did not identify the group, or specify the extent of the potential investment, or of Oyston's future involvement with the club, if any. Most fans I speak to shrug their shoulders. Just another Oyston smokescreen to buy time, they say.

From the top of Blackpool Tower, Bloomfield Road rises from the urban sprawl like a gleaming white shrine to the beautiful game. On closer inspection it is a smart ground with a hotel and conference centre, and modern stands with a capacity of 17,338 which is currently four times more than required.

At least away fans are no longer singing in the rain. The old uncovered East stand, dubbed the Gene Kelly stand because that's where they were exposed to the elements, was replaced by covered seating in 2010 in time for the club's debut in the Premier League.

I am in the club shop to meet retired postman John Cross, a member of both supporters' associations and liaison officer of a former players' group, who is firmly in the boycotting camp.

A memento of happier times gazes down at us in a large framed print of Blackpool fans in fancy dress on their way to Wembley for the cup final in 1953. They include a fish dock worker dressed as an Indian Maharajah, who for reasons best known to himself took along a duck painted orange with fish dye, and gave it the freedom of the pitch before kick-off. Those were the days.

For all John is determined to stay away from home games, one of his best mates is Chris Beveridge who can't imagine missing one. The two of them are chatting about old times when I arrive, and it's obvious they have not allowed conflicting views to wreck their friendship.

Chris is the club's disability liaison officer, and he's uniquely qualified for the job as he has been confined to a wheelchair since childhood with spina bifida. This has not prevented him from competing in marathons on a chair with wheels emblazoned with the Blackpool club crest. Unsurprisingly, his nickname is Wheels.

'I can't get to away games because I'd need lifts, but I couldn't miss one here,' he says. 'I don't know how John does it. I've signed myself out of hospital because there's a game on. They were putting things in my leg and stuff like that, I was quite ill at the time and they were worried about my white blood cells.' Happily he survived the 90 minutes and returned to hospital to ensure he'd still be around for the next match.

Chris has been assisting disabled spectators and visitors as an unpaid volunteer for 28 years, and says he'll carry on doing it no matter who owns the club. 'I'm happy to show people round if they ask, I'm proud of this club. The one thing it never is is boring.'

John has no problem with this. 'Each to their own, there are still lots of people I know who still come and I'm not going to fall out with them because they have a different opinion to me. I respect that, and if the Oystons ever do go then I'll be back here like a shot.

'I go to some away games and I still find a game to go to every Saturday. I watch a lot of non-league football so I've got my fix but it's not the same, it's not like watching Blackpool, it never will be.

'Many fans want us to lose every game, because they want them to sink as low as possible to force the Oystons out. They're not bothered what sort of level we're at as long as they're gone. But I can't be that, I love the club and always want us to win. You've got to support your home-town team. I've always had great admiration for fans in Bury, Rochdale and Oldham, minutes away from Man Utd and City, who support their home clubs. So I'm a Blackpool fan for life, no matter how we do.'

Not for the first time, I am reminded that the loyalty of diehard fans outlasts iffy owners and always will. Thankfully.

Personally, John would like to see the Latvian banker Belokon taking over. 'He might be as big a rogue as the Oystons because he's made so much money, but he's a great bloke, I've met him a few times.'

Notably in Latvia, on four occasions when Blackpool played pre-season friendlies and John went along. He recalls Belokon being accompanied by a couple of bodyguards, and on a windy day their jackets flying open. 'Guns on both of them. I thought bloody hell, what's this guy been up to he needs bodyguards with guns? Turns out he was a sniper in the Russian army. I'm amazed Oyston hasn't been bumped off.' Note to Oyston: this was a joke.

We repair to the hotel restaurant overlooking the pitch where the first team is having a final training session before tomorrow's match. Normally they would be at Squires Gate, their spartan training ground near the airport, but they're enjoying the rare luxury of the Bloomfield facilities because it's the last home game of the season.

'The training centre is a joke,' John says. 'They don't even have a hut there. The players change here and drive down in their cars. There are no showers or toilets and the last I heard they were talking about getting a portaloo. It's an absolute joke.'

Former Blackpool defender Alex Baptiste once reminisced on the joys of Squires Gate: 'No balls in training, having to run on the beach because the pitch had been frozen for two weeks, no food after training, leaks in the portacabins, having to buy our own weights, just random stuff like that. It was definitely an experience.'

The former players' association still organises Legends Nights dinners, charity football matches and golf days, but John admits its hospitality box isn't as popular as it used to be. 'I used to host it, but it was getting more difficult to get the players to come because they didn't want to be seen supporting the regime.'

John's dad was a lifelong Seasider who began taking him to reserve games as a boy, instilling the belief that you support your home-town team no matter how bad they are. 'It's very different from the Premier League. I watched every game we were in it and it's not football, it's a business. They don't understand the real world. Arsenal fans complaining about Wenger should come and support Blackpool for a few years and see what shit is. They're just deluded, they make you laugh. Man City lost at Man Utd and there's people crying, get a life. You don't get that here.'

His favourite memory is beating Arsenal in a third-round FA Cup replay in 1971. 'We drew 1-1 at Highbury and brought them here on a Thursday night and went down 2-0 and came back to win 3-2 in extra time. A few Arsenal fans were sat down crying at the end, and our fans were laughing at them.' The euphoria didn't last long and Gunners fans had the last laugh. 'Typical Blackpool, having beaten them we got drawn against Fourth Division Mansfield and lost 2-0.'

John doesn't care much who takes over the club as long as the Oystons go. 'I'm of the opinion I'd rather have Saddam Hussein in charge, it's as bad as that. Other clubs have issues with owners, but they all pale into insignificance in comparison to us.'

So here we are on the eve of the last home game of the season, in the eye of a gathering storm, and everything in the besieged citadel seems calm and normal. The Oystons' corporate headquarters are in a suite of offices next door, but so far there are no signs of barricades.

The first team comes into lunch and manager Gary Bowyer spots John and comes over to say hello, and I am introduced. He doesn't appear to be affected by the bunker mentality, and readily joins us for a chat.

Bowyer knows the game from the grassroots up, having begun playing professionally at full-back alongside his dad Ian (ex-Man City and Notts Forest) at Hereford United before moving to Rotherham. Retirement through injury led to a coaching career at Derby and Blackburn, and in 2016 he became Blackpool's eighth manager in little over three years after they were relegated to League Two. He promptly brought them back up with a 2-1 victory over Exeter in the play-off final, and so far this season has achieved something of a miracle under the circumstances by pushing for a top-half finish.

He credits his players for focussing on each game as it comes rather than the background turmoil. 'The team's done wonderfully well considering what we've had to contend with off the pitch. We concentrate on what we can control in training and playing, and make sure the boys work hard and enjoy it. I can't affect who's behind the club so we don't focus on it.'

I ask if, nevertheless, the boycott has affected the mood in the dressing room, and he gives an honest answer: 'No. Well, I'm saying that. As long as they're getting paid they're alright generally. It might affect them every now and again, but it's down to us to keep the focus on the football.'

The team's resurgence is all the more remarkable given the relative financial muscle of opponents like Blackburn and Wigan. In a local newspaper interview a few weeks before, in what appeared to be a message to any potential buyer, Bowyer said, 'We've had to compete against teams with unbelievable budgets. The club has got to understand to get to the top level there has to be significant investment.'

Having said all that, he is enjoying himself. He has a refreshing boyish enthusiasm for the game, despite its constant pressures and concerns about how long careers will last. 'There's far worse jobs than managing a football team, that's for sure. I love it. The game is the best in the world, so to be involved in it is brilliant. Of course there's pressure, everybody wants everything short-term, but once you go into the profession you know that's the way it is and you just get on with it and concentrate on what you can control.

'There will be people who worry and panic about their contracts, but that has an impact on their performance, whereas if you just concentrate on doing the best that you can every day it looks after itself. That's what I say to these players. It is hard, of course it is, but ultimately there are sacrifices involved.'

Bowyer has done the best he can but admits he will be glad when the ownership dispute is resolved. 'For everybody, for the whole town, not just us as players but the town because look at the potential that we've got here. What we've done in these two years is lay massive foundations and we've got to build on them.'

Good luck with that I say, and he joins his players who seem to be in good spirits and looking forward to the game. At the end of the day they're footballers and tomorrow's Saturday.

In the afternoon I'm shown around the stadium by Derek Duckworth, a general dogsbody who runs the club lottery, helps find players' accommodation, hangs framed shirts and prints on the walls, and shows visitors around. A lifelong fan, there's no danger of him turning his back on his club, but he admits the atmosphere among hard core fans is toxic. 'It's nasty. There are lads who grew up together and played Sunday league football together who won't talk to each other, just turn their heads away.' I ask how he feels personally: 'We just get on with it. We tell people how good we were and how good we will be again. If we were on the Blackpool Big Dipper we'd be at the bottom, but we've been at the top and we'll come back. We're a good Lancashire Championship club.'

Meantime he shows me images of the glory days on corridor walls, notably a huge print of the champagne celebrations after the play-off final to reach the Premier League. 'That was the greatest day in Blackpool's history. The losers got the gate receipts and we got £110 million.' At the start of the next season Derek placed a framed photograph in the trophy cabinet, showing Blackpool top of the league after winning their first game at Wigan 4-0. This historic table-topping exploit lasted for almost three hours until Chelsea won their opening match 5-0.

He has fond memories of his club's brief campaign among the Premier big guns. 'We did the double on Liverpool and Newcastle,' he recalls proudly. 'It's different at that level. When you're watching Man Utd with Alex Ferguson yelling on the touchline you don't feel the cold, but if it's Gillingham or Hartlepool you feel every bit of it.'

In those days the club was drawing big crowds, but Derek says many faded away with relegation. 'They weren't Blackpool fans, they'd rather sit in the pub than watch us at Doncaster on a wet Tuesday night.'

The man is a treasure trove of little-known facts, including the origin of the current strips. Before the war Blackpool played in blue and black stripes, until a director went to the continent to watch Holland, was dazzled by their flowing teamwork, and decided his team would look good in Dutch orange but called it tangerine.

The club was flying high in the war years, largely because the town served as an RAF base and was able to recruit the service's best players, notably the two Stans, Matthews and Mortensen. In his office Derek has their contracts which shows Matthews's wage was £10 a week and Mortensen's was £8. 'I'm told Mortensen wanted to know why Matthews was getting paid £2 more and he was told it was because Stanley was a better player. But it was Mortensen who scored the hat-trick that won the cup.'

Another contender for a pub quiz is that Bloomfield Road is the only football ground in the country where murder has been committed. It happened in 1974 when a Bolton fan stabbed a Blackpool supporter in the old Kop stand and got away with it.

The stadium is silent and empty on the eve of the match and it's not only the famously boisterous home fans who will be missing tomorrow. Advertisements in the ground are few and far between, the largest are for an estate agency and a magazine owned by Oyston, and Belokon Holdings. 'Nobody will sponsor us,' Derek admits ruefully.

At least the hospitality packages are cheaper. In the Premier League the main suite was packed with 500 guests paying £300 each for a three-course lunch with wine, a match ticket and reserved parking. Now it's on offer for £55. Derek is philosophical. 'There's still a few of us who love the club. I think we're all cut from the same piece of Blackpool rock. We'll come back.'

Saturday, matchday, the skies are bright and clear and a soft breeze carries a hint of spring. My guest house is in a quiet street near the sea, north of the piers, and I go for an early morning jog along Queen's Promenade. It runs by a massive sea wall, and the only other early risers are a few fishermen waiting for the tide to come in.

I ask one of them what he hopes to catch and he reels off a long list that I remember included plaice, whiting and dogfish. 'If you're lucky,' another fisherman calls with a laugh. The sea seems far out on sandbanks, but he says they'll have two and a half hours of rising tide and the same on the ebb, giving them five hours of fishing. It seems like a pleasant way to pass the day. It is bliss to enjoy the sea air and the cries of gulls far from the tacky tinsel town around the piers. On my way back I pass a man with a couple of dogs collecting litter who turns out to be a local councillor. I ask if he gets paid for it and he says no, he's a volunteer and a member of a civic group that maintains public gardens. He seems happy tidying the refurbished promenade and his dogs are enjoying the walk. There's hope for Blackpool yet.

Later the sun comes out and the town puts on its happy clown mask for day trippers and the weekend party crowd. The seafront around the piers is packed, the coach park is full and long queues are forming outside the tower. A scantily clad chap dancing through them in speedo trunks and a cowboy hat is cheered by a bunch of sparkly dressed girls in a horse-drawn Cinderella pumpkin carriage. Gay cowboys and princesses off to have a ball, it's midsummer madness in April. My host Simon tells me it's the start of the wedding season when stag and hen parties converge from all over the north. 'People come on holiday to Blackpool because it has something for everybody,' he says. 'You can't be too critical.'

Driving up Lytham Road leading to the ground, I pass knots of police watching crowds in Hawaiian shirts and straw hats with beach balls and inflatable palm trees spilling out of a couple of pubs. It turns out they're Shrewsbury fans, indulging in festive celebrations at the end of a successful season. There are police on big horses, looking ominous as if they are about to charge, but the worst that happens is a beach ball bounces off a horse's backside.

Mike recommended the New Albert pub, a short walk from the ground. I'm pleased to find it fairly relaxed with no cops outside or bouncers on the door, and a scattering of older men with Blackpool scarves inside supping pints. I introduce myself to a group of three and learn they are members of a 'secret society' in Leyland Trucks. Tom Snape builds trucks and his pals Austin Senior and Ian Southward used to build buses until they retired. Tom says they got together when they discovered they were all Blackpool fans, mostly because their fathers were. 'We're surrounded by Preston, Blackburn, Wigan and Bolton. To support Blackpool we got a lot of shit, but we've kept the faith all these years. It took years to find each other behind enemy lines.'

Having braved the scorn of Preston supporters, they're not about to desert their club when it's under fire from its own fans. 'We're Blackpool supporters,' Austin says. 'We can't do anything about who owns the club. The protesters can shout and bawl all they like, but they should go and support the team.' Ian agrees: 'I understand the boycott, but we were going long before Oyston and we'll still be going after he's gone.'

They don't believe the half-empty stands are entirely due to the unrest. 'Every time we got relegated we lost fans and we had back-to-back relegations,' Ian says. 'To blame it all on the Oystons is a bullshit excuse.'

The Leyland society has fond memories of Premier League and Championship days, and is saddened by the change in fortunes. Tom says, 'The ground was jumping with fantastic support, now it's as quiet as death. Fans against fans, it's been horrible, and it's had an effect on the community. There used to be a working men's club along the road that was packed on matchdays, now it's closed down.

'We're hoping by the time we come back next season we'll have a new owner and can kick on.' Anything else? 'We hate Preston.'

I wander up to the ground, and there are no signs of protests. For an extra few quid I have one of the best seats in the house, directly behind the home dugout. There are plenty of empty seats around me, and only a scattering of home fans in the Jimmy Armfield stand. The former Gene Kelly stand is closed and empty. The away stand by contrast is crammed to the rafters with singing, chanting Shrewsbury fans playing drums and trumpets and chucking beach balls. It is as if the Tangerines are playing away.

With the visitors assured a place in the play-offs and Blackpool comfortably mid-table, neither side has much to play for, and it promises to be a low-key, end-of-the-season affair. In the match programme, Bowyer thanks fans for their 'fantastic' support and says the team and coaching staff will return to the pitch after the full-time whistle to show their appreciation.

The club's Community Trust participates in an Amnesty International 'Football Welcomes Refugees' initiative, and for a few years it has been helping refugees and asylum seekers to rebuild their lives in a new country. Today, 50 have been invited to the game, with a stadium tour before kick-off, and for some it is their first experience of live football. Senior sports participation officer Michael Brown says in the programme, 'Football can give people a sense of purpose and belonging, and football clubs are at the heart of our towns and cities and have an important role to play in welcoming refugees and helping to promote respect, understanding and integration.' It is a ray of sunshine penetrating the gloom of Bloomfield.

Most of the stands are still half-empty when Bowyer comes out and signs autographs and poses for selfies with children before kick-off. Even with the presence of the Shrewsbury carnival crowd the attendance is given as 5,825. The pre-match talk around me inevitably is of who's going to be in charge next season, and whether players out of contract will stay on.

I finally catch a glimpse of Owen Oyston. He is sitting in the back row far above me, a sinister figure with a pinched face and long, grey hair straggling from beneath a black fedora hat. A goatee beard and dark sunglasses complete the image of a dodgy character from a Harry Potter novel. Which reminds me, the claret and amber of Motherwell FC are probably the best-known football colours in the world, because Potter wears them on his scarf.

If this is a meaningless end-of-season match with nothing at stake, somebody forgot to tell the players. Fast-paced attacking football produces chances at both ends before Shrewsbury's Sam Jones is given time on the ball on the edge of the box and drills home in the 20th minute. Occasionally Bowyer is out of his seat and on the touchline remonstrating with his players, but the Shrewsbury fans are making such a racket I can't hear him. It's almost half-time before home supporters find their voices with a brief chorus of 'Come on 'Pool'. Their team is playing decent football and creating chances, but missing them with poor finishing. Fans behind me are bemoaning that striker Kyle Vassell was injured in the warm-up: 'He'd have put these chances away.' He's sitting just in front of us, and as he gets up at half-time somebody calls out, 'You'll sign next season Kyle?' He just smiles.

Blackpool come out for the second half fired up, swarming at the visitors, and after ten minutes striker Abayomi Delfouneso levels with a powerful header from close range. A linesman initially flags offside, but is overruled by the ref and this finally sparks a ragged chorus of the Seasiders' victory chant, 'Glad all Over' by the Dave Clark Five. The Tangerines are on the front foot, scything through a weak defence, but a culmination of poor finishing and superb goalkeeping deny them the win they deserve.

Honours shared, a point apiece, and the Shrewsbury fans head off happily with their beach balls to the seafront pubs and amusements, looking forward to a tilt at the Championship (they lost 2-1 in the play-off final to Rotherham).

The Tangerines come back out to exchange applause with their depleted following, but it's hardly a lap of honour as there are only a few fans left in the main stand.

In football, loyalty defies logic and survives the worst of times. Walking away from the empty ground, I hear a chorus in Blackpool ranks: 'See you next season, mate.' Owners come and go, but fans are in with the bricks.

Forest Green Rovers

If the football's terrible there are sheep in that field that can entertain you all afternoon.

Founded:	1889
Ground:	The New Lawn
Average attendance:	2,772
Honours:	FA Vase winners 1981/82

YOU COULDN'T make it up. An erstwhile hippy traveller who used to live in a caravan rescues a Cotswolds village team from financial meltdown, and against ridiculous odds takes it to play-off finals at Wembley and into the Football League.

Along the way he transforms it into the world's first vegan professional football club and provides it with an organic pitch mowed by a solar-powered robot that freaks out badgers. Welcome to the wacky world of Forest Green Rovers, 'the little club on the hill'.

The hill in question lies on the outskirts of Nailsworth, a picture-postcard village tucked peacefully into a wooded valley in Gloucestershire.

This is traditional rugby country, boasting 74 clubs affiliated to the county Rugby Football Union. It is not a place to attract big-time soccer stars.

A narrow road winds steeply up the hill to Forest Green, a hamlet of post-war houses with a school, a community centre and a compact stadium that is home to the eponymous football team. It is arguably the most rustic setting in the Football League, overlooking rough pasture dotted with sheep, and occasionally llamas. The road beyond is a meandering single lane with passing places, bounded by hedgerows and meadows overlooking a great sweep of hills around the Stroud valleys. On calm, sunny days it is a pastoral symphony sweetened by birdsong, and for visiting fans from gritty northern towns it must seem like somewhere over the rainbow.

A mile up the road the blades of a lone wind turbine spin lazily in the unbroken blue sky of a bright spring day. It is at once a symbol of New Age technology, and of the unlikely transformation of Forest Green Rovers. The windmill was erected by Dale Vince, the former itinerant hippy who used to park his caravan nearby, as a first step in creating a renewable energy company that grew to make him a multimillionaire and bought him a football club.

Vince is not your average football fan. He never followed a club, though in his former life he and his mates would go to somebody's caravan at Glastonbury, hook up an old black and white television to a battery, and watch England stuttering to defeat in the World Cup. 'I don't have happy memories of watching England in those days,' he admits.

But after setting up in business, he liked what he saw when Rovers invited him to a friendly Conference game in 2010. 'I thought it was a lovely place and lovely people, and the chairman said they just needed £30,000 to get through a cash-flow problem. I was looking at a local football club with a long history and some good people behind it and it just seemed a shame for it to go bankrupt for want of £30k. We are a local company and it seemed the right thing to do, it wasn't a fortune, and I'm a football fan, so it was a good fit.'

The compelling final ingredient was the name. 'Green' was a perfect fit for Ecotricity, his ecological energy company based nearby in Stroud. He soon found the cash hole was bigger than he thought, ended up buying the club, and transformed it into a flagship for his environmental and vegan ideals.

For an entrepreneur based in a rural backwater, it was a stroke of marketing genius. Overnight Forest Green Rovers and their unconventional chairman attracted international media attention, culminating in a FIFA accolade as the world's greenest football club. The fortunes of Vince and his team duly improved. Over a few seasons they worked their way up the Conference until they beat Tranmere Rovers 3-1 in a play-off final at Wembley in May 2017, to join the EFL for the first time in their 123-year history. It was *Roy of the Rovers* stuff, fantasy football in the Cotswolds.

So Forest Green were first on my planned fixture list, along with the equally romantic rags-to-modest-riches tale of Accrington Stanley. An added incentive was discovering that Rovers play near the childhood home of one of my literary heroes, the poet, traveller and writer Laurie Lee. If you haven't read *Cider with Rosie* or *As I Walked out One Midsummer Morning,* do yourself a favour and do it now.

Winter in Glasgow has been brutal as usual, and it's a blessed relief to step out of Bristol airport in warm spring sunshine. I love the wild beauty of Scotland, but there is a softness and gentleness in southern England that is deeply comforting. I invariably seek roads less travelled and get lost, which is fine with me because as often as not in the rural heartland of Anglo-Saxons there's a village pub around the corner or over the hill to provide home-cooked food and directions to where I'm going.

With the sun at my back I cruise happily out of Bristol through a maze of minor roads and single-track country lanes winding up hill and down dale, by sloping meadows dotted decoratively with sheep, and men building dry-stone walls much as their ancestors have done for centuries. This is England's green and pleasant land in spades, a bucolic haven of peace and plenty that seems to breathe deep contentment in tune with seasons that ripen with harvests of grain and tourists. By a minor miracle I find Nailsworth swathed in woodland at the bottom of a steep hill with a little river running through it, and at first sight it is a life-size toy town (population 6,000) of solid stone houses and ancient woollen mills that look as if they have been there forever.

In fact, the mills date from the 17th century when the town and its neighbour Stroud were the centre of a thriving wool-weaving industry – Stroudwater Scarlet was the cloth that provided the army of the British Empire with its distinctive red uniforms that formed ranks in the Zulu Wars and the Indian Mutiny. A couple of centuries later the cloth industry collapsed and through time the empty mills were occupied by engineering works and meat processing plants, until they too went out of business and gave way to gentrification with myriad small businesses, quirky shops, cafes and decent restaurants. My landlady recalls that when she arrived in the 1980s Nailsworth was a grimy, industrial town with lots of blue collar workers who would have been Forest Green supporters. 'It was like a proper northern town,' she says.

Now it is a middle class arcadia of well-tended gardens and happy dogs, with narrow streets and lanes blissfully free of high street chains, named by *The Sunday Times* as one of the best places to live in Britain. It is a civilised community where people greet each other with friendly hellos and good mornings, and a brass sculpture of what looks like folded wings in the town centre bears an enigmatic inscription: 'In Memory of Short and Bright Lives'. The window of the information centre is filled with notices for art exhibitions, plant and seed swaps, creative writing and gardening groups, and countryside rambles with pub lunches. The only apparent concession to modern commerce is a small supermarket, where the notice board alerts shoppers to the tenth anniversary of the Amberley Cow Hunt for 'wonderfully dressed' cows hidden around the village, and homemade cake in a vintage tea tent. Other upcoming events in *Cotswolds Life* magazine include puddle jumping championships and live lambing. Not your average football town then.

And it's nowhere near Gatwick Airport, as misguided fans of Worksop Town discovered years ago when they turned up at another Forest Green in Surrey for an FA Trophy match.

My wife, who is my gifted personal travel agent, has booked me for the first couple of nights into a bed and breakfast in an even smaller and impossibly quaint hamlet in a bustle of hills above the town. Box Village is a huddle of stone houses with steeply pitched roofs snuggled into a wooded glade that looks like a grown-up version of Hobbiton in the Shires. Cue Bilbo Baggins sharing a pipe and reminiscences with his old pal Gandalf. I have a sense I'm going to enjoy this trip.

On Saturday Rovers are at home to Chesterfield, currently bottom of League Two and fighting for their lives with only four games to play. Rovers aren't safe either after only one win in 14 matches has left them precariously eight points above their opponents and only six above Barnet. A win is vital to ensure their hard-won first season in the Football League isn't short-lived.

Tonight I've arranged to meet Ian Crawley, chairman of the supporters' club and retired town councillor, in a local pub to find out how his village team has progressed this far and is managing to compete with the likes of Luton and Notts County. It can't be easy with average crowds of less than 3,000, but Rovers have come a long way since they were founded in 1889 by a nonconformist minister, Reverend E.J.H. Peach. In 1906/07 they had the distinction of finishing bottom of the Stroud & District League with zero points (although they had won one game they had two points deducted for fielding an ineligible player) and more recently they toiled for 19 seasons in the Conference (renamed National League in 2015/16) before winning promotion through play-offs at the third attempt. In a subsequent interview, manager Mark Cooper suggested they had become victims of their own success: 'We've had a lot of animosity towards Forest Green. When I played for them they were a friendly little club, part-time, and everyone loved them because they weren't a threat. Once they became a threat nobody liked them, so I'm just chuffed for the chairman.'

The chairman, Dale Vince, is also chuffed and has big plans, including a new stadium designed by award-winning architect Zaha Hadid with the aim of playing in the Championship within five years. The 'little club on the hill' is getting bigger, and striving for pastures new.

The Village Inn in Nailsworth is a cosy warren of rooms offering local ales and live TV football. It doesn't serve food, but there is a chippie next door and patrons are welcome to bring in their fish and pie suppers to enjoy with a pint. This strikes me as an excellent symbiotic relationship, and a perfect place to begin my Rovers research.

Ian Crawley came late to Forest Green. Born near White Hart Lane, he was a season-ticket holder at Spurs until a career move took him to Bristol and a home in Nailsworth.

'I didn't know Forest Green Rovers existed,' he admits. 'Years before Tottenham I used to go to local non-league. I was always fascinated by clubs like Bishop Auckland that appeared at Wembley out of nowhere, so I was delighted when I discovered there was quite a good Conference team in the village where I'd bought a house.'

Ian was soon seduced by the easy-going friendliness of his new club. 'The great thing about the game at this level is that the players come into the club lounge after the game and stay for a drink and a chat. So you get to know them and feel for them in a different way.

'It's not about winning or losing any more. The attraction is the honesty of the footballers on the pitch. You know they're not paid massive salaries and they're often condemned as journeymen footballers, but it's fascinating to watch quality players at the fag end of their careers and talented lads on their way up. The older guys may have lost their pace, but they still have that innate quality, it's a joy to see.'

Ian cites examples in Isaiah Osborne, a midfielder who played with Aston Villa in the Premier League, and Ethan Pinnock, a young centre-half who has just signed for Barnsley. 'Everyone said Osborne had a fantastic future when he was at Villa, but he lost his way and we got him on a free and he's brilliant. He's got time on the ball, left foot, right foot, he's kept us in the league. We got Ethan from Dulwich and he's the most perfect footballer I've ever seen. He's perfectly balanced and whatever he does with his left foot he can do with his right, and he's brilliant in the air. Straight away you knew he was going to play in the Premier League and that we had him at best for one season. But when you love football it's a joy to watch lads at the beginning of their careers improving in the time they're with you.'

Recruiting a blend of youth and experience is one thing, but as any manager knows forging them into a successful team is the hard part. 'I've always thought football manager must be the most difficult job in the world. With new players coming in every season you've got to have them in the right positions in the right team with the right tactics that work against a particular team on matchday. It's an absolutely impossible job, it's far easier being prime minister of a country.'

Ian admits that stepping up to the EFL has been tougher than expected. 'A lot of people gave us a false sense of security, saying there wasn't a lot of difference between the top of the Conference and the bottom of League Two. Well maybe there wasn't in the past, but there is now. We struggled because Mark likes small, two-footed, quick ball players, particularly in midfield, and when we started in League Two we were just bullied off the pitch.'

The arrival of Osborne on a free, followed by three robust centre-halves in the January window, strengthened the midfield, and a few decent results have kept their heads above the stormy waters of relegation.

'A lot of players won't come here because we're not a city or even a town, we're just a village really, so if top players choose to play for Rovers at this stage in their careers you appreciate that and thank them. At Tottenham I never wanted to lose our best players to someone else, but here if a young lad goes on to a big club you want to be pleased for him. It's all part of being closer to the players than you'd ever be in the Premiership.'

Vince has not been slow to splash the cash in pursuit of success, paying out more than £70,000 on agents' fees in 2017, one of the most in League Two. By contrast, Accrington paid less than £10,000. (The top spenders were Coventry City at £113,620.)

Yet Ian concedes not everyone is happy about Vince's patronage. 'There are some fans in the town who don't want any more to do with the club because they feel it's become a rich man's plaything. Admittedly the chairman has been using the club to promote green values and his renewable energy business, but that's fine with me because personally I believe in them, and the new support we've gained is a hundred times what we've lost. I think it's exceptional in any walk of life when you have someone who is really idealistic and wears their values on their sleeve, and there's not many people you can say that about.'

It is a sentiment I hear often over the next few days, mixed with bemusement among villagers who would no more go to a football match than miss the local flower show. It is a moot point whether Rovers or the Amberley Cow Hunt is more popular among Forest Green residents fed up with fans disturbing the peace of their Saturday afternoons.

The matches don't seem to bother the bees and the butterflies, however. There are lots of them buzzing and fluttering around Rovers' stadium thanks to planting of native trees and wildflowers as a haven for wildlife. The banks of hazel and ash, and clusters of spotted orchids and cowslips, are highlights of an 'Ecotrail' created by the chairman, along with an electric car charging bay and a system for recycling waste cooking oil as biofuel for the club tractor. Needless to say, the stadium is largely powered by the sun and wind, and water that goes into the organic pitch is collected by drainage pipes and used again. Visiting fans can read all about the green initiatives on information boards on the approach road to the stadium – rechristened New Way – and are advised that if they look around carefully they may spot a lizard or a slow-worm. At least it makes a welcome change from looking for ticket touts.

I'm at the stadium to meet Rambling Man, the author of amusing essays in matchday programmes on his travels to away games with his pals Compo, Foggy, Deep Throat and Sir Tomcat. Most of them are National Trust members, and for years they've been making the most of expeditions to far-flung opposition grounds by visiting NT properties and other places of interest along the way. Rambling Man, *aka* author and retired surveyor Chris Gardner, told club officials he'd happily write about away fixtures, but don't expect him to say much about the football.

In a recent programme he took readers on a trip to Accrington via Ramsbottom Station, a scenic stop on the East Lancs railway, in time to see the 12.15pm steam train from Bury enveloping sightseers in clouds of steam, 'a unique aroma that all old-uns will never forget'. On to Stanley's Wham stadium, which he found 'old fashioned, small, homely and populated by some of the friendliest people I have ever encountered in sport. The weather might have been Arctic, but there were more than 2,000 of the warmest hearts in England in the venue.'

The hospitality extended to piping hot Lancashire Hot Pot with mushy peas, and despite losing to two late goals, the Rovers contingent left in good spirits. 'As we fled the gathering snowstorm, home supporters complimented Rovers' quality of football and we thanked them for their exceptional hospitality. Defeat still left good memories.' I try to imagine a Chelsea fan writing this about visiting the Emirates, and give up.

On a previous historic occasion Chris and his pals travelled to York for Rovers' final match in their promotion-winning National League season in an 'FGR Special' vintage train. It so happens his wife is marketing manager of a local 'period' railway company and her boss is an FGR season-ticket holder, and by coincidence it was running a tour from Gloucestershire to Scarborough and back again through York, arriving about 90 minutes before kick-off.

The ramblers were duly invited on board, and with the enthusiastic agreement of the train's paying customers it was billed as an FGR Away Day Special with a Rovers scarf emblazoned across the driver's windscreen. Chris recalls, 'The return train picked us up too, giving ample time to enjoy the York National Railway Museum. A wonderful day that lives long in the memory.'

The New Lawn is a tidy little stadium offering the best of old and new, with a seated stand and three banks of terracing with views of the surrounding countryside. It can hold 5,147 fans, which is pretty much the population of Nailsworth, but the rival attractions of agricultural shows and arts fairs means it's never full.

Since supporters are welcome in the main function suite before and after games, most will have seen a legend emblazoned in large letters above the staircase in the main stand. They are the immortal words of Bob Hunt, a commentator for BBC Radio Gloucestershire, in the euphoria of Rovers' victory over Tranmere at Wembley in 2017: 'Let me tell you this Cheltenham, Swindon, Newport, you are going to eat HOUMOUS next season, because Forest Green Rovers are in the Football League.' As a warning of Rovers' prowess it may leave something to be desired, but it gets across the chairman's message.

It's too early for a vegan lunch, so Chris offers me a coffee in the directors' lounge overlooking the pitch. He is a likeable, articulate man who talks enthusiastically about the club's green revolution. 'When Dale came in it's probably fair to say the average age of supporters was high. When you read the births, deaths and marriages column you began to worry about the support. And the one thing that's really difficult, no matter how hard you try, is to make a club cool for young people.'

The answer lay in a pilot scheme by Norwich City, which handed out club shirts to every new primary school pupil in the area, after a survey showed that if you catch children when they're young they might move away, but they never lose their team loyalty. 'When you do the maths it's very cheap marketing. When Dale heard about it we did it and its worked like a dream.' Rovers took the idea a stage further with a hugely successful 'ambassadors' programme, in which pupils are recruited to act as club representatives in dozens of schools at primary, secondary and tertiary level, liaising with players who visit for talks and award ceremonies. Chris reckons it has been the main factor in increasing gates from an average of 900 to close to 3,000. 'What's happening is that the ambassadors bring their friends, but better still they bring their parents and grandparents, so you get people with time on their hands and a bit of money coming to matches with the kids.'

The enduring appeal of Rovers, and of other lower league clubs, he says is their intimacy and community ties. 'I know it sounds crazy, but lots of supporters know each other here, and at the end of every match everyone tends to head for the hospitality suite, along with the players and their families, and we do man-of-the-match presentations. There's a closeness in this club that you never want to lose.

'I think there's growing awareness that some of the best morals in football are actually in the lower leagues. We don't get loads of money thrown at us like the Premier League, so we have to work much harder to get schemes going and interest young people to survive. You go to Accrington who exist on crowds of 1,500, or Morecambe or Hereford, they work their arses off in their communities to help charities, and it's really an act of faith.'

He admits Rovers have been fortunate in acquiring a wealthy benefactor in the Green Czar of Stroud, whatever people may think of him and his penchant for casual wear and ear studs. 'People will look at Dale and the way he dresses, and draw all sorts of conclusions, but he doesn't half make some good decisions. He's a visionary, he's not a chairman who's in it to make loads of cash, but to satisfy his interest in football and promote the things he believes in. You'll never convince some people, but he's convinced me.

'He's always had the knack of being ahead of trends and overcoming closed minds, revelling in the impact of his less conventional appearance. The big-spending tag has long since been consigned as we now invest in young, lower league talent and are able to sell on a player or two for big money every year. Dale's a one-off but 100 per cent genuine. I don't think it's an exaggeration to say that Ecotricity and to some extent Forest Green Rovers have become to the Stroud area what Norwich Union is to Norwich. It's put us on the map.'

Chris has written a couple of highly readable books about Rovers' rise to fame and fortune, and in one of them the chairman writes frankly about the rationale and driving force behind it. 'I don't do short term, no matter what world it's in, football is no different,' he says. I think and plan very long term. I think that the further we travel up the leagues of English football the louder our eco message will be and the more people will pay attention to what we're doing and the more fun we can have along the way. Life is really short, at least that's what I think, and it's best to make an adventure of it so that's what I'm up for. I'd like to see Forest Green in the Championship; that's the goal.'

Having put Rovers firmly on the map, he plans to move them to a new all-seater stadium eight miles away, beside junction 13 of the M5 motorway. A vision of the future lies in a glass case at the head of the stairs in the main stand, a model of a 100-acre sports and green technology 'Eco Park', incorporating a wildlife conservation area and the only stadium in the world built almost entirely of wood, designed to seat 5,000 fans and to extend to twice as many depending on the club's success. With outdoor and indoor training pitches and leisure facilities, it is a mini sports city with provision for orchids and earthworms.

The rationale is that Rovers have become too big for their Forest Green boots, and to attract new fans beyond the Stroud valleys they have to move. So one day perhaps it won't be 'the little club on the hill' any more, and the fairy tale will be over. Manager Cooper alluded to the problem after guiding the club into the Football League: 'People talk about us having a lack of fans, but you've got to remember we're on the top of a hill in the middle of nowhere.'

Chris agrees a move is probably inevitable. 'The sentimental part of me and a lot of others thinks it will be sad to leave Forest Green. A big fear of any traditional fan is their club losing its sense of identity, but I think most of us don't see a choice really. Football's the same as any company, you grow or you die, and we're in a little football bubble in rugby country here. The growing population is out there in big expanding towns along the A38, and if we're going to grow as a club it's logical for us to move there.'

For the time being matchdays at the New Lawn are lively affairs with legions of excited children sporting Forest Green shirts and bringing along mums and dads and grandparents, making the stand pretty much a family section. The man behind the youthful fan club is Phil Butterworth, a retired head teacher who began supporting Rovers after the previous chairman bought him chips at a Conference game. 'I really like things like that,' he says when we meet at the stadium. 'It was my first time at the club. I wrote something in the local paper about how much I enjoyed it, and the club secretary rang me up, though he didn't know me, to say thank you. From then on I became a keen supporter.'

Phil is now club vice-chairman and a member of the supporters' club board, but his biggest contribution has been the school ambassadors scheme. 'As a head teacher I was fed up seeing Man Utd and Chelsea shirts everywhere, and no

Forest Green shirts anywhere in the community. So I had a word with the chairman and said can we do something about that, can I take players into schools, and we started taking them to different schools every week. It was very popular, the children and the players loved it, but what nagged me was there was nothing left behind, the kids weren't coming to matches or anything. So I started the ambassador scheme to try and have a pupil in as many schools as possible who would spread the team message, have a notice board, talk about Forest Green and enthuse about them.'

A simple, successful idea that began as a pilot project in eight schools, at the last count had recruited 80 young ambassadors – tomorrow's season-ticket holders – in 53 schools. Every Forest Green programme has match reports by children, and a profile of one of the ambassadors who also provide the ball boys and girls.

It's mainly families that make up the crowds now, Phil notes. 'If anything the girls are even keener than the boys. The great thing is the kids grow in the role, it gives them confidence and enthusiasm to stand up in front of the class, and often they'll give presentations before the whole school. And because of the green message, schools love it.'

For the price of free shirts and season tickets for seven-year-olds, Rovers' match attendances have rocketed with a new generation of potential supporters. But will they still come to the new ground? Phil is confident they will. 'In an ideal world we'd stay here and improve the stadium, but Dale's vision is more than just being in Forest Green, he wants to put us on the map in the South West as a big club, not just for the football but for the green message with a wooden stadium. And it's only ten minutes away, it's not really far. I don't see it as an issue at all.'

Meanwhile, Rovers still attract curious visitors to their home on a Cotswolds hill. Leaving the ground, I meet a character wandering around with a vaguely bemused look. This is not surprising as Robert Newey is a Crystal Palace fan who reckons he'd enjoy watching Rovers just as much for a fraction of the cost. 'We're on holiday here and I just thought I'd take a walk up the hill and have a look,' he says. 'I've read the stories about Forest Green and wondered what it was like. I'll bet it's lovely in there on matchday. If I lived here I'd love to support this club.'

Robert is a loyal Eagles fan who loves Premier League football, but is falling out of love with what he has to pay for it. 'Every year it gets more difficult and expensive to support Palace. Five years ago our seats were £450, now they're building a new stand and asking for £1,400, and £500 a season for the car park next to the stadium.'

On Saturdays Robert has lunch at home with his wife, then his brother comes over and they set off for the match together like they've always done. Now the club is saying if they want to keep their seats behind the dugouts in the new stand they'll have to take out corporate memberships, dine in a hospitality suite, and be in the car park by two o'clock for health and safety reasons.

'We always get there at a quarter to three, we have a pint after the match and that's it. It's been our routine all our lives. We don't want to get there at two o'clock and have a big lunch, it doesn't appeal to us at all. I think we'll get thrown out basically if we don't buy that package, and I don't know where we'll end up sitting.'

Robert understands the club demanding top prices for premier seats, but it's a familiar story of fans being priced out by corporate deals to pay inflated wages of players and their agents, and he's unimpressed by the antics of some of them. 'The behaviour of quite a lot of players irritates me. It's not their fault what they earn but I can't quite get to grips with it. I've always done quite well in life so I'm okay financially, but still most Premiership footballers earn more in a week than I used to earn in a year. You wonder what do they do with it? And when you see people you respect like Jamie Carragher spitting out of his car window at somebody it disappoints me a lot.'

If ever Robert finds himself living closer to the New Lawn than Selhurst Park, it wouldn't faze him to support Rovers. 'We love being in the Premiership. I love sitting there and watching all the stars, even the referees and the managers they all walk right past in front of us. But I don't think the emotional part of it would change if this was my team, I'd still get just as excited and I don't think the quality of the football would make a huge difference to me, because I watched Palace when they were in the third division and I enjoyed it just as much.' Spoken like a true fan, and I leave him wandering around, musing on what the atmosphere will be like on Saturday.

The sun is burning off early morning mist, and I decide to go for a stroll in a valley 'narrow, steep, a channel for the floods and a jungly, bird-rammed, insect-hopping sun-trap whenever there happened to be any sun'. The Slad valley a couple of miles from Stroud remains as it was described by Laurie Lee, who spent his childhood there and portrayed it in his autobiographical novel *Cider with Rosie*. I first discovered Lee in a second-hand bookshop that had an old copy of *As I Walked out One Midsummer Morning*, an account of wandering across Spain with a violin and a blanket on the eve of the Spanish civil war. I was instantly charmed by his lyrical writing and wry humour, and now I'm delighted at the prospect of retracing his steps in the valley that set him on his way.

The hamlet of Slad straddles a winding country road to Painswick with a small parish church, a pub, a schoolhouse and a scattering of farmhouses in a green valley. Blink and you'll miss it, but park in a lay-by just beyond and you'll find a five-mile 'Laurie Lee Wildlife Way' meandering through woods and nature reserves that are a timeless vision of an English rural heaven.

The sun is beaming from a cloudless sky in accordance with Lee's recollections as I descend on a footpath through ancient woodland of pollarded beech trees, ash and hazel. Nailsworth is hardly a bustling metropolis, but it is a joy to ramble through woods where the only sounds are a gentle sigh of wind in the trees, birdsong and the occasional rattling of a woodpecker. The sun-dappled path seems to be leading me into the quietly beating heart of countryside barely disturbed by man, and the chorus of tweeting and chirruping grows louder as if the woods are greeting their lone visitor.

A shimmering pond and a brook teeming with small fish and mayflies invite me to rest and meditate on the extravagant beauty of nature, before a stiff climb leads to a panorama of limestone grasslands flanked by more woods. The slopes are too steep for modern farming, so they are rich in wildlife and the beech woods are full of spring wildflowers. Descending again, my map guide says there is a pile of stones here that are the ruins of a brothel. I can't find them, but muse briefly that few customers of such establishments could have enjoyed such an idyllic setting. Shortly afterwards I run out of waymarks and become happily lost, and ramble along a ridge enjoying views of scattered stone farmsteads that look as if they are rooted in the land.

Eventually a farm track leads to my destination, the Woolpack Inn. Lee returned to live in Slad in his 50s, and this was his pub. It is a cosy warren of low-ceilinged rooms, and I am relieved to find it has not been transformed into a tacky literary shrine. A large portrait of the author as a young man hangs above a piano, but he is outnumbered by a photo gallery of other departed pub regulars. I arrive five minutes after the kitchen has closed, but the barman rustles up a cold pork pie and a bag of crisps to wash down with a pint of cider – what else – and I stroll out to a terrace with views over the valley probably unchanged since they inspired Lee. It is late afternoon and the only other customer is a pretty, flaxen-haired girl sitting on a wall with a drink and a book, and I discreetly christen her Rosie.

The Wildlife Way is interspersed with wooden markers bearing glass panels, inscribed with excerpts of Lee's poetry. One of the poems is *The Wild Trees*, which ends:

O fountains of earth and rock,
gardens perfumed with cucumber,
home of secret valleys
where the wild trees grow.

Let me return at last
To your fertile wilderness
To sleep with the coiled fern leaves
In your heart's live stone.

He got his wish. He is buried in the little churchyard across the road from the pub.

Back to the football. Ken Bolton is a sprightly, silver-haired gentleman in his late 70s who wears his advancing years lightly. He's been driving buses for more than half a century, including the Forest Green team bus when they were playing in the Beazer Homes Midland League and supporters travelled with them to away matches. He had his own bus company then, and ended up taking over as short-term chairman a couple of times and becoming a life member.

We meet in a Nailsworth café where I've bagged a courtyard table in the sunshine, and over a pot of tea he shares a few memories. 'Driving the team and supporters together for about six years was brilliant,' he says. 'It was different in them days, the players played for the love of the club instead of money, and we had genuine supporters who wanted to help the club through bad times. There was an unbelievable atmosphere on the bus, it was all good humour, the wives of some players would come and make sandwiches, there was a tea machine and even the chairman would make me a cuppa.' Officially Ken is retired, having sold his company, but he kept a bus for himself and still drives the supporters. He says he's just passed his MOT to continue driving and intends to go on as long as he is able.

A highlight of his away-day adventures says much about changing attitudes in the game. It was in the late 90s when they were travelling to an FA Trophy match at St Albans, and on the bus was a young reserve goalkeeper who had just joined from Melcham Town. 'We were on the M6 and when we pulled into a service station the chairman offered him a contract. The lad said, "I don't know, what's it all about, this contract?"' The chairman told him how much he'd get paid, but the lad said he'd never thought of a contract, he'd just enjoyed playing. Well you'll be better off, the chairman said, and he got the paperwork out and said sign here. And the lad did, which was just as well for us.

'Our keeper at the time was a gravedigger, and he'd dropped a headstone on his foot. He was in a bit of pain but he said he'd give it a go. He wasn't the brightest, but he was a good keeper. But he had to come off and the young lad went on and the first thing he did was save a penalty. We went right through to the final at Wembley and he was in goal.'

They lost 0-1 to Kingstonian but it was an historic occasion, one of the last finals to be played at the iconic old stadium before it was torn down and rebuilt. Ken remembers it well. 'I've been driving coaches since 1963, but to drive through the arches of Wembley towers with a cup final team was unbelievable. They'll never take that away from me.'

Around the corner from the café I have made an interesting discovery, a sign pointing to a muse of my youth. Above the stream that runs through Nailsworth a lane of old stone cottages winds up to a mini-suburb called Watledge, and for a few years one of them was the last home of a tramp given to poetry and philosophy who penned lines that struck a chord with me as a young man and have remained an inspiration ever since:

What is this life if, full of care,
We have no time to stand and stare ...

The 14-line poem entitled *Leisure* goes on to wax lyrical on the pleasures of stepping off the whirling roundabout of life to contemplate wonders of nature like '*... in broad daylight, streams full of stars like skies at night ...*'

It was written by W.H. Davies, an Anglo-Welsh poet who spent much of his life bumming around America, and tramping the byways of England on a wooden leg, having lost most of one train-jumping on his way to the Klondike gold rush. At the age of 52 he married a would-be prostitute half his age he'd met at a bus stop on the Edgware Road near Marble Arch, and love brought his travelling days to a close when they settled in rural Kent, where he penned the poem that made him world famous. Later they moved to Nailsworth where they lived happily ever after, at least until he died in 1940.

The lane also seems to be a haven for old cars, notably Morris Minors and Citroen 2CVs, attesting to the free spirits of their owners. My first office car as a trainee sports reporter was a black Morris Minor and I've owned two 2CVs (one repainted in the claret and amber of Motherwell FC), so this was a pleasing stroll down memory lane. Davies's last abode on Earth was Glendower Cottage, a humble, low-stone dwelling reminiscent of a Thomas Hardy novel. After he died the house lay empty for years and was in danger of becoming derelict, until volunteers and local builders backed by the district council stepped in and restored it. But homes often reflect the character of the people living in them, and Glendower seems sad and forlorn, as if the life went out of it with the passing of Davies.

A plaque by the door is inscribed with the opening lines of *Leisure,* and in tribute to their author I stand and stare, but there isn't much to see because the views over the valley are obscured by the house opposite. So I carry on to the top of the hill where an imposing manor house built by mill owners maintains an aura of Victorian wealth and privilege. In front of it, a low-stone wall straggles above a sloping meadow and provides a perfect perch for me to sit and stare to my heart's content at wooded hills across the valley. I am no poet like Lee and Davies, but sitting here, lulled by late afternoon sunshine, drowsy buzzing of bees and cooing of wood pigeons, I breathe deeply and share their sentiments. For an appreciation of their love of rustic countryside read Davies's poem *The Green Tent.*

There are ancient footpaths everywhere in the Stroud valleys. One leads down through woods from the manor house to an old railway line that is now a pedestrian and cycle path by the stream and the mills that it once powered. The mills may have been dark and satanic in their day, but under new owners they have been transformed into smart homes, an upmarket hotel and an arts and craft centre. The ponds that once drove the mill water wheels are now wildlife havens for wetland plants, tufted ducks, kingfishers and dog walkers. Needless to say I stand and stare quite a lot.

I'm told Nailsworth's mayor is a Rovers supporter, so I pop into the information centre and ask if they have his office number. A nice elderly lady obliges with his mobile, and he promptly agrees to meet that evening in The Britannia, a venerable alehouse serving decent food in the village centre.

'I'll be easy to spot,' he says. 'I'm tall and bald.' Jonathan Duckworth is also a pleasant, easy-going character who cares for his community and its football team. Before Vince came along he was a volunteer helper at Rovers, painting a corridor in the stand, taking frost protectors off before matches, and drawing on his background in retail to advise on stadium operation and marketing.

When Rovers went to Wembley to win promotion to the EFL, the mayor of Tranmere had a seat in the royal box with the directors, but Jonathan was down near the front row with a ticket he'd bought online. 'My one regret is that I didn't have the mayor's chain with me, I don't know if it's insured to go to a football match. But I should have been there with the chain on, I'd probably have been swinging it around my head.' It is a glorious image, and if ever it had been recorded it would have gone down in the annals of Wembley history.

The team has put the town on the map, he affirms. 'When I go somewhere and people ask where I'm from and I say Nailsworth, mostly they look at me blankly. Then I say Forest Green, and they say "oh yes, I've heard of them".'

Originally from the London area and a Watford fan, he's enjoying the more intimate match atmosphere at the New Lawn. 'Even when you're in the stand the furthest away you are is a dozen seats, so you're pretty close to the action. It's touchable. I've been to West Ham at the London Stadium, and Wembley, and sometimes you're so far away you feel you could reach out and pick up the players by hand, they're so small, it's like playing Subbuteo.'

He recalls his brother coming with him to a Rovers match and observing with interest a curious animal grazing in the field beyond the away terracing.

'That looks like a llama,' his brother said.

'It is a llama,' Jonathan replied. In fact there were several of them.

While the green dawn of the Vince era heralds a bright future for the club, Jonathan has reservations about the vegan crusade. 'A big part of going to football was to have some really revolting food,' he says regretfully.

Of more concern is the planned move to a new stadium. As mayor and Rovers fan, he is uneasy about it and reckons opinion in the town is divided. 'Communities like this are made up of pieces, and if you take away pieces from the jigsaw like the football club it becomes less. You can stop people in the street and they'll complain about traffic on a Saturday, but you should be careful what you wish for. Take the team away and a big piece of the jigsaw and the town's identity has gone.'

His fear is that New Lawn and jobs at the club will be lost to a housing development, and Forest Green will become a suburban dormitory for people employed elsewhere. And he doesn't see the point.

'You've got 127 years of history here with an effectively brand new stadium with 5,000 capacity, and they're planning to build another stadium with 5,000 capacity which is accessible to more people but not as accessible to its current community.'

Jonathan finds himself going to fewer matches now because it feels as if he's supporting the move, and he's unsure if he'll follow Rovers to their new home. 'It's a difficult decision. At the moment I can walk up the hill for the game and have a few pints and walk back. It's a drive to the new ground.' He might end up watching the town's other team Shortwood United, playing in the Toolstation Western League. Its Meadowbank Ground is less than half a mile away across the valley as the crow flies.

Friday morning, back at the ground to meet a man living the dream. One of the teenage fans who travelled on Ken Bolton's team bus in the 1980s was Ashley Loveridge, whose ambition was to become a journalist. Years later he ended up as sports editor of the *Stroud News and Journal*, where his main brief is to report on the ups and downs of the team he has always supported. We arrange to meet before the manager's pre-match press conference and take coffees into the empty stand.

'It's not what I thought would happen in my life,' he says. 'I've got to keep reminding myself it's a bit of an honour.' The money in local journalism is not great, but he counts himself lucky to have kept his job for 16 years and has no ambition to go anywhere else. 'I've always been satisfied. I'm not a country bumpkin, just a happy person. From my office in Stroud I drive to work across the common, it's lovely.'

It's pretty much a dream job, and with Rovers' promotion to the EFL Ashley earns a bit of beer money with reports for the Press Association, but his most vivid memories go back to his youth, and away games in the Beazer Homes League.

'There were ten of us travelling with the players. These guys had jobs in Stroud, we had a taxi driver in the team and a factory worker, one was a school teacher, you'd often see them around town. It was a real non-league club. But when you're a teenager they're your Kevin Keegans, they're your heroes then, you're singing out their names during the match and asking them for a wave. They were big stars to us.'

'They always will be,' he says. 'I'm still in touch with players who won the FA Vase, and I always thank them for what they did, and remind them they're true heroes. That's one thing about the new regime, they need to think about the past a bit more. When they move to this new stadium they need to have a museum to show and respect how they got to this point.'

I ask if there is a danger of Rovers losing their sense of identity by deserting their rural hilltop. 'There's always a fear of that, people don't like change, do they? But I think you've got to look forward. The club has a dream of getting to the Championship, and doing a Fleetwood [currently in

League One]. I think you've just got to embrace it and move with the times.'

Ashley agrees that Vince's takeover was not universally popular. 'I wouldn't say he was welcomed to the club with the way he implemented his vegan beliefs, but people have warmed to him. There's nobody quite like him. The access road here used to be called Smiths Way, after the company that did the groundwork for the stadium, and he changed it to Another Way. It sums this guy up really. One of the interesting things he said to me once was, "I used to lie in bed at night thinking about windmills, now I think about Forest Green." I thought it was quite a nice little line.'

Rovers may have struggled to survive in their first season in League Two, but this seasoned journalistic observer believes they have the talent and the resources to climb higher.

'The manager has them playing on the deck as much as possible, and most opposing managers say it's the best footballing team they've played, so for them to be where they are is a false position really. Vince comes out with some stuff, but he's a positive person. I'd never have thought, back on the coach with the players in the Beazer League, that one day they'd be in the Football League, I'd have laughed. Now League One is a definite possibility, Vince has the clout to get there, and maybe even the Championship. Burton have done it, haven't they? So maybe in my lifetime, why not dream?'

If the dream comes true, Mark Cooper's pre-match press conferences will probably be a lot busier. Today the press pack in a small meeting room comprises Ashley, a local radio reporter and myself. If anyone can take Forest Green to a higher level, Cooper has the credentials and experience to do it. The son of Leeds United and England full-back Terry Cooper, his midfield playing career took him to 17 clubs, including a spell at Rovers as club captain and supporters' Player of the Year, and he managed four before returning to take charge at the New Lawn. Along the way he guided Darlington to the FA Trophy, but now he's preparing for a relegation dogfight with Chesterfield.

In answer to questions, Cooper makes the point that with four games left to play the visitors must win to give themselves a chance of survival. 'We've got to be wary they'll come at us with all guns blazing, we have to be ready for it, but it might leave some openings for us to exploit.'

He says he is not discussing contracts until he knows they're safe, and he repeats the mantra that as a player or manager in football you're only as good as your last game. 'The carrots are stay in the team and earn a new deal with a good progressive club.' Like Accrington Stanley. Cooper is full of praise for the Lancashire club sitting on top of the table with a shoestring budget. 'John's got a team full of Scousers and that creates a team spirit. They've done fantastically well and they deserve all the credit and accolades they're going to get. Fair play, good luck to them.'

On that note of lower league fraternity, the press conference winds up and Cooper invites me into his office for a cuppa and a chat. He tells me he was at Notts County on a short-term contract when Vince lured him to Forest Green with his vision of the future. 'Basically he wanted me to oversee it, which is what I was looking for, having been at a couple of clubs where I didn't really have autonomy. What he told me about where we could take the club with a new stadium and training complex was music to my ears really. He sold it to me, and he's been true to his word.'

The challenges of football are the same at any level, he says, it's all about recruiting the best players because the best coach in the world can't win without them. And this has been a problem for Rovers. 'Recruitment was really difficult last summer. We're competing with Coventry, Notts County, Luton, Lincoln, Swindon, Cambridge, big clubs in big places to live, and we're asking players to come and play in the middle of the Cotswolds among a bunch of sheep on top of a hill. So we have to either pay lots more money or recruit in a different way.'

With the chairman's backing, he is hopeful of strengthening his squad at the end of the season, and sees the planned move as a positive step towards higher goals. 'When we move to the new stadium we'll open up a new catchment area and get more people through the gate, so we can sign better players. That's our vision, we're not going to get away from that. Look at Burton Albion in the Championship, look at Bournemouth, a smallish town getting crowds of 11,000 in the Premier League. Why can't we dream about getting Forest Green in the Premiership once we're in the new stadium, why not? I think we should aim for that, it's certainly my goal.'

He's a long way from signing players of the calibre of his boyhood heroes at Leeds United, the likes of Johnny Giles and Billy Bremner, but he is determined to recruit the best ball players his budget will stretch to. And the long-ball game is definitively not his style. 'We can get out of this league by playing good football like Accrington and Luton, and we're going to play even more football next year.'

Forest Green is still a small club with one part-time scout, and Cooper oversees coaching, recruitment and checking the opposition, but more staff are being hired and with a five-year contract and the support of his chairman he feels as secure as anyone ever can in the modern game. 'You have to live and die by your results, I get that, but the chairman can see the big picture. I think I'm in a lucky position compared with other guys who're out if they lose four or five games.'

Rovers have lost more games than he would have wished this season, but like their fans Cooper is singing when they're winning. 'When you've got three points on a Saturday at teatime the feeling is fantastic. I can't envisage ever living without that.'

At least they'll have a decent pitch to play on tomorrow. It's a bit bare in patches after a hard winter, but generally it's in good end-of-season shape thanks to a groundsman well versed in plant biology and his badger-repelling robot mower.

Adam Witchell, a strapping West Country lad with a passion for plants and football, learned his trade at a local authority sports centre that didn't have much money, so instead of buying chemicals he studied biology to produce plant-based fertilisers. He won a string of awards for his efforts, and for Vince's green revolution he was a natural recruit. But it's been hard work greening a heavy clay pitch of landfill that doesn't drain well. Taking a break from painting the lines for the match, he says, 'The previous groundsman put a lot of carbon in so it's hard to get the roots down, but we got there. Except for a couple of areas where we've got blocked drains, it's not looking too bad. We've had the worst winter in 60 years they say, we've had snow, frost and a lot of rain, but we're one of the only clubs in the league that hasn't lost a game. It's been hard, it's really taken a toll on me, but I love it. I wouldn't be able to do it if I wasn't passionate about the club and the ethos behind it.'

His pride and joy is the solar-powered mower that chugs happily around on its own, stopping every few hours to recharge, and cutting the pitch in three days. As far as Adam knows, the only other professional football club to have one is Bayern Munich. An unforeseen benefit is that it freaks badgers who have a habit of digging big holes before matches. 'They're looking for worms and grubs and we promote earthworms here, but the movement of the mower and the sound of the blades going round spooks them and keeps them off the pitch.' Sometimes after a fight. Scratches on the machine attest to episodes of badger resistance. At such times, and if a sprinkler pops up and knocks it on its head, the mower sends Adam a distress signal in a text message. The problem is that this can happen at any time, day or night. 'Try and explain to your partner at two in the morning it's your robot that's calling you. It sounds like the worst excuse in the world. At first she was going mad, but she's got used to it, kind of.' With his robot and seaweed fertiliser, Adam was nominated for FA Groundsman of the Year last year, and he has mixed feelings about leaving the New Lawn he has nurtured. He loves the pitch, he says, but it will be nice to have a new one that isn't a landfill clay pit.

Saturday is a bright spring day and the town is getting into the swing of weekend activities. The organic fruit and veg stall is busy, an art exhibition has opened in rooms next to the library, and a fiddler and his daughter on guitar are playing lively Irish jigs outside the newspaper shop. The sunshine has brought out classic car enthusiasts, and a Triumph Herald and an early Alfa Romeo Spider cruise by with their tops down. Anywhere there are trees, which is pretty much everywhere, there are choruses of birds tweeting, warbling and cooing. As a prelude to a football match, this is a novel experience.

I have been advised to arrive at the ground early to beat the crowds up the hill and find a parking place, and am pleased to find I have been allocated a place in the car park by the ground. It is one o'clock, but already the hospitality lounge named after a former director is buzzing with a lively crowd. At this point on matchdays I'd normally be queuing at a stall for a greasy Scotch pie, but the lounge is like a smart restaurant serving strictly vegan fare. I opt for a Quorn pie with mash and peas washed down with a pint of Budding Ale from the Stroud Brewery, and readily admit it's the best, tastiest meal I've had at a football ground.

Thus fortified, I spot a couple of ladies draped in Forest Green scarves at a corner table and ask if I might join them. Jackie Totterdell turns out to be a retired newspaper reporter who interviewed Dale for the *Stroud News and Journal* when he put up his first wind turbine, and Penny Smith is a checkout operator who helps out in the club reception when they're short of staff. Both have lived in London and supported variously Arsenal, West Ham and Leyton Orient, but have been won over by the charms and gastronomy of Forest Green.

'The football's different,' Penny says. 'There are fantastic players in the Premiership and there's nothing like going down the Wembley Way if you want big crowds, but it's much more gutsy down here, more earthy. It's more real somehow. It's small and friendly, and look at the view. If the football's terrible there are sheep in that field that can entertain you all afternoon.'

Her highlights were the play-off finals at Wembley that were David versus Goliath affairs against the relatively mighty Grimsby Town and Tranmere Rovers. 'That's the thrill of the game, when you have such a small community pitched against the whole of Grimsby at Wembley. It was amazing. We lost because of two goalkeeping mistakes, but as we came away a Grimsby fan said to us, "Don't worry, you'll be up next year." That's lovely about this level of football, and he was right.'

Jackie remembers Vince as a scruffy hippy erecting a 42-metre windmill on top of a hill amid protests from local villagers that it was a noisy eyesore. 'He stood his ground, and that commitment in him to try something different has led to this, the ultimate green football club. There's very few organisations that can be this proud of their green ethos, and all power to him for that.'

As vegetarians, both are deeply grateful to Vince for his culinary fare, having been presented with more cheese sandwiches and omelettes and chips at football grounds over the years than they care to remember. And they're looking forward to leaving the confines of Forest Green. 'There's nowhere to expand here,' Jackie says. 'It's lovely and very Paddington Bear with rabbits in the field, and when we move we'll miss this. But hopefully with a bit of cleverness some of that ambience and family feeling can transfer as well. If we want to work our way up the leagues with more fans and more exciting football we have to move to the motorway and compete with Bristol. I think it will be a big bonus for Stroud and the area to have a bigger, greener football club. I think it will be great.'

From a table behind us I overhear a club official asking a family if they're enjoying their first visit. Curious, I wander over and find the Nelson family from Derby tucking with relish into vegan pies and fajitas. James, a submarine engineer, says he was intrigued by the Forest Green story when they were promoted last season and by the vegan ethos, although they're not vegetarians. 'I phoned the club a couple of times and they were very friendly and welcoming, and we've enjoyed the vegan food. This might be the start of a beautiful relationship with Forest Green Rovers. We'll have to see, but so far the impression is very favourable.'

His wife Caroline says all her family are Derby fans, but James supports Nottingham Forest. 'When you go to a game between them the rivalry can get a bit too much, sometimes it can feel a bit aggressive, and I don't like that aspect of football. I like this small-club ethos, it just seems a lot more friendly to me.'

Kick-off is approaching, so it's time to check if there's any simmering aggression among the away fans. I find them outside in a marquee bar erected for them next to an Indian takeaway stall offering inventive cross-cultural cuisine with onion bhaji wraps and aloo tikki burgers.

Far from being up for a rousing dogfight, the emissaries from Chesterfield are not in good spirits. For football fans, optimism leads to death by a thousand cuts, and this season Chesterfield supporters have been cut to ribbons. Steve Hatton, a site manager, has driven two and a half hours to be here but is resigned to his team's fate. 'I don't think we'll survive, we don't deserve to,' he says gloomily. Steve has mixed feelings about rags-to-riches stories in basement leagues, with millionaires funding meteoric rises of teams like Fleetwood. 'A lot of clubs with limited resources don't like it. But if someone's prepared to invest in a club like Forest Green for altruistic reasons, fair play to them.' Today he arrived on a park-and-ride system set up by Rovers to alleviate parking problems. 'It was a strange approach coming up the hill, not what you're used to in the league. It'll be good practice for being in the National next year, I suppose.'

The main stand is rocking when I take a seat in the second front row, as close to the action as I can be without kicking a ball. The rows behind are pretty full with a lively, good-natured crowd spanning at least three generations. With sheep grazing beyond the away terracing, it is like waiting for the main event at a village fair. When Rovers take the field the sheep are startled by a crescendo of childish cheering.

Mark Cooper was right. Chesterfield start as if their lives depend on it, which in a sense they might, and they're unlucky to see an early strike cannoning off a post with the keeper beaten. Rovers reply with a similar effort that bounces out from the underside of the bar, before going ahead with an angled drive from 25 yards. Neither side can afford to lose, but credit to both for trying to keep the ball down and entertaining us with flowing, incisive football. Balmy soccer in warm spring sunshine, the crowd is loving it, and the visitors get something to cheer about when they level from the spot in the 36th minute.

At half-time a lady in a white hat appears with a trolley of Indian vegetarian food, and long queues form at outlets for Quorn pies, veggie burgers and chip butties. Milk for tea and coffee is a choice of soya or Swedish oatly on cartons labelled 'wow no cow'. A local butcher used to advertise at the stadium, but when he sent in his money as usual after Vince took over, it was sent back. Phil Butterworth told me about it. 'I think it's a shame because he had been a great servant of the club, but Dale lives by his principles and values and he felt he couldn't accept it.'

For the second half I join the home rhythm section on terracing behind the Chesterfield goal, a tightly packed herd of youthful fans belting out a chorus of chants like singing sardines. They're in high spirits, having a laugh, but not all of them favour playing out from the back, and there are occasional despairing cries of 'F...ing lump it!' The stewards don't have much to do other than chatting with fans they seem to know and among themselves, and a couple of cops spend the second half watching the game from outside the dressing rooms. It's probably the easiest shift money they'll earn.

With 15 minutes to go, Cooper makes an inspired substitution. On comes Dayle Grubb, a midfielder signed from Weston-super-Mare in January, and two minutes later he slides the ball to striker Christian Doidge, who finishes with aplomb for his 23rd goal of the season. The former Dagenham and Redbridge man is second top scorer in League Two, and understandably Cooper rates him highly: 'If you had a dozen of him in your squad you wouldn't go far wrong.' Four minutes into extra time Grubb gets on the scoresheet himself with an impish piece of skill, and Doidge adds insult to Chesterfield's injuries a minute later when he sticks away a penalty.

The final result of 4-1 is unfair to Chesterfield, but the Rovers choirboys don't care, subjecting the away terracing to rousing renditions of 'we're staying up, you're going down'. For a whimsical encore, they chant 'finished up we're better than you'. There is no response from the dispersing Chesterfield contingent – they've seen it all before this season, more times than they care to remember. Rovers, having virtually rubber-stamped their league survival, trot around a lap of honour, and by the time they're posing for selfies with fans and signing autographs, their dejected opponents have left the field. Chesterfield had their chances and near misses, Rovers' keeper made vital saves, and the result could easily have been different. By such fine margins are the fates of clubs and careers decided.

Back in the hospitality lounge, it seems half the crowd is packed into it with celebrating officials, players, their wives and a fleet of prams to watch the man-of-the-match award and school ambassador prizes being presented. A small, white-haired figure looks vaguely familiar, and she turns out to be a moderately successful local author.

Jilly Cooper, world renowned doyenne of bonkbuster novels and long-time Cotswolds resident, is a Forest Green fan and she's been chatting with players and staff for material for another bestseller, set in the world of football. Jilly contributed a lyrical tribute to the club in one of Chris Gardner's books, saying she had been drawn to the game by an inspiring dinner speech by Sir Alex Ferguson about involving young people in the game, and falling in love with her local team 'whose chairman is another visionary like Sir Alex, a man of principle and great generosity'. In Chris's book she recalls being invited to a semi-final play-off against Dover, and writes, 'Most football clubs are part of big towns, attracting large, belligerent crowds of supporters. Forest Green turned out to be ravishingly rural, surrounded by rolling hills, meadows and grazing sheep. The setting sun was casting great tree shadows over a perfect pitch, kept green by rainwater alone.' She is equally impressed by her reception, saying home games are like 'a wonderful party enhanced by the delectable vegan food'. She calls it

'Cordon Green'. By now a passionate Rovers fan, Jilly goes to the Wembley final against Grimsby Town and shares the sense of loss: 'David lost out to Goliath and nothing could've been more heart-rending on the greatest day in little Forest Green's history than to see our brave players slumped in post-defeat desolation on the hallowed turf.'

Jilly goes on to muse poignantly on the passion roused by players and managers who never know if they will be in a job tomorrow, and her resume is included in the epilogue of this book. I have her permission, because I have just asked her for it. She's leaving the lounge when I introduce myself briefly, say how much I enjoyed her contribution to Chris's book, and ask whether I might quote from it in my own. 'Of course you may, it would be an honour for me,' she says graciously. I guess this is the equivalent of Lionel Messi saying he'd be honoured for me to wear his shirt.

For the past week I've been trying for an interview with the chairman, and finally I've been told he might be able to spare a few minutes after the game. He's not hard to spot, a slim figure in a black t-shirt, skinny jeans and sparkly sneakers with an ear stud and a haircut suggestive of an ageing rock star. He looks like a renegade Millwall fan. I edge through the crowd, ask if we can have a few words, and we sit at a corner table where I can just about hear him above the babble of the crowd and constant interruptions by fans congratulating him. One of them is from Chicago, and he says there are lots of Forest Green supporters in the city because of the environmental and vegan principles. This is music to Vince's ears. 'I don't feel like an owner,' he says, 'I get to run the club and try to change the world by creating a different club with the environment at the heart of it. We're not preaching to the choir when we come into football to talk about ecosystems and animal rights, you know what I mean? It's a challenge, I like that, but it's a chance to broadcast our views on environmental stuff and being super ethical and family friendly. We get to show people another way to live.' Vince reckons coverage of the Forest Green story on TV, radio, print and online has reached millions around the world, and a few months before he was invited to address a United Nations conference in Bonn on climate change. 'They put us in a room with all sorts of sports bodies, including the San Francisco 49ers and the German and Japanese FAs, and they all knew about Forest Green and wanted to know how they could develop their clubs with the same message. For me this is incredible, suddenly our influence is reaching the world.'

A few months later Rovers are presented with a Momentum for Change climate action award in New York, after the UN recognise them as the world's first carbon neutral football club. The Executive Secretary of UN Climate Change says, 'These activities ... are proof that climate action isn't only possible, it's innovative, it's exciting, and it makes a difference.'

After decades of non-league obscurity, Forest Green Rovers have become an international flag bearer for a green crusade, aiming to move to a bigger stage to attract more converts. Vince agrees it won't be the little club on the hill any longer, but insists, 'I don't think we'll lose our identity. We won't change the name, and I think our identity will grow at this new location with north Bristol and south Birmingham as our catchment area. Our all-wooden stadium will be amazing, we get to design from scratch something that's never been done before. It'll be a wonder, people will want to come and see what we've done.'

No doubt, and I'll be among them, but personally I sense the quirky, friendly wee club on the hill is about to lose some of its magic. But not yet.

The car park is almost empty as I drive out, but I have to pause because the man of the match, still in his tracksuit, is kicking a ball around with a little boy in a Forest Green shirt bearing the player's name on the back. I find I'm smiling all the way down the hill.

Final whistle

THE SEASON ended with inevitably mixed fortunes for the clubs on my fixture list.

Accrington manager John Coleman was right about fairy tales. His team defied the odds to be crowned champions of League Two, above more fancied rivals Luton and Wycombe, gaining promotion to the highest level in its history. Billy Kee kept banging in the goals to finish the league's top scorer but sadly he retired two seasons later at the age of 29 with continuing health problems.

At the other end of the table, Forest Green survived their first season in the senior leagues by the skin of their teeth, a single point above the drop zone that consigned Barnet and Chesterfield to the National League. Grimsby were also saved by a late rally that took them five points clear of relegation, and Cambridge ended safely in mid-table.

In League One Argyle came agonisingly close to the play-offs, falling only three points short of a tilt at the Championship. Blackpool ended the season in mid-table, and Oyston's 31-year reign ended in the High Court a year later. The first match under the new owner, a local asset manager and lifelong Tangerines fan, drew a sell-out home crowd.

In Scotland, Queen's Park's brief sojourn in League One ended when they lost 3-2 on aggregate to Stenhousemuir in the play-offs, and financial pressures decreed they were fated to lose their stadium and amateur status a couple of years later.

The border raiders of Berwick lived to fight another day by finishing eighth in ten-team League Two, but their days in the senior ranks were numbered. A year later they dropped to the (Scottish) Lowland League after a 7-0 aggregate loss to Highland League champions Cove Rangers.

Epilogue

Here is the stuff of heroism

SO NOW we know.

Clubs with big hearts survive at grassroots levels of the professional game through bonds with the communities that sustain them. Faith and hope from fans are reciprocated by charity from clubs with health and welfare schemes that make everyone feel part of a big family. The ties established over generations run deep, club colours are in the genes, and when the administrators are called in the extended family instinctively rallies to help.

Raffle tickets, sponsored walks, volunteer car washes, anything it takes to save the club, and thousands of pounds lying in the boot of a car while the fundraisers take a break for a curry are a measure of devotion to clubs that are more than football teams.

In the absence of foreign billionaires, hard-headed local businessmen step up to the mark to rescue clubs in financial trouble, and if they weren't fans before they are now.

When fans and local folk need help, or just cheery company, they can find it down the road at their team's ground. Men rebuilding lives in Glasgow after drink and drug addictions are coached for Sunday league games, old timers in Plymouth get together for tea and outings, and teenagers in Cambridge are given advice on how to cope with stress.

There is an intimacy in these symbiotic relationships that few teams in higher leagues, if any, can match. Accrington's star striker joins fans and the chairman for a pint in the club bar after the game, Cambridge players chat with fans at a training session, Forest Green's man of the match has a kick-about with a young admirer in the car park. Easy familiarity between men trying to make the most of short, precarious careers and the fans who pay their wages.

The refrain is much the same from Glasgow to Plymouth: '… there's a closeness in this club that you never want to lose … they work their arses off in their communities to help charities, and it's really an act of faith … I like this small club ethos, it just seems a lot more friendly to me …

'… it's much more gutsy down here, more earthy. It's more real somehow … it's not about winning or losing any more. The attraction is the honesty of the men on the pitch … some of the best morals in football are actually in the lower leagues …

'… it's fascinating to watch quality players at the fag end of their careers and talented lads on their way up … when you love football it's a joy to watch lads at the beginning of their careers improving in the time they're with you …' And so on.

In towns blighted by economic decline, football clubs help to preserve civic pride, and occasionally give their supporters something to cheer about: '… this place is on its rear end, the team's about the only thing it's got going for it.'

So here's a thought. Next time your mate's Premier League team is playing at the other end of the country, or he's complaining about how much it costs, suggest he gives the Sky 'live' game a miss and come down to your local club for real live football, and bring his kids. It will be a different experience, chances are they'll enjoy it, and your club will be glad to see them. Because it's Saturday.

I leave the summing up to two eloquent fans, novelist Jilly Cooper in a contribution to a book on Forest Green Rovers, and Grimsby poet Gordon Wilson in a lyrical tribute to his beloved Town.

> *People continually moan that footballers are paid too much. I think they deserve every penny for the pleasure and excitement they bring to the world. A bad defeat may cast their fans into a week's black gloom but this will be transformed into a week's euphoria after a good win. Their careers can also be so fleeting with injury or age kicking in at any time and, like glorified slaves, they can be bought, sold or sacked at a manager's whim and often a manager's career is just as precarious. How resilient they have to be to cope with blistering invective from media and fans both on the terraces and the website. While even the greatest player must rise above defeat, particularly if his missed penalty, careless finish or let-in goal deprives his team-mates of promotion and untold riches. Here is the stuff of heroism.*
>
> – *Jilly Cooper*

EPILOGUE

ON SATURDAY

These wordless bards draw in such crowds
as those with pens can only dream on
We gather along the wings,
awed by elegant crafters of legend and myth
whose drama is uttered in passes and runs,
in stops and blocks and crosses and shots;
dribbling their soliloquies – these disbelieve suspenders,
this timeless troupe of hope inspirers,
rage inducers, joy creators,
this priceless chorus of passion purgers

– Gordon Wilson

Postscript

THE SEASON has just ended when a friend posts a petition on Facebook from a group of Syrian refugee footballers.

'Football was our way of life, but the war destroyed football clubs and stadiums, and dispersed Syria's football players across the world. For us, football has been a pillar of stability, offering us camaraderie, joy and laughter even in the darkest days. We have seen the unique power of sport to bring people together and inspire the values of respect, integrity and unity.

'Since the Christmas truce of 1914, where soldiers played football between the trenches, sport has proven to be a powerful catalyst for peace. This summer, as the football community heads for Russia, it could be one again. We believe that the World Cup should be harnessed as a force for good in our world.

'That is why we are calling on all world leaders to urge President Putin, the World Cup host, to declare a ceasefire in Syria, and bring greater peace and security to Syrians ahead of the opening ceremony on June 14th. We need a World Cup of Peace.'

The petition has been signed by almost 20,000 people.

Pissing in the winds of war I suppose, but a reminder that football can be a powerful weapon for good and that sometimes in life there is more at stake than winning trophies.